MAGGIE OLIVER

FIGHTING FOR JUSTICE

SURVIVORS

One brave detective's battle to expose
the Rochdale child abuse scandal

JOHN BLAKE

Published by John Blake Publishing,
The Plaza,
535 Kings Road,
Chelsea Harbour,
London SW10 0SZ

www.facebook.com/johnblakebooks ⬤
twitter.com/jblakebooks ⬛

First published in paperback in 2019

ISBN: 978 1 78946 085 8
Ebook: 978 1 78946 102 2

British Library Cataloguing-in-Publication Data:
A catalogue record for this book is available from the British Library.

Design by www.envydesign.co.uk

Printed and bound in Great Britain by Clays Ltd, Elcograf S.p.A.

3 5 7 9 10 8 6 4 2

John Blake Publishing is an imprint of Bonnier Books UK
www.bonnierbooks.co.uk

For Norman,
who encouraged me to reach for the stars,
and my four beautiful children who helped me
come through the heartache.
I love you.
Xxx

Although this book is based on real people and real events, many names, places and identifying features have been changed in order to preserve their anonymity.

Contents

Freezer 46

Gripping the clipboard in his hand, the police officer yawned as he ticked off another forensic exhibit from the list. It was another day at the station and a routine review of Greater Manchester Police exhibits that all needed to be checked and accounted for. He slowly ticked off one after the other – samples of blood and saliva – all stored and frozen in time, waiting for pending prosecution cases. Checking his watch, the officer smiled to himself – only another couple of hours left to go. With his day almost done, he lifted the lid of Freezer 46. An icy blast made the hairs on the back of his neck stand on end as a cold shiver ran through him. Digging a hand deep inside the chest freezer, he continued with the checklist, slowly sifting through the samples.

Suddenly his hand came to rest against an unfamiliar square-shaped container. The officer shrugged, a little bemused, as he picked it up to take a closer look. The container had been sealed inside a forensics bag so he used a forefinger to brush away some ice crystals that had formed on the outside. The container was much larger and had felt much heavier than the others. He wondered what on earth he'd just found at the bottom of Freezer 46. Condensation from the warm exhibits room had clouded the outside of the bag, but its contents were still visible. A blurred crimson and pink object nestled inside ominously. Curious, the officer used a thumb to clear the label so he could read what its contents were. The description was short and blunt:

Aborted foetus.

'Jesus Christ!' he gasped as he reeled back in shock.

His fingers fumbled in horror as he tried not to drop the container or the dead baby inside. Once he'd managed to compose himself, he strode over to his desk – his arm outstretched the whole time, trying to keep a distance between him and the foetus – and gently rested the bag on the side. He wiped his hand thoroughly against his uniform, picked up the phone and dialled an extension number. His heart thumped loudly against his ribcage as he held his breath and waited for an answer. Finally, someone picked up on the other end of the line.

'Boss,' he began. 'We've got a problem...'

*

The aborted baby would trigger one of the biggest criminal investigations in British history: the wide-scale child sexual exploitation of white girls by Pakistani men. The investigation, by Greater Manchester Police, would later become known as the Rochdale Grooming Scandal. The Rochdale case would not only lead to one of the biggest scandals the UK has ever seen, it would lead right to the heart of the British government.

POLICE OATH OF ATTESTATION

I do solemnly and sincerely declare and affirm that I will well and truly serve the Queen in the office of constable, with fairness, integrity, diligence and impartiality, upholding fundamental human rights and according equal respect to all people; and that I will, to the best of my power, cause the peace to be kept and preserved and prevent all offences against people and property; and that while I continue to hold the said office I will to the best of my skill and knowledge discharge all the duties thereof faithfully according to law.

Chapter One

Beginnings

❝ This is life
and I decided
to live it ❞
— Anon

My first day at police training school, in October 1997, was a monumental one. It had taken me five years to get to this point – to enter a new career at the ripe old age of forty-one. I felt a mixture of pride, fear, amazement, uncertainty and excitement all rolled into one. But I'd done it, in spite of all the odds. No longer just a wife, mum, parent governor, or cleaner, I'd now become a police officer and would embark on a new career, carrying out one of the most important roles of my life.

I walked into class on my first day at Sedgley Park Training School in Prestwich, Manchester, to see a dozen or so other would-be officers sitting there. Immediately, I felt like the underdog. Not only were the other recruits half my age, they were mostly ex-military and super fit to boot. But I had a burning desire to be a good police officer and to make a difference to other people's lives, so

I pushed away all my self-doubt and took my seat among them. I wanted to give something back to my community and I was determined to give this my very best shot.

My life experiences up to that point meant I understood what people wanted from a police officer. Following a motivational but scary introduction from our class trainer – a seasoned police veteran – we were told to go and collect our uniforms and then trek up an enormous hill to what would be our digs for the initial two weeks' training. I puffed and panted as I dragged an enormous box full of uniform, hats, handcuffs, belts and riot gear along with me. To make matters worse, I was surrounded by the other younger and fitter recruits.

What on earth have I got myself into? I wondered, totally out of my comfort zone as I trailed behind.

We were told the first fortnight would be spent in the classroom, where we would learn the basics, like how to polish our shoes until we could see our face in them, how to put the numbers in our epaulettes and how to write in our pocket notebooks. That first fortnight I'd gone from being a student to feeling as though I was on the set of *Z Cars*. Unlike the ex-squaddies, I'd never experienced such regimented learning.

Although the police uniform was smart, I decided to add my own little touches to reflect my individual character. I started with an objection to flat shoes. I'd never worn them, not ever. I was determined not to compromise and maintain my own sense of style – a battle I was destined to lose from day one. My preferred footwear had a little bit of a heel which, when the training sergeant first clocked them, raised an eyebrow.

'You need flat shoes,' he insisted, 'not bloody ballet shoes!'

As the days went by, my heels became lower and lower. I bought first one, then two, and finally, three pairs of shoes until, eventually, I accepted defeat and settled on a pair of boring, plain black brogues. I wasn't happy, but by then I had another battle on my hands: the length of my hair. I'd had shoulder-length hair – a sort of *Charlie's Angels* Farrah Fawcett-Majors style – since the year dot. My hair was my identity and now I was told it was unsuitable.

'Your hair must not touch your collar!' the training sergeant barked when he spotted my blonde locks. I had no choice but to cut it short for the first time in my life.

Then there was the make-up.

'No make-up!' the training sergeant added gruffly.

'But why not?'

He sighed, stopped and turned back to stare at me with an icy glare as though it should be obvious. 'Because, when it rains, all that muck will just run down your face!' he said, flicking his hand towards my blushing cheeks.

I was mortified, but determined I wasn't going to lose my fight to retain an element of femininity in the male-dominated world of Greater Manchester Police.

'No problem, sarge,' I answered, 'I'll just wear water-proof.'

He shook his head as though he'd given up the will to live, but then I saw an unexpected smile hovering around his eyes and I knew I'd be okay.

*

Perhaps I was always a rebel. I grew up in the Lancashire mill town of Bacup, with my parents and my younger sister, Di. We were a typical family – Dad worked hard as an electrician, while Mum was a stay-at-home housewife. The only unusual thing about us was my mother was Austrian, which, during the post-war years, meant we stuck out like a sore thumb.

Mum was born in the 1930s in Graz, the second-largest city in Austria after Vienna, and spent the war years growing up in Linz, in the northern part of the country, which had been almost bombed to destruction by the allies. She had many stories of the terrible scenes she'd witnessed. In the early 1950s she left Austria and travelled to England in a bid to improve her English. Back then, jobs were plentiful, especially in the cotton mills of Bacup. My dad was Lancashire born and bred and had led a sheltered life, largely untouched by the Second World War, so they were polar opposites. But Dad was smitten and the two had a whirlwind romance ending in marriage after Mum found out she was pregnant with me.

From a very early age I was acutely aware of coming from a different family. It made me sensitive to bullying, prejudice or injustice of any kind. In short, I always fought the corner of the 'underdog'. This didn't diminish, not even when Dad was promoted and our family moved to Sale, in Manchester. It was clear from the start that I was fairly academic and I absolutely loved school. I passed my 11-plus and went to the local grammar school, but I was always very shy and would blush horrendously at the smallest thing.

I grew up like this until the age of twenty, when I met

a lad called Norman. Through him, I decided I was far too young to settle into the domesticated life my parents had planned for me and instead I rebelled. Norman was to become my co-conspirator and, boy, it was going to be one hell of a journey.

I enrolled at Salford College of Technology (now Salford University), where I studied French, German, Spanish, shorthand and typing. As the eldest daughter, my parents expected me to get married and settle down. They assumed I'd have children, not a career. But I wanted both. My younger sister, Di, had been dating a guy called Kevin, so, one weekend, I decided to tag along. The nightclub – The Blue Rooms in Sale – was hot, noisy and full of people smoking and chatting as music blared away in the background. As soon as we walked in, I spotted him – a slim, good-looking, curly-haired guy, talking to a group of people over the far side of the room. As he turned, he noticed Kevin and headed across the dance floor to speak to us.

'Hello,' he said, looking so intently at me that I felt myself blush. 'And who do we have here then?'

Good-looking, but with a real confidence and sense of danger about him, I felt an instant attraction. I wasn't looking for a relationship, but when Norman showed an interest in me I felt my resolve begin to weaken.

As soon he began to talk, I realised not only was he charming, but he was totally different to any man I'd ever met. He was also football-mad. A builder by trade, he'd left school without a single paper qualification, but he knew his job well and there was very little he couldn't do. Norman played for Manchester City's youth team, although ironically, he actually supported Man United. He was a man's man and liked to have a drink with the lads. The attraction was immediate and the connection between us electric.

'You want to watch him, Margaret,' a friend later warned me. 'He's a bit of a lad, that one.'

With her words ringing in my ears, I decided to steer clear. But it didn't last long. A few months later, fate decided to throw us together when I went on holiday to Devon with Di and a friend of ours. We travelled over to Newquay and were strolling along the seafront when a familiar face approached from the opposite direction.

'No, it can't be...' I mumbled as my heart began to flutter. I felt my stomach somersault with nerves as he grew closer.

'So, what are you doing down here?' Norman asked.

'I might ask you the same,' I replied, even though I knew he'd been working down in Newquay over the summer season.

We chatted for a while before Norman suggested taking us all for a drink. As we sat down in the pub, I studied him. He was a larger-than-life character, so much so, once you'd met him, you'd be hard-pressed to forget him. His parents were equally memorable, too. His father was a staunch Conservative, while his mother had been a life-long Labour supporter, so they were at opposite ends of the political spectrum, with their son at the centre of their world.

That summer – 1976 – was one of the hottest summers on record but, sadly, I had to return to Manchester. I was young, happy, sun-tanned and single. But Norman had other ideas. A complete curiosity and the opposite of anyone or anything I'd ever known before, he and I began dating. At that time, I was working as a bilingual secretary as my parents were keen I should improve my secretarial skills as it was a job I could fit around a husband and children. But I had other ideas. I'd always been pretty smart at school and thanks to my Austrian mother, I was multi-lingual and spoke French, Spanish and German. Mum and Dad had wanted me to settle down with a successful businessman. Needless to say, as soon as Norman returned from Newquay, I took him home. My dad hated him on sight. However, Mum warmed to him. He was a typical working-class, popular lad and the life and soul of any party – the absolute opposite of what my parents considered 'marriage material'.

By summer 1977, I'd managed to find a summer job in Newquay. Dad was horrified when I packed in my steady job to become a waitress in a hotel. But I didn't care: I couldn't bear to be parted from Norman, nor he from me. We travelled down to Newquay and spent every spare hour together. I was twenty-one and I felt as though my life had just begun. It was a wonderful summer, helped by the fact my job came with live-in accommodation, which meant that all the money I earned was mine to keep. Norman returned home earlier than me – just in time for the football season – and I followed.

The following year, we travelled back to Newquay, but the year after, we daringly decided we would go and work the summer season in Jersey. I found a temporary job as a secretary straight away. By now, we'd been going out for almost three years and so we decided to find a place together. We'd been renting a room in a house for around a month or so when there was a tap at the door. It was our landlady, Mrs Simpson.

She looked a bit awkward and I suspected she hadn't expected us both to be in.

'Norman,' she whispered almost conspiratorially, 'There's been a girl come to see you and she left you this... it's a letter.'

I was confused. Who was this girl? How did she know Norman and where had she got hold of our address? I watched as Norman stood there holding the letter in his hand. He tore open the envelope, his eyes flickering across the page, searching for a name. He read one side of the letter, before turning it over.

'I can't believe it!' he mumbled. 'It's from Lesley, my ex-girlfriend.'

My heart froze. Lesley had been his first love and someone he'd held a torch for since schooldays. They'd had quite a serious relationship until Lesley's family decided to uproot and emigrate to Canada.

'But I thought you said she lived in Canada?'

He looked over at me and back down at the letter.

'She did. I mean, she still does, but it says here,' he said tapping the letter with his finger, 'her grandma has died so she's back in England, well, Jersey, and she wants to see me.'

I felt sick as Norman's face broke into a huge smile.

'All right,' I said standing up, 'you can, and you should see her, but I'll come with you.'

'No, you can't,' he said, 'I'm going alone.'

His words had been so unexpected that they felt like a punch to my stomach. I looked him square in the eye. My voice was clear and calm and then I spoke.

'Okay, it's your choice. But if you go without me, then I'm telling you, don't bother coming back.'

As soon as the words left my mouth, I felt sick because I knew they'd change everything. We'd been going out for three years and while it had been great fun, Norman hadn't fully committed to me. Now he was planning to go and visit an ex-girlfriend without me. It told me all I needed to know about the state of our relationship.

'Don't be stupid...' he began, trying to reason with me.

But I was adamant and turned my face away. Norman huffed, grabbed his jacket and stormed out. I noticed that before he'd left, he'd shoved Lesley's letter inside the pocket of his jeans. After he left, I sat there, heartbroken. I pulled out one of his bags and began to pile his clothes inside it. Within the hour, two bags were waiting for his return.

'What are these?' he asked when he finally came back, pointing down at them. I could tell he was shocked that I'd followed through with my threat.

Before he could say another word, I grabbed my coat, headed towards the door and left for work. By the time I returned, Norman was gone. He reappeared the following night and every night after that for a week. I think he hoped I'd calm down and change my mind, but the more he knocked at my door, the more resolute I became. I convinced myself our relationship had run its course. There was no commitment, no engagement, and now that he'd buggered off to meet his ex-girlfriend alone, well, there was no trust and no relationship – not anymore.

'You're wasting your breath,' I told him. 'You're not coming back.'

In spite of my bravado, I was utterly heartbroken. Up until that moment, we'd been inseparable. It'd been us against the world, but now I was alone. Returning home at night to an empty room made me feel even worse, so I called around until I managed to secure work in a hotel – one that offered live-in accommodation. With a roof over my head and a new group of girlfriends, I moved out of our old digs. I was young, proud and stubborn. I also had a good work ethic, so instead of spending my evenings moping around after Norman, I landed myself a second job in a nightclub. But the long hours eventually caught up with me and I decided I needed a complete change of scene.

With a new determination, I picked up a copy of *The Lady* and applied for a position as a nanny. My new employers lived in Jersey, but they were millionaires and owned a six-seater plane, an enormous villa in Florida and a golf course in France, so they were always travelling. It really was how the other half lived. In spite of my inexperience, each day I had two children under my charge: a two-year-old girl and her five-year-old brother. It was up to me to cook, clean and care for them.

Just weeks into my new job, we travelled to France to stay on their golf course for a few weeks, but I felt lonely and isolated, so, when one of my friends told me he was travelling to Germany for work, I decided to hand in my notice. Together, we headed off to Germany, where I found work in a guesthouse, waiting tables and improving my knowledge of German. At that point in time, I had no intention of going back to Manchester or of ever seeing Norman again. But then fate stepped in again. My sister got in touch to say she and Kevin were expecting their first child, so I booked a flight home. My nephew was born in early September 1979 and I flew in to meet him. I didn't know then, but Kevin had told Norman I was back home and he immediately picked up the phone and called my parents' house. I'd only been back a few hours when the phone rang in the hallway. Mum went to answer it.

'Norman's on the line!' she shouted upstairs to me.

Nerves gripped me as I took the receiver from her hand, but I was also still very angry. However, as soon as he began to speak, I could tell that Norman sounded like a different man.

'I'm sorry, Margaret. You've got to believe me,' he began, 'I've changed. The last thing I wanted to do was hurt you. I've had six months to think about things. I've thought of nothing else and I know it's you I want, you've got to believe me.'

Although this was exactly what I wanted to hear, I was naturally reticent.

'But what about Lesley?'

'I know what I did was wrong,' he said. 'It was the biggest mistake of my life and I've regretted it every single day since. I love you and I want us to get engaged. I want to spend my life with you. You've just got to believe me, I've made the biggest mistake of my life...'

Norman wasn't one to wear his heart on his sleeve or speak about his feelings, so this was completely out of character for him. When he begged me to meet him later that night for a drink, I agreed. As soon as I saw him, my heart melted. My feelings for him were still there and as intense as they had always been. I knew then that he'd meant every word he'd said on the phone.

'I was out of order,' he said, putting our drinks down on the pub table.

Norman took my hand in his and looked across at me. 'You've got to believe me, it was the biggest mistake of my life. I realise that now. Please, let's give it another chance. I want us to get engaged.'

That six-month separation, hard as it had been, turned out to be the absolute making of us. It brought home just how much in love we were and how we truly couldn't live without each other.

Chapter Two

Arabian Nights and Manchester Days

❝Jobs fill your pocket.
Adventures fill your soul❞
— Jaime Lyn Beatty

When Norman told me he'd booked a three-month trip to Gran Canaria and insisted I go with him, I was ecstatic. Two weeks later, we stunned everyone when we announced our engagement. A month later, we flew out to Gran Canaria, where we travelled to the south of the island – a place called Playa de Tauro. We pitched up a tent and lived in a 'commune' on the beach with other backpackers for three blissful months. We had a camping stove – a relative luxury in 1979 – and soon became the most popular members of the camp. In the evening, we'd sit on orange boxes and eat fresh food cooked on the stove, staring out towards the sea. It was almost a honeymoon if we'd not had a pittance to live on.

There was a couple in our mini commune who owned an old converted single-decker bus they lived on. The man,

Brian, his wife and their baby boy were touring Europe and we soon became friends. One night, Brian announced they would be leaving the camp and heading for Morocco. Then he made a suggestion: 'I'll tell you what, Margaret,' he said, 'if you can get ten people to pay £100 each, I'll take you all with us.'

By the end of the week, Norman and I and eight others boarded the bus. We caught a ferry across the Bay of Biscay to Cádiz in Portugal and drove along the south coast into Spain. From there we caught another ferry and docked in Ceuta in North Africa, before driving the short distance to Tangier. It was the beginning of 1980 and travelling to remote countries like Morocco and North Africa wasn't something people did in those days, especially not girls like me. But I immersed myself in the whole adventure and adored every moment of it.

Everything in the bustling Tangier kasbah felt magnified in the blazing heat. The air was thick, peppered with a heady aroma of spices. I could smell and almost taste cumin, cayenne, turmeric and paprika, mixed with the scent of spiced teas. The kasbah was crowded, chaotic and buzzing with life. As we passed through, billowing robes fluttered against cluttered, colourful market stalls in an explosion of colour. Deep scarlet, ochre and burnt orange clashed loudly against cobalt blue and emerald green, with too many humans, and often camels, crammed into the small, winding streets. It was organised chaos, with the pushing and shoving of crowds, shoulder to shoulder, as Moroccan Arabic and French voices rose high in the air. Market stallholders raised their voices and moved their hands dramatically as they bartered with the crowds.

It was intense – the volume turned up to maximum – a percussion of noise and energy throbbing below us. I'd never felt so alive.

We continued our journey and arrived in Fez, an exotic historical kingdom, the old city entered through a set of grand golden gates that looked as though they'd come straight off the set of an old Hollywood movie. Norman held my hand as we walked over the rooftops to a tannery, where we watched men curing leather in the blistering heat. Like mountain goats, the men leapt from one rooftop to another, dipping the leather in a foul-smelling vat of liquid before laying it out to bleach and soften in the midday sun. The smell was acrid, overpowering, and it caught at the back of my throat, making me choke.

The locals had never seen a mixed band of travellers quite like us, it seemed, for wherever we went, they would appear and bring out their coats, spread them out on the floor and cover them with an assortment of spices, which they'd grown and ground inside their own homes. One day, as we were travelling through a particularly barren patch of desert, I spotted what I thought was a horse running alongside in the distance. Another appeared and then another.

'Look,' I said, turning to Norman and a couple of others on the bus.

'Camels!' Brian called from the front of the bus. 'They're wild camels. You get them around here.'

We were so astonished that a few of the lads insisted on getting off the bus to try and catch one so they could attempt to hitch a ride.

'Don't be daft!' I howled, as I fell about laughing.

Unsurprisingly, they failed to rustle a single camel. Four legs, it seemed, were much faster than two.

That night, we and the rest of our group decided to pitch our tents up on the outskirts of a town. Up until then, no one had bothered us and we'd had no trouble. We were all fast asleep when suddenly we were woken by the sound of a man screaming incoherently outside. Suddenly, the sky appeared as the tent roof ripped above our heads. Then I saw the flash of something – the glinting edge of metal – as it stabbed against the fabric roof, slicing it open. The face of a menacing-looking stranger – a Moroccan – hovered above us.

'Quick!' Norman shouted, grabbing my hand.

We were petrified but jumped to our feet and dived outside within seconds. That's when I saw it – a long, sharp knife in the man's hand. He continued to shout and slash our tent to ribbons before moving on to the next one.

Brian was fast and bundled him to the ground and the pair tumbled awkwardly over into a ravine. Some of the other lads rushed forward and helped him pin the knifeman to the floor. I was terrified one of them would be stabbed to death but, somehow, they managed to hold him until the commotion brought a few locals running over to lend a hand. Someone must have alerted the police because they arrived shortly afterwards and carted the man off. Afterwards, Brian slumped to the floor, nursing his right arm.

'My shoulder is killing me!' he groaned.

Brian's wife put his arm in a sling and I tentatively approached some of the Moroccans to ask who the man was and why he'd targeted us.

'He's high on drugs,' one explained in perfect French.

He circled a finger against the side of his head – a universal language – to indicate that the man had lost the plot.

The following morning, despite his arm now being in a sling, Brian insisted on driving the bus. I don't think he trusted a bunch of twenty-somethings to drive what was, after all, his pride and joy.

The sheer anarchy of the kasbahs could only be matched in power by the vastness of the Atlas Mountains. We trekked our way through them in the bus, stopping off at small villages along the way. But Brian's shoulder continued to trouble him. Sling, or no sling, he finally admitted defeat and pulled the bus to a halt.

'That's it, everybody off! We're pitching up here. I need to rest my shoulder.'

A dislocated shoulder and the fact he didn't want anyone else to drive his bus meant we were now well and truly stuck. Fortunately, we'd stopped in paradise – a lush and leafy oasis which rose from the middle of the desert called Meski Springs.

If I'd thought the oasis was spectacular, I wasn't quite so enamoured with the lavatory arrangements – a black hole in the middle of the ground. In the dead of night, when I was bursting for a wee, I nipped to the 'loo'. I was just perched above the hole and about to have a pee when something unexpected jumped out of it. I screamed at the top of my voice. My cries were so loud that I'm sure they must have heard me as far away as Cape Town.

'Margaret, are you alright?' A voice called out in the darkness. A figure came running towards me from the shadows before stopping and gasping for breath. It was Norman.

'Something's just jumped out of that bloody black hole! Oh my God, what is it?' I shrieked.

Norman went over to investigate and reappeared moments later, crying with laughter.

'Was it a snake?' I asked, my heart hammering inside my chest.

'No, you daft bugger! It's just a frog, it won't hurt you.'

But I didn't care because that wasn't the point. All I knew was I'd almost had a heart attack and that would be the last time I'd squat over that bloody hole in the ground in the pitch-dark. From then on, it was behind the bushes for me.

*

During the first couple of days at Meski, I spotted the cutest little boy, aged about five years old, who had been hovering around our camp. He had the biggest brown eyes I'd ever seen and the most beautiful skin. He was naturally shy but, because I started to speak to him in French, he slowly warmed to me and we became friends. I'd always loved children, long before I had my own, and I discovered I had a natural ability to communicate with them and gain their trust. My heart melted one morning when I came out of my tent to find him, dressed in shabby clothes, waiting patiently for me. He was holding a little present – a camel he'd woven from rushes growing nearby. After that day, his face would light up and break into a huge smile every morning when I stepped out of my tent. One day, I walked out into the blazing sunlight to find my little friend waiting there. He shyly asked if I would like to visit his home and meet his mum.

'That would be lovely,' I replied in French, adding, 'I'd be honoured.'

As his new 'special friends', Norman and I followed him out of Meski and through a desert landscape to a pressed sand opening that led underground. As we descended, we entered a labyrinth of tunnels dug into the earth, each leading off what could only be described as a circular room in the middle of an underworld. The room was full of smoke and chickens and goats wandered around freely. I wondered where the smoke was coming from and then I noticed it – a large kiln – in the centre of the room. It had the most delicious smell of fresh bread.

The little boy brought his mum over to meet us and she insisted on gifting us some of her freshly baked bread. She refused to take anything from us in return, though it was obvious they had very little themselves. We were totally overwhelmed by their kindness. It was an early lesson in life for me that happiness doesn't depend on wealth and riches, but kindness, sharing, friendship, family and love. This journey was bringing me into contact with people from vastly different backgrounds and lifestyles to my own, helping me to understand different points of view, and when the time came to move on, I felt so sad to say goodbye to my little friend and leave him in his underground home.

It was the beginning of the eighties – a whole new decade – and anything seemed possible. As we left the springs to continue into deepest, darkest Morocco towards Marrakech, life felt good. There was a main square in Marrakech where everyone from snake charmers, jugglers, beggars to pickpockets gathered. Robed men sat inside shaded tea houses, putting the world to rights, as traditional music blared away in the background. It was the unknown – exotic and magical.

'Pinch me?' I whispered to Norman.

He turned to me, a puzzled look on his face.

'Pinch me,' I repeated, 'because I can't actually believe I'm here!'

*

We continued our adventure, travelling to places I'd never even heard of, except for Casablanca – which I only knew because of the Humphrey Bogart film. We slept on the beautiful beaches in Essaouira and dipped into the hustle and bustle of the capital, Rabat, until it was finally time to leave the magical land and head home. We'd been travelling for five months and by now it was April 1980. By the time we reached Paris, Norman and I climbed off the bus completely starving but hopelessly skint. We found our way to a McDonald's on the Champs-Élysées, which was relatively new at that time. Neither of us had a penny so we decided to sit and wait for someone – anyone – to leave a scrap of food. When they finally did, we were there like a shot, devouring the leftovers.

Travelling the world and, later, living hand-to-mouth made me appreciate what was important – and that was my life with Norman. Brian took us to Calais, where we caught the ferry back to Dover and drove on to London, where we had to say our goodbyes as everyone prepared to go their own separate ways. Distraught that this amazing chapter in my life was coming to an end, I sobbed as we hugged each other tightly: these people had become like family to me.

Back at home, my dad had a job waiting for me: he needed help in the office because the lad who usually did the wages at his electrical firm had died suddenly from a diabetic hypo. Everyone was really upset and my father needed someone so I agreed to help him out temporarily. Norman also found work with a local builder and, by the end of the year, we'd managed to save up enough deposit to buy our first home, a small two-bed terraced house in Altrincham. It was as far removed from the hustle and bustle of Morocco as you could get, but we'd had our adventure and, for now, it was time to settle down and build a future together. Norman decided he needed qualifications to evidence his skill as a joiner, so he enrolled on a course at college, while I worked and supported us both. Then he got a job as a joiner. Life was good, but just as we'd settled into a routine I began to feel unwell. Once again, fate had another surprise in store for us.

I'd run out of my contraceptive pill when we'd been in Morocco, so I'd decided to give my body a break. Looking back, we'd played Russian roulette with my birth control, so I suppose it was inevitable I'd eventually fall pregnant, which I did. However, the timing couldn't have been worse because Norman had just been laid off from his steady job. We'd always wanted children, just not in these circumstances. Once I realised I was pregnant, I let the news sink in for a day or so before I decided to tell him. Deep down, I suppose I wasn't quite sure how he'd react.

'I've got something to tell you...' I began hesitantly.

'What is it?' Norman asked, glancing up from a football magazine he was reading.

'I'm pregnant.'

I was prepared for shock, I was prepared for panic, but what I wasn't prepared for was laughter. Norman was beaming.

'I heard you,' he said, 'and it's…well, that's fantastic!'

In typical Norman style, he took the news completely in his stride but I was adamant we'd get married and do it properly. In the end, we were hitched at the registrar's in Sale just six weeks later. The reception was at a local pub and it was a small affair with just a handful of guests. I wore a lilac dress and carried a small bouquet – nothing fancy at all. It was a special occasion, of course, but in those days to be expecting a baby when getting married was still slightly frowned on. The wedding and reception was followed by a cheap but romantic weekend honeymoon in Blackpool.

Our beautiful son, Steve, was born in November 1981 and we were besotted with him. I became a devoted mum, which is the most important job I've ever done in my life. Norman became the best husband and father I could wish for, seeing a life he'd never dreamed of now opening up before his eyes. He'd gained his professional joinery papers, we'd bought a house and now he had a son. The same man, who only a few years earlier had been Jack the Lad, had turned into a devoted husband, father and friend. After losing his job, Norman became self-employed. He was already doing 'foreigners', jobs on the side, and so he continued with these and grew his own business, never going back to work for anyone. He started doing a lot of work for The Children's Society, especially on one of their residential homes called Ingledene, in Bowden. He enjoyed the company of the troubled young people living in the home, and a couple of these became regular visitors to our home. The first Christmas he worked there, he discovered that one young boy called Leslie was to be alone there over the festive period, so we invited him to stay with us, and over the years he became like an extra son to us.

I absolutely loved being a mum and felt I'd found my niche in life. Within a few short years we had three more children: Danny, born three years later in July 1984, followed by his sister Vicki, in September 1986, and Matt, who was born in April 1989. I spent the whole of the 1980s being pregnant and I loved every minute. We were a family, often struggling to make ends meet, but totally happy with our lot.

I enjoyed caring for people, particularly children. When my kids were small, I worked part time in the Lil Stockdale Centre in Sale, a residential home for severely disabled children. I would go in early on a Saturday and be back for 1pm, in time for Norman to go to his football. I'd feed the children, play with them and generally look after them because they needed twenty-four-hour care. Before that, when I was much younger I'd often go up to a local old people's home and help out there with whatever was needed. From an early age caring was part of my nature. As my kids started to grow up and meet friends, our house became like the local kindergarten. It was always full of kids and that was never a bother to me – I loved them being around.

After Vicki was born, I became a parent governor at the kids' local school and then chair of the governors. I discovered that I had a knack for being able to talk to and reason with people from different backgrounds and on different levels. I'd always been a bit of a workaholic and I liked being busy, so I decided I'd try to become a teacher, but that meant I'd need a degree.

I enrolled at South Trafford College in my mid thirties and took two A-levels in English and Sociology. I had a burning desire to help other children and was determined to get the qualifications I needed so I could work with them. After passing both A-levels, I enrolled on a BA Hons degree in Humanities. It was something I'd wanted to do since I was sixteen and now, with Norman's support and encouragement, I was able to achieve it. I chose my modules carefully so that they fitted around the school day. It was often very stressful, juggling family life and study, but not only did I gain my degree, I was awarded the highest mark out of my whole year group for my dissertation. I felt proud at my graduation ceremony, at Manchester Bridgewater Hall, dressed in my cap and gown with Norman and the kids cheering me on. I was forty – a life-changing age in many ways – when I applied to do a PGCE. I was all set to follow my planned career path, but suddenly I had a rare moment of doubt.

'What if I don't get on the course?' I said to Norman late one evening after the children had gone to bed.

'You will,' he insisted, looking over the top of the paperwork he was doing.

'But what if I don't?'

'Well, if you don't, then what else do you want to do?'

I thought for a moment. Matt, our youngest child, was now seven and I'd spent the past fifteen years looking after my kids. But the years spent at university had opened my eyes to a different world, a world full of possibilities.

'I think I'd like to become a police officer,' I announced. The words had left my mouth before I'd even considered them but, instinctively, I knew this was a role that would suit me. I wanted to help people, to be useful in the community and to make a real difference to people's lives. There were no other police officers in my family and everyone was shocked at my decision. Although I knew the police force would give me a good career until retirement, I wasn't in it for the money. I thought it would fulfil my strong social conscience because I would be able to do something worthwhile for people and the communities they lived in.

Norman stared at me. 'What? A police officer? Are you serious?'

Not being the biggest fan of the police, Norman was shocked. He'd seen friends have run-ins with officers in his youth, and he always considered them heavy-handed. That said, he was always supportive of every decision I made.

'Yes,' I said, 'I think I'll try for that, and then maybe I could work in Child Protection. First thing tomorrow, I'm going to apply to Greater Manchester Police.'

It was a decision that was to change the course of my entire life.

*

Taking my entrance exams for the police reminded me of taking my eleven-plus for grammar school, only they were thirty years apart and totally nerve-racking. There was a psychometric test, a sort of maths test, an observation test and interview – all of which I passed with flying colours. The final hurdle was the physical test. I hated running with a vengeance but, on this occasion, it was a necessary evil. There was no getting around it, the 'bleep test' was compulsory and I had to pass it. This test was to establish a certain level of physical fitness and it comprised a series of electronic bleeps which marked time between two points. You started by walking between the two markers and each time the gaps between the bleeps shortened, so that eventually you were going hell for leather between each bleep.

I was panicking, my stomach was tied in knots, and when I got home it was all I could talk about. As always, Norman listened to me rabbiting on, then he put down his brew and disappeared upstairs. I could hear him rooting through the kids' old toy boxes before he reappeared in the kitchen holding one of their old toys: an old-fashioned battery-operated kiddies' tape recorder. I hadn't seen it in years. But now he had it in his hands, bright yellow and blue, with big, red, shiny buttons.

'Right,' he said, 'stop moaning and get your trainers on! We're going over to the field.'

I stared at him in total disbelief.

Twenty minutes later, I was standing in the middle of a freezing-cold field as he marked out the necessary distance with two T-shirts that he'd positioned one hundred metres apart. Then he pressed the huge red buttons of the toy tape player and a huge 'bleep!' sound came from the speaker.

'This is nuts!' I moaned, but he refused to listen.

I tried to keep up as the pace speeded up through the different levels. But instead of getting faster, I fell further and further behind until, eventually, I couldn't run anymore.

But Norman refused to let me wallow: 'Come on, get

a grip!' he urged. 'We'll come every night until you do it. You can do this, and you will.'

True to his word, he was there, night after night, as he encouraged, cajoled and generally spurred me on through rain and snow. I ran in the cold and I ran in the dark; I ran every night as soon as he came in from work. My husband never once doubted me. Instead, he'd make me trudge over the deserted field. Sometimes he'd even take the kids to cheer me on.

I was breathless, sweating like a pig, with my heart almost leaping out of my chest and legs like jelly. I wanted to strangle Norman, who was the hardest personal trainer I'd ever met. But even though I was loath to admit it, he knew what he was doing. In the end, with his commitment and encouragement, and my sheer hard work, I did it, reaching level seven every time. I was elated, although it'd been total teamwork, with me and my fabulous family all pulling together.

Then it was on to police training school and despite juggling the commitments of family and a new job, by the end of October 1997 I was ready for my swearing-in ceremony. This was one of the proudest moments in my journey to become a police officer. After all the struggles and sacrifices of recent years, I was filled with amazement that I had reached this point.

I was able to invite one person to witness this occasion and, of course, as always Norman stood by my side and watched on, on what was actually my forty-second birthday. He had supported me every step of the way on my journey to this point and he shared this special moment with me too.

SURVIVORS

As I stood in front of all these senior police dignitaries and the police chaplain in my shiny shoes polished to within an inch of their life, wearing my smart police uniform with short hair (*and* make-up!), I repeated my Oath of Attestation – the one you've read at the front of this book. They are the most important words a police officer will ever say and I believed without a shred of doubt that that was what I was being paid to do – to uphold the law and protect the public.

Chapter Three

Destination Moss Side

> ❝ Do not judge me by my successes, judge me by how many times I fell down and got back up ❞
> — Nelson Mandela

A week after my swearing-in ceremony I transferred to Bruche, a national training college for police officers from all over the north of England. It was a whole new world with legal studies, public order training, long runs on Friday mornings, physical fitness, traffic directing, life-saving and role plays. The list of new challenges was endless, but I loved every minute even though it was the hardest thing I had ever done in my life. Just like everyone else, I had my own room at the police training college, but at night I was the only one who'd dash home to see my husband and kids.

I was a square peg in a round hole, especially when it came to the weekly fitness runs. Pitched against a bunch of fit and mostly ex-military men, I always came last, but at least I ran. In my mind I truly believed that although I was

29

fit for my age, my life skills were the reason I was useful to the police, not my running.

By now, I'd swapped my 'ballet shoes' – as the sarge had put it – for a pair of sturdy Doc Martens, but I had to wear the same regulation boots as everyone else for riot training. They weren't just heavy, they rubbed my feet raw and gave me blisters as well as shin splints. My police overalls – a body suit of armour – with a heavy belt, boots and shield, were hard enough to move in, but then they made us run up a bloody hill! I couldn't run anyway, but I was close to a snail's pace, dressed in my riot gear.

Another lesson involved directing traffic, which I was also useless at. Under pressure from the watching sergeant, I soon got my left mixed up with my right. I cringed when I noticed him rolling his eyes. But it didn't matter how many times I messed up, deep down he knew it was all I wanted to do. In fact, the more I seemed to fail, the more determined I became to pick myself up, dust myself down and try harder.

When it came to the classes studying law, doing role plays and interacting with members of the public, I excelled. This was my strength and what I had joined the police to do. I wanted to deal with serious crime, rapes, domestic violence, murders, witness protection and working in the community, not public order, riot training, traffic or undersea diving. I knew I could do it and be good at it, as long as I could get through my probation.

With winter fast approaching, the roads iced over, which slowed me up even more in the mornings. I'd promised the sarge I'd be in class every day for 8.30am sharp, but more often than not, I wouldn't be able to find a parking space, so I'd abandon my car on double yellows in the car park or on the grass verge. Parking on double yellow lines at a police training school isn't to be recommended and I'd often return to find my car plastered with parking tickets. I was hauled in front of the training school inspector on more than one occasion for a good telling-off. It became such a regular occurrence that it was soon a bit of a standing joke. At the end of training we had a passing-out parade and celebration night. In recognition of my 'skill' of collecting parking tickets, I was awarded a unique certificate for being the 'Parking Ticket Queen'.

After a couple of months, the time came to be posted to our own division and put 'in company' with a tutor constable. We were sat in class as the Sergeant stood at the front with the all-important list that would determine our fate. I sat there holding my breath as I heard him read out the names of each of my mates and the division they would be posted to. I heard names like Sale, Altrincham, Didsbury, Chorlton and other lovely leafy areas where I had imagined I'd be posted. When he finally called out my name, my heart felt as though it would leap out of my chest. I was crossing all my fingers and toes at the same time, hoping for a good placement.

'You,' he said pointing straight at me, 'you're going to Moss Side.'

My mouth fell open; I was totally lost for words.

Back in the 1990s, Moss Side, an inner-city part of Manchester, was a no-go area – an area that thrived on an underground economy funded by drugs. It was one of the most deprived areas in the country, never mind Manchester. Moss Side was a place of riots, shootings, drug dealings and gangs such as the Gooch Close gang,

Doddington gang and the Pitt Bull Crew. It was a place run with guns by people who had an in-built mistrust and hatred of the police. A place you wouldn't want to be on your own during the day, never mind at night.

Moss Side? I had four kids, for Christ's sake!

But it was too late. I'd been posted to a place otherwise known as 'Gunchester' and I didn't have a clue what was about to hit me.

Moss Side was the place where I saw my first dead body. Thankfully, it was laid out on a mortuary slab at a post mortem and not in the street. As a serving police officer with only a few weeks' training, I wasn't allowed to do very much, only observe. However, Keith, my tutor, had decided it was time.

'Ready?' he asked, as he approached the door that led into the mortuary.

The door was hidden at the back of Manchester Royal Infirmary, an old Victorian building long past its sell-by date. In fact, it was so decrepit, it reminded me of nineteenth-century Whitechapel during the days of Jack the Ripper. It was eerie to say the least.

Back then, the body wasn't kept behind glass as is often the case today so, unfortunately, I had a bird's-eye view of the whole proceedings. It was my first post mortem, my first time in a mortuary, and my first time seeing an old man's naked dead body – I was a novice on all counts. I was terrified. I am a bit squeamish, I don't like blood and didn't know what to expect. I was the mum who couldn't even remove a splinter from Steve's finger without crying myself. But I knew I had to grit my teeth and get through it, or lose face in this very macho world I had just joined.

As soon as we entered the room, Keith opened up a container of Vicks VapoRub, dabbed some under his nostrils and urged me to do the same.

'What's it for?' I asked.

'The smell,' he replied, screwing the top back on tight.

The overwhelming stench of death was so strong it made me feel nauseous, so I did as he said although I tried not to breathe in too deeply. I thought I was doing well at keeping it all together until the pathologist began to cut into the body. That's when my legs turned to jelly and I had to grab the guard rail by the window to stop myself from keeling over. Along the edges of the room were a series of metal sluices and sinks, and collections of jars and exhibit bags, holding human body parts. Strangely, it reminded me of a butcher's shop, because when human organs such as a liver, kidneys or a brain are removed from a body they no longer look human.

This was my first brutal introduction to death. It felt gruesome to suddenly be behind the scenes and witness what happens to the body of someone who has died unexpectedly. Before I'd joined the police, I'd been a housewife, a stay-at-home mum and then a university student. Norman always had the interesting stories to tell, but now it was my turn. Soon, he couldn't wait for me to come through the door and say what I'd been up to that day.

'Well?' he asked later that night, 'how was your day?'

So, I told him the lot.

Norman glanced at the sandwich he'd been eating, put it down and pushed his plate to one side.

I was always frank with him, but the further into my training I got, the more problems I began to experience at home. Suddenly, and quite unexpectedly, our marriage became a little shaky. Neither of us had anticipated just how intense and draining my police training would be. Even though he was still working as a self-employed joiner, Norman and I had effectively switched roles. Now it was up to him to sort out the kids when I wasn't back from a shift. Sometimes I'd be totally worn out after working seven nights, so getting the shopping in wasn't as high on my priority list as before. By the time I arrived home at 8am and I'd taken the kids to school, slept a few hours during the school day and picked them up at 3.30pm before making tea, I was totally knackered. Then I'd have to help the kids with their homework and put them to bed before returning to work for another ten-hour shift.

Once the novelty of his wife becoming a police officer had worn off, Norman became less interested in doing the mundane jobs I'd been doing for years. He was supportive in that he never once asked me to give up my new career, but neither did he want it to change his own routine.

'You've got to share the responsibility with me,' I told him in no uncertain terms.

By now, I was exhausted and close to breaking point. I'd always been a good mother, but now I was a police officer and I had to deal with all the demands that went with that. Something had to give. It was time for him to step up to the mark. But he wasn't lazy, far from it: he was happy with the old ways and too laid-back for his own good. Initially, he dug his heels in and that led to a stand-off. Inside, I was burning with resentment because Norman had carried on with his head buried in the sand.

In spite of the difficult times, we still loved each other and life apart was just something neither of us could ever imagine, even when the chips were down. We sulked, argued, stood our ground and fought like cat and dog, but eventually worked through it and Norman reluctantly conceded defeat. He agreed, among other things, to take on the weekly shop. However, he had a secret ally in the form of our beautiful, capable and very determined ten-year-old daughter, Vicki, who had her father wrapped around her little finger. From the age of five, she had been the main lunchbox maker and, each night, she'd turn out amazing packed lunches for six.

Once the kids were in bed each night, I'd sit down to study law for my upcoming exams. The training was intense and the workload relentless. To make matters worse, I felt as though my line manager had it in for me, but I was fearful of voicing my concerns and being accused of being unsuitable for the role of police officer. I knew I was a woman in a predominantly male environment, but I also knew he had me down as some middle-aged do-gooder, which I certainly was not. I also felt he was a misogynist, which really bothered me. I even questioned if I was out of my depth and wondered if I should just walk away. I was an intelligent, capable and hardworking person, but I began to witness an organisation that was stuck in the Dark Ages – a place where discrimination, bullying and antiquated beliefs were able to flourish, virtually unchallenged. Yet I knew if I could survive Moss Side, I could survive anything. Each of the five groups there had its own inspector and each trainee had been assigned a tutor constable and a sergeant, who were meant to help, encourage and generally guide them. Unfortunately, my sergeant turned out to be someone with a point to prove. To make matters worse, the acting inspector was his best mate.

During my initial period in company I'd trained with Keith, a tutor constable. A hard taskmaster in many ways, he had always been fair and did his best to give me a good grounding. However, by the time I'd reached the end of the first few weeks, I was told my next tutor constable would be a guy called Geoff. As soon as Keith said his name a snigger went round the rest of the group. I didn't understand why, but it soon became clear.

We were driving through the barriers the next day when a car approached from the opposite direction. Keith stopped and wound down the window. By way of introduction he said: 'Geoff, this is Maggie. You're going to be her tutor when she next comes back from Bruche.'

I peered past Keith and smiled at the other guy.

'Hi, Geoff, pleased to meet you.'

He looked me up and down with what could only be described as complete disdain and then he spoke.

'Nothing personal, sweetheart, but I'm fucking not!'

To say I was shocked would be an understatement. I felt my new career and faltering confidence plummet like a stone.

It turned out Geoff was ex-military with a reputation for being a bit gung-ho. I'd also been told by officers that the powers that be felt he wasn't very strong at doing paperwork. As a last resort, a decision had been made: he would be tasked with tutoring a probationer and focusing on paperwork rather than running around after burglars. It felt unfair because the last thing I needed was to be saddled with someone who wasn't trained in that particular role or someone already identified as in need of development himself.

I never blamed Geoff for this, though. In fact, we got on really well, but he just wasn't suited to being a tutor. In my opinion, the blame lay firmly at the door of the sergeant. He was my line manager and I felt he'd forced Geoff into a corner. I also secretly believed he wanted me to fall flat on my face and be kicked out of the service.

One evening, I was sent to an incident in Manchester. A businessman had been involved in a fracas with a bunch of drunken students. He had been enjoying a meal out with his girlfriend when the students became obnoxious. The man had repeatedly asked them to tone it down but, instead, they became louder. He approached them and lashed out, clipping one of the lads round the back of the head. Unfortunately, the student's head lurched forward, hitting his coffee cup and chipping his tooth. As the man left, another student took down his car registration and called the police.

My opinion was there was no need to put the businessman in the back of a Black Maria. I'd make an appointment for him to attend the police station, interview him and go from there, so that's what I did. The guy was reasonable, he had never been in trouble with the police in his life and regretted what had happened. I decided the best way forward would be to interview him under caution, by appointment – all perfectly lawful and reasonable, given the circumstances. However, the sergeant saw things differently. Before the man had even arrived at the police station, he insisted that

I put him in the back of the police van and transport him to the custody office, over at Platt Lane station.

'But he's willing to just come in,' I explained.

It didn't matter – the sergeant seemed determined to force me to do something I felt was completely unnecessary, just to prove a point. Of course, the real loser was the businessman, who was mortified when I put him in the back of the van. I felt bad for him and I told him so. He later admitted to a Section 39 assault (a minor assault that can be just a bruise), which was his first ever offence, so he was given a caution. But I was raging: he accepted he'd done wrong and while I couldn't condone his actions, there had been a certain level of provocation. I also felt we'd alienated a decent guy when common sense should have prevailed.

Geoff made it clear he wasn't a tutor and would regularly disappear to chase round the streets on more exciting jobs than sitting with me and filling in paperwork. Consequently, my confidence reached rock bottom. One day, I got a call to go to the local supermarket following a report of shoplifting. I was 'out of company', which meant I went on my own and not with a tutor. I walked to the manager's office at the back of the store, then opened the door to find four tear-stained eleven-year-old boys waiting for me.

'What did they take?' I asked, looking along the line of guilty little faces.

The security guard turned around solemnly.

'A sausage roll – but they ate it as they walked around the store.'

I tried not to laugh. It was hardly the crime of the century, but I knew if I arrested them it would mean we needed four 'appropriate adults' to chaperone the boys.

I'd also require four police vans and eight officers, because they'd all have to be transported separately. On top of this I'd need custody office staff and potentially four solicitors. I did a quick calculation in my head – it would cost thousands of pounds of taxpayer's money, all for the price of a 30p sausage roll.

Common sense told me the best thing to do would be to call their mums, explain what they'd done, get them to pay for the 'stolen' goods and send them home for a good telling-off. So that's what I did. But the incident had been recorded and been given a FWIN (Force Wide Incident Number), so when the acting inspector saw how I'd dealt with this job, he wasn't happy. Neither was the chief inspector, who tore a strip off me and threatened me with dismissal.

In spite of protocol, there were plenty of good officers who had devoted their whole lives to carrying out their duty, trying to make a difference while juggling home life, responsibility, pressure and danger. One of the most respected bobbies on my sub division was 'Bob the Dog', a real character and a complete nutcase. Back then, every group had its own dog handler and Bob was ours. He was a real tonic – the life and soul of the group – who was only too ready to have a laugh and a joke in a bid to brighten everyone's day.

One day, Bob walked into a briefing room of around twenty officers, wearing full leather chaps and a Stetson. He was in full YMCA cowboy mode.

'YMCA...' he sang, doing all the moves as everyone fell about laughing. Even some of the miserable buggers had a chuckle.

Bob was totally hilarious and always ready for a laugh,

especially when the chips were down. Not long afterwards, he found himself trapped alone in the heart of the Curry Mile – a mile-long strip of south Manchester that is home to many of the city's Indian restaurants and takeaways. He was caught in the middle of an angry mob, shouting for urgent assistance.

Visions of PC Keith Blakelock and his brutal murder during the 1985 Broadwater Farm riots in Tottenham, North London, ran through my head. Needless to say, every officer, including me, broke the speed limit that night to go to Bob's assistance. That's how much he was loved and respected. Yet after almost eighteen months, I was still wondering whether being a police officer was actually the right job for me. I was starting to seriously consider my future when something happened that knocked me sideways.

Norman and I had just returned with the kids from our annual holiday at Eurocamp in Spain. By now, Vicki was eleven years old and due to start at Altrincham Girls Grammar School so I'd booked her in for a routine eye test. The optician checked one eye and then the other again and again. A knot formed in the pit of my stomach: something wasn't right. I glanced at the clock on the wall – we'd been in the room ages.

The optician pulled himself away from the machine and looked directly at me.

'I'm not certain, but something is not quite right. I'd like you to take your daughter to the eye hospital today.'

My stomach constricted with fear. It was Saturday morning. Opticians didn't usually tell you to go straight to hospital on a Saturday morning, particularly not on a Bank Holiday weekend. It was still early morning, but I was due to work an afternoon shift that day, starting at 3pm. I rang Norman to ask him to meet me at the hospital and then I called in work to explain the situation. I'd not had a single day off throughout all my training, but this was an emergency.

'I'm not sure how to deal with this,' I told the sergeant on the other end of the line.

'It's fine, just go and sort it out. We'll see you when we see you, but don't worry.'

I thanked him and set off for the hospital. Vicki was examined straight away by a consultant, who explained that our daughter had a detached retina which could lead to blindness in that eye. It was a crisis and it had only been by pure chance that I'd booked a routine eye examination, something that hopefully might have just saved her sight.

'We need to operate in the morning, so she'll have nothing to eat after midnight tonight,' the consultant explained. 'There are the beginnings of a detached retina in the other eye, too. It's extremely serious. If we don't operate then I'm afraid your daughter could go blind.'

The hours that followed were some of the worst and longest of my life. Vicki underwent emergency surgery the following morning. Thankfully, it was a success.

Heavily bandaged and a little groggy, we brought Vicki home to recover the next day. She was a brave and tough little thing, so she didn't complain once. Throughout that nightmare few days, I'd kept my supervisor fully informed of what was happening. I'd missed four shifts when I unexpectedly received a call from my sergeant.

'Me and the inspector are coming to see you,' he announced.

I knew him well and I knew this wasn't a social call. Shortly afterwards, I heard a knock at the door. I opened it to find both men standing on my doorstep.

Vicki was lying on the sofa, her head heavily bandaged. It was plain for anyone to see that she'd just had major surgery. I knew full well they'd come to check up on me and catch me out. They both sat down on the sofa opposite me. I felt as though I was on trial. My sergeant glared at me as I spoke.

'But I rang in,' I tried to explain. 'I've been in daily touch with the station...'

He put a hand up to stop me mid-sentence. 'It's not your place to tell us you're not coming in. You *ask*, you don't *tell* us.'

I shook my head in total disbelief, but he wasn't finished.

'Anyway, why are you at home? Your husband should be at home, not you.'

I opened my mouth to protest, but no words came. I was on the verge of tears. I also knew what this meant. The message was loud and clear: they could get rid of me any time before the end of my probation and this could be another nail in the coffin of my career.

Later that week, I returned to work and on my first day back I was given an appraisal. A week later, I was given a copy of it, which I read in complete shock. Instead of the four-month period it covered, the whole document had been based on the day I'd returned to work following Vicki's operation. My stomach was knotted and I was blinded by my own tears because it seemed totally unfair. It also felt like the last straw – my sergeant had finally broken me, he'd won. I couldn't handle the constant chipping away at my confidence, I was crumbling before my own eyes.

During all this, Norman was totally supportive of me. He just wanted me to be happy and enjoy my job. Whatever I chose to do he was next to me, and told me not to worry about the finances. We would manage as we always had.

I had a few days off before I started my next shift, but instead of relaxing, I spent the next five days sitting at my computer, writing my response to my 'unfair appraisal'. In it, I mentioned the businessman I'd been forced to put in the back of the van. I explained I'd been made to feel worthless and that I hadn't been assigned a trained tutor constable. I knew I was effectively signing my own death warrant.

Ever since I was a little girl I'd hated to see anyone bullied and I'd always jumped to their defence. Now, for perhaps the first time in my life, I felt I'd been bullied. Deep down, I'd known for months what was going on, but I felt unable to stand up for myself. Now, though, I'd found the strength to fight my own corner. Though I was ready to walk away from my new career, I was determined my swansong would be to expose what had happened so that no one else would have to suffer. The following day, I felt all churned up inside as I walked into work. After the morning's briefing, I stopped my sergeant.

'Can I have a word in private?'

He seemed surprised, even though he must have known I wouldn't take his criticism of me lightly.

'I don't feel I've been treated fairly or equally by you since the day I arrived in Moss Side,' I said as I handed over my written response.

As he began to read it, the colour drained from his face.

I could tell he was shocked that I'd dared to challenge him. He also realised it was now official and not just a verbal conversation between a supervisor and a powerless probationer. After a moment, he managed to compose himself.

'I'll have to pass this to the inspector,' he insisted.

My stomach dropped to the floor because I knew they were best mates – I didn't stand a chance. The sergeant stood up and left the room, gripping my report in his hand. Around thirty minutes later, the acting inspector walked into the room. He could barely contain his anger towards me.

'What's all this about?' he said, waving the piece of paper in front of me. 'You do know that you've just made the biggest mistake you can make in this job by putting pen to paper?'

'I wish that hadn't been necessary,' I said, looking him square in the eye. 'But my appraisal has been put down on paper and I feel I have to respond to the points you made in it.'

The inspector told me they were grounds for a grievance and, as such, he could send my complaint through as an official matter. I told him that wasn't what I wanted, but I did want it dealt with. He said the matter would be referred to the superintendent. I knew then it was serious – the super never usually got involved, but he also knew of me and he knew I wasn't a troublemaker.

Later that same day, I got a call to say the super wanted to see me. As I climbed the stairs to his office on the top floor, I clenched my hands into nervous fists. The super's response shocked me to the core: he couldn't have been more supportive. I have nothing but good words to say about Superintendent Andy Holt, who not only supported me on that occasion, but later helped me on my journey into Serious Crime by entrusting me with my first Witness Protection job.

'You've done nothing wrong,' he insisted.

The anxious breath I'd been holding inside my lungs came rushing out as a sigh of relief.

'Now,' he asked, 'how would you like this to be progressed?'

I explained I didn't want any trouble, I just wanted to be treated fairly like everyone else.

The following week, I returned to his office. As soon as I walked in, I noticed my sergeant and line manager. He was sitting there like a naughty schoolboy inside the headmaster's office. The super began by explaining my job wasn't under threat in any way. He went on to say my sergeant would no longer be my line manager and that he had assigned someone else with immediate effect – a newly promoted sergeant called Steve Bailey, who was a great guy. I felt like punching the air because I felt vindicated. But that wasn't all.

'As an indication of how much we value you, I'm going to allow you to go into the Child Protection Unit for two weeks,' the Super went on. 'This will give you a glimpse of the posts open to you once you reach the end of your probation.'

This was totally unheard-of during probation, but an inspired move by the superintendent. Without his support and encouragement, I would have walked away from Greater Manchester Police that day, but now, for the first time in ages, I felt I had a future there.

Chapter Four

Working on the Front Line

> ❝ The hardest challenge
> is to be yourself in a
> world where everyone
> is trying to make you be
> somebody else ❞
> — e e Cummings

Just before I started in Child Protection, I was in the van with another lad – a young copper called Colin – when a job come through over the radio, a suspicious death. We listened as the radio operator explained that a concerned neighbour had rung in to say she was worried about an old lady who lived next door and asked if we could go and check it out.

'C7324 en route,' I responded, using my collar number, as Colin put his foot down and we drove over to the woman's address.

As soon as we'd pulled up outside the house I knew something was amiss. There were countless milk bottles lined up outside the door. It was obvious no one had opened the post in days either, because letters were hanging out of the letterbox.

'Right,' I said, climbing down from the van, 'let's go and see if we can get an answer...'

The words had barely left my mouth when another call came over the radio. Colin was a lovely lad, but he also had a reputation for being a bit of a wimp. The van door slammed loudly as it closed abruptly behind me. I stood there in shock as the van sped off into the distance, taking my colleague with it. He'd buggered off sharpish and now I was all on my own. I was dressed in uniform, so, to the outside world, I looked every inch the well-seasoned, calm and professional police officer. But I'd never attended a suspicious death before, only a post mortem, and that had been bad enough. The bottles of curdled milk and reams of unopened letters told me I probably wasn't going to find the little old lady sitting there alive and well and sipping a cup of tea.

I took a moment to compose myself. The house looked deserted as I approached. Suddenly, the concerned neighbour appeared at my side. She held out her hand and a key to the old lady's property, which meant I didn't have to put the door in.

'This is Mrs Cooper's key,' she said, handing it to me. 'I was too frightened to go in because no one's seen her for a few days. I was scared what I'd find.'

'Right,' I replied, trying to take control, even though my legs had turned to jelly.

I unlocked the door, pushed it slightly ajar and edged inside.

'Hello,' I called out into the darkness.

It was pitch-black inside as my eyes strained, trying to make out shapes and doorways.

'Hello, it's the police…' I said again, as I inched my way along the darkened hallway. My hands were shaking and I purposely took tiny steps so that I didn't inadvertently trip up over a dead body on the floor. I located a light switch but didn't turn it on; I was certain the old lady was dead and therefore her house was now a potential crime scene. Everything was still and quiet. It was *too* quiet, there was no sign of life.

'Hello?' I called, hoping she would answer. But all I could hear was blood pulsing around my head and inside my ears.

There was a closed door that I guessed led into the front room. I nudged it open with my arm, careful not to touch the handle. As soon as it swung open the light burned against my eyes and a searing heat scorched my face. The room was roasting with the gas fire turned on full. Lying in front of it on a little brown rug was the old lady. She was dead, possibly as a result of a heart attack. However, because she'd fallen directly in front of the fire, her skin had started to melt. A pungent smell overwhelmed me and I clasped a hand against my mouth to stop myself from throwing up. I wanted to turn off the fire, but protocol meant I couldn't touch a thing. I radioed in for supervision and Scenes of Crime Officers (SOCO) to attend. Then I turned and left. As I stepped outside, I took a huge gulp of fresh air. When I opened my eyes, I saw the neighbour standing there, waiting for news.

'Is Mrs Cooper alright?' she said, trying to push past. 'It's just I haven't seen her for days…'

I put my arm out to stop her.

'I'm sorry, you can't go in there. I'm sorry to have to

tell you this, but it appears your neighbour has died.' At this the neighbour began to cry, dabbing at her eyes with a hankie.

I remained there, guarding the front door, until back-up arrived. The whole house had to be sealed off so Forensics could carry out their work. Thankfully, the pensioner had died from natural causes. A subsequent post mortem examination estimated she'd been lying there for at least two days. That haunting image stayed with me long after the event had passed, but it wasn't the first and it wouldn't be the last thing to shake me to my core. The job, I was slowly starting to discover, was full of surprises and no two days were ever the same.

Although I was furious with Colin, I knew that he wasn't a bad lad. In fact, he didn't have a nasty bone in his body – he was just one of life's panickers. That day, he'd not only panicked but had buggered off, leaving me all on my own. I didn't report him; instead I tackled him myself. I was never the type of officer to make a complaint. If I was unhappy with something or someone I would deal with it myself, face-to-face.

Back at the station, some of the other lads grew tired of his flakiness and decided to get their own back with a massive wind-up. One day, Colin was called out to a job. Unbeknown to him, the lads had grabbed the spare key to the squad car he was driving. They followed him to the address, where they found the vehicle parked up outside. With Colin busy inside the house, they moved the squad car around the corner and sprinkled broken glass on the road where it had been and then they waited. When Colin came out, he saw the squad car was missing, spotted the glass and went into a blind panic. Everyone was in on the joke, even the inspector, when Colin rang in sheepishly to say his car had been stolen and could he get a lift back to the station. By the time he'd finished his shift later that night the poor lad was mortified, wondering what on earth would happen to him when he came back to work. The following evening, he was quiet as a church mouse when he arrived for his next shift.

'Car trouble?' A voice piped up from the back of the parade room as everyone fell about laughing.

Colin looked around, saw us all killing ourselves laughing and that's when the penny dropped.

He'd been well and truly stitched up.

'You fucking bastards!' he laughed, shaking his head.

He knew he'd been had and the look on his face was priceless, if not well deserved.

*

There was a lot of mickey-taking at the station and a great sense of camaraderie, which relieved the stress of the job. The lads and girls I worked with were brilliant, but sometimes I felt like a mum looking after a bunch of naughty schoolchildren. I was organised and very good with paperwork – I didn't leave a stone unturned. As a result, I started to deal with a lot of what we called the 'Missing from Homes' (MFH) – both kids and adults who'd gone missing. No one else wanted these jobs because they were time-consuming, but I loved helping other people. In fact, I became so good at dealing with these cases that following the death of a young man who had been reported missing, I was asked to work closely with an inspector for a couple of months and review all our procedures. Officers had failed to follow protocols and so hadn't forced an entry into his home, which may have saved his life. I therefore visited the Missing Person's Helpline in London, where I spent two days and the suggestions and advice I brought back with me were incorporated into our revised Missing from Home (MFH) forms that we redesigned.

I started to feel as though I was really beginning to make a difference – the reason I'd joined the police.

*

The nature of our shift patterns meant you'd get partnered up with a different colleague each set of shifts. Not long afterwards, I was 'partnered' with Pete, an ex-military lad and a great copper. In the good old days there was a canteen and billiards room at Moss Side station – unfortunately, now long gone. However, if you were on late shift, the canteen would be shut. Instead, you'd have to go out and buy your own food. It had been a reasonably quiet evening, so Pete and I drove to a local garage to pick up a sandwich. We walked in and I was just thinking what to have when I spotted a guy paying for petrol. I can't explain it, but there was something not right about him. In fact, every fibre in my being told me he was definitely 'dodgy'.

The security guard nodded as we passed, but as soon as he'd clocked us, the man at the counter seemed uneasy and kept looking over his shoulder. He'd just started to walk away when the cashier held up his bank card.

'Your card's not working, mate,' he called after him, but the man started to run towards the door we'd just come through.

The security guard turned and gave chase, but the man picked up a bin and threw it at him. Pete and I legged it outside, but the lad climbed into his car and started up the engine. However, Pete was fast: he ran over and tried to grapple the keys out of the ignition through a half-opened window. The engine roared as the thief slammed on the accelerator, dragging Pete with him. I winced as the car swerved, throwing Pete to the floor, narrowly missing his leg by millimetres. Clutching my walkie-talkie, I radioed in. Thankfully, that particular area of Manchester is covered by University Security Services, so it's blanketed with CCTV cameras.

The man escaped, but I knew he'd be caught, and he was. The car was later found abandoned, but Forensics managed to get some partial DNA from a baseball hat found underneath the dashboard. Both Pete and I were called to give statements and the incident was crimed as an assault. By 'crimed', I mean that it was officially recorded, and a crime report submitted onto the system containing all the details. Of course, the bank card turned out to be stolen, but we got a match on the DNA. I was called up to an identity parade, where I picked him out straight away.

The man was arrested and later pleaded guilty to burglary, assault and obtaining property by deception – a triple whammy. We'd had a result, even though I never got my sandwich. Although delighted the lad had been caught, I knew without doubt this type of policing wasn't what I'd joined the force to do. Instead, my skills lay in a completely different area – talking and working with people. I wanted to do more missing persons' work and deal with children, which happened sooner than I'd thought.

I was sent to a report of a child missing from home. By now, I was routinely given most of these jobs. When I arrived, the mum – a working prostitute – was utterly distraught. She'd left her baby girl with a 'friend' – another prostitute – while she'd gone out to work. She'd returned to find both the friend and child missing, so she'd called the police in a panic. Her daughter was only two-and-a-half years old, with curly blonde hair and the face of an angel. I knocked on all the doors in the block until I found the child sitting in a basement flat, along with the caretaker. As soon as he unbolted the door, the hairs on the back of my neck stood up. My maternal instincts told me there was something not right about him or the situation. I took the child and gave her back to her mother, who was beyond relieved. As soon as I returned to the station I ran a check on the man with Scotland Yard (back then, it was the only way you could check on someone because the Sex Offenders' Register didn't exist). Sure enough, my instincts had been bang-on: the man was a convicted sex offender.

'Never leave your child with that man,' I made the mother promise me.

I couldn't tell her why, but I needed her to understand that he presented a real danger. Then I submitted a full report to social services, who advised her. Thankfully, Child Protection overrode the need to conceal his previous conviction.

I always tried to avoid a situation where a child would be taken into care. There was one young boy in particular whose story haunts me to this day. His name was David and he'd been placed inside children's homes at just eleven years old. It left him to mix with teenagers much older than him and, because he was extremely vulnerable with no family, he welcomed their friendship. Care workers in these children's homes knew what was happening, but if any of their children went missing, they'd simply report it to the police. Their attitude was they had fulfilled their obligations. This caused a lot of bad feeling with the police as the general view was no one was missing from home, they were out on the streets because they wanted to be. We'd spend hours searching for the children and, more often than not, find them in Piccadilly Gardens, in Manchester, where they were being abused. This is in the centre of Manchester and was (and still is) a notorious place. It was regularly patrolled by police, who dealt with many sad people struggling with life in general, including homeless men and women, prostitutes and vulnerable children, all of whom seemed to be drawn to this place, a fact that is still true today.

We'd return them to the home only for the whole process to be repeated the following weekend. In short, children were not being protected. I found it scandalous; however, I was still relatively inexperienced, so powerless to do anything other than submit reports and express my concerns.

For years, David had been passed around the system, slowly becoming more and more damaged. We all knew he should have been in secure accommodation, but that was seen as 'too expensive'. Often I'd sit down and talk to him before writing a report, asking for him to be moved. He was tiny and looked much younger than eleven. Yet he had a cheeky smile, and I just wanted to hug him and take him home with me. The poor kid was a tragedy in waiting. I could never understand why he had been placed with older teenagers who were pulling him into a life of crime and abuse because that was all they knew. The authorities may as well have signed his death warrant, he was vulnerable from the word go

A few years later, David was found dead from a drug overdose. Just sixteen years old, he had been a tragedy waiting to happen. Tragically, his wasn't an isolated case. It was a scandal that he and other children had been denied proper care just to save money and a real eye-opener for me.

One day, we received a report of an attempted abduction. A young lad of nine, living on the Hulme estate, was leaving home to go to the shop when a van had pulled up alongside. The driver offered to give the boy a lift but, thankfully, he had more sense. He'd bolted home and told his mum, who'd called the police. When the call came in, I was in the area so I drove around looking for the van. I was stuck in traffic when I spotted a vehicle matching the description ahead of me. It was the same colour and make, and the vague description of the man also seemed to match the driver. I watched as the van suddenly pulled a sharp left. The driver was acting odd, as though trying to hide his vehicle. I followed and found him in an enclosed residential car park nearby, so I parked up and approached.

The man told me he was a council worker – a plumber – but again, there was something about him that set my teeth on edge. I took his details and rang them through for a PNC (Police National Computer) check. But he wasn't wanted so I had to let him go. Then I went to interview the child, whose description matched the strange man. Back then, before the Sex Offenders' Register existed, some crimes were recorded on a stand-alone system with Scotland Yard, so I couldn't cross-reference easily for more information. However, as soon as I carried out some deeper checks my instincts were proven right yet again: the man had previous offences for child abuse, yet somehow he'd landed a job with Manchester City Council, going in and out of tenants' homes largely unchecked.

I contacted the council and that's when I discovered there'd already been questions asked about his behaviour. When I dug a little deeper, it became clear he'd lied on his original application and hadn't revealed previous convictions for sexual offences. I pressed on and on, and eventually, he was sacked – I couldn't just walk away and leave it or him because I knew he was a potential risk to children in their own homes, a place that should be their sanctuary. I was given a commendation for my work, but I didn't care about the award or recognition – I just wanted to protect children from predatory paedophiles.

As soon as I was out of my probation, I applied for, and was granted, a three-month attachment to the Child Protection Unit (CPU). Unlike the rest of the police force, CPU was mainly staffed by women police officers. Like me, most of them had children, so the job suited them perfectly because the hours were mainly Monday to Friday, nine-to-five. I'd already served two and a half years as a police officer and I was a mum of four, so, to me, there was very little that was more important than child protection. As an officer, you can not only make a difference, I firmly believe you can change young lives for the better. I went into CPU at the beginning of 2000.

One of my first jobs was to investigate reports from a

thirteen-year-old girl, who'd accused her step-father of sexually abusing her. She'd told her mother he'd tried to humiliate her by forcing her to wash his feet, that he'd touched her sexually, and she also claimed he'd physically abused her too. Mum and the step-father had broken up, so by the time the case reached court, the step-father's defence barrister claimed the child had been primed by her mother to lodge allegations against his client. The jury chose to believe him and he was acquitted. After the case, I felt gutted. It was, and remains, the only case in my entire career where the defendant was acquitted. Although I felt devastated for the poor girl and her mother, I didn't have time to dwell on it because another job came through almost immediately afterwards.

A mother had called in to report the suspected abuse of her five-year-old daughter, Chloe, by a cousin, who at that time was twelve years old. The case was complex because the boy, Joshua, had learning difficulties. Things were further complicated by the powers that be, who deemed the little girl was too young to be believed or interviewed. I understood the mother's frustration because I was a mother as well as a police officer, so I refused to accept we should just 'leave it' when there was a possible risk to both her and other children.

'I can't believe a five-year-old could, or would, make something like this up,' I insisted.

Eventually, and through my persistence, the detective sergeant running the CPU backed down and I was allowed to conduct an interview. However, first, I took the child to St Mary's Sexual Health Centre, where she was spoken to by a doctor and then examined – although not intrusively.

I set up the interview the following day. I was already an advanced 'Achieving Best Evidence Interviewer' so I asked the mum if she would bring Chloe in. As Mum could become a potential witness, she wasn't allowed to listen to her daughter's interview. Instead, I asked for an 'Appropriate Adult' to chaperone the child.

The room was set out like a living room at home, with sofas, a coffee table, curtains and pictures on the wall to make children feel at ease. Microphones and video equipment were set up discreetly to capture everything evidentially. I sat down on the floor with Chloe, a notepad and paper, and then handed her a drink, some paper and different coloured crayons so she could draw. I began by asking her a few gentle questions.

'What did you do today, Chloe?'

'I went out with Mummy,' she said, glancing up at me briefly before starting to draw some pretty flowers.

'Do you go to school?' I asked, trying to establish if she knew the difference between truth and lies.

She nodded her head.

Slowly, I began to build a rapport. Once she seemed comfortable, I moved on to more in-depth questions.

'Why have you come in to speak to me today?' I asked her.

Chloe stopped drawing her flowers and paused for a moment. Although she answered, she didn't look up at me.

'To talk about Joshua,' she said quietly.

'Is your cousin called Joshua?'

Chloe looked up briefly and nodded before returning to her drawing.

I purposely kept my questions light and open because I wasn't allowed to use any leading questions.

'Where were you when you last saw Joshua?' I said. 'Can you draw me a picture?'

I watched as she used the crayon in her hand and began to sketch out a new picture. This time it was a room. In it, she sketched herself and a boy.

'Who was in the room with you and Joshua?'

'Only us,' she said.

'Can you describe your picture to me? What did you do?'

Chloe looked up at me with innocent wide eyes.

'Joshua put his peeny weeny in my tum tum,' she said, pointing at herself in the drawing.

Chloe didn't have to say anything else, it was clear what he'd done to her. I was devastated that a child so young was having to deal with this, but spoke to her as gently as I could because I didn't want to frighten her. My attitude was that we needed her to tell us what had happened so I could take it further and protect other children and the boy himself. It was never about a prosecution for me, but about enabling her to feel safe to talk about what happened.

Afterwards, I started to make inquiries into Joshua. It transpired that he'd previously suffered brain damage to his left frontal lobe. As a result, it meant he had absolutely no inhibitions. Joshua's doctors also believed his mental age didn't match his chronological age, which meant we had a problem because the criminal age of consent was ten years old. However, I didn't want to leave it there because I felt he presented a danger to other young children too. He also needed professional help himself. I called a meeting with Social Services and then I met with his headteacher.

'We're so glad you're here,' the headteacher said as soon as I sat down and explained the nature of my visit. 'We've been banging on the doors of Social Services for two years about this child.'

I was stunned. It seemed this hadn't been an isolated incident, although police had no record of any incidents. According to the headmaster, he'd received complaints from five other girls, who had said Joshua had touched them 'inappropriately'. Armed with this information, I called him in for an interview. However, instead I was duly handed a prepared statement from his solicitor. In the end, we were unable to take legal action; however, Joshua was moved to a special unit with appropriate support as much for his welfare as it was for other children. It had been a good outcome given the difficult circumstances, but I also realised my hands would always be tied by whoever was in charge – usually Social Services. In this case, the family's social worker held all the cards and all she would say was she was 'working with the family', so it was frustrating to say the least.

Also frustrating was the growing realisation about gaps between different police departments. The Child Protection Unit (CPU) only dealt with abuse, neglect or sexual abuse by a parent, carer, professional or family member – in other words, an offender who had 'care, custody or control' of their victim. Such cases would be dealt with in a joint investigation by police and social services. Often I felt frustrated because social workers would always say they were 'working with the family', in which case the police had no further involvement. I found it hard to accept because I couldn't just walk away if I knew in my heart that a child was being abused. However, if something was classed as a 'stranger' rape, it would then be investigated by the CID

(Criminal Investigation Department) because it would be classified as a 'serious crime'. Yet detectives didn't work with Social Services, so the knock-on effect of this meant officers were often not equipped to deal effectively with the abuse of children. CPU also had a stand-alone computer database that wasn't connected to CID or the Greater Manchester Police Opus system, either. In short, there was no crossover or sharing of vital information between the two systems unless someone had been charged. The gap between the departments soon became huge, but no one had thought to link the two together. This was evidenced by the case of the Soham murders and Ian Huntley in 2002. This man was the caretaker of the school attended by Holly Wells and Jessica Chapman, both aged ten. As they passed by his house one summer's afternoon, he lured them in and murdered them both. Huntley had been known to police previously, but the information had been recorded on CPU stand-alone systems only, which meant he was able to slip through the net when it came to CRB (Criminal Record Bureau) checks.

The significance of this became apparent again many years later in a way that would not only shock the nation to its core, but shame countless police forces who chose to ignore a major epidemic – the grooming and sexual exploitation of children.

Chapter Five

Changes

❝ It is only during a storm
that a tree knows how
strong it is ❞
— Dalai Lama

The Child Protection Unit (CPU) had felt like a whole new world to me and it was exactly what I'd always wanted to do. I attended regular meetings with sexual health workers, schools and Social Services and we worked together as a team to discuss and protect individual children. Social Services were primarily there to protect at-risk children and as police officers, we were there to prosecute the offenders and share information of risk with other agencies.

During my time in CPU, I met lots of social workers – some good, others not so good. This proved to be a source of growing frustration. As a mother and a police officer, I knew I couldn't just walk away if I felt a child was being abused, but in some cases I was unable to change things even with all the will in the world. Disillusioned, I left CPU and headed back to Moss Side. I'd only been out of my probation period a matter of months when I got a call to go back to the station and see the super. When he told me a Witness Protection job had come up that he wanted me to take on, I was absolutely thrilled. The super, who had supported me during those dark days of my probation, believed in me and I was determined not to let him down.

The job was to protect a mum, dad and five kids in a major gangland kidnap and murder case. A man had been bundled into a car boot and set on fire. A member of the public walking their dog had interrupted the attack and the offenders had run away, allowing the victim to escape. The victim was now the key witness to this crime and had to be protected. He was already in Witness Protection, but he came from a large Asian family and the other members of the same household were also deemed to be at risk. I was drafted in to move his brother, sister-in-law and their children to a safe house in a different area of the country. Once moved, they'd not only have to change their names and take on new identities, they'd also have to register their children at a new school and with a new doctor and dentist. It was a big ask, but I spoke with the family and got them on board. It was a massive responsibility for which I'd had no formal training, but I approached it as though I was moving home with my own family. Honoured by the trust and responsibility given to me, I was determined to do a good job.

I knew I loved working with people, especially families, so, on the strength of that job, I decided to apply to become a family liaison officer (FLO). It would mean I'd be working on the most serious of crimes with the best detectives, but I'd also be playing to my personal strengths.

I'd be an investigator, but also the primary link between the families of murder victims and the investigation. Being a FLO was the perfect role for me because my strengths were being able to talk, work and generally gain the trust of members of the public. I knew, without a shadow of a doubt, it was what I wanted to do from now on.

During my time there, I worked with many families. I was appointed FLO in the gangland shooting of Aeon Shirley, in Longsight, Manchester in April 2002. Both Moss Side and Longsight were rife with gang culture and it was difficult for lads such as Aeon not to get caught up in it. Aeon hadn't been a bad lad, he just happened to be caught in the wrong place at the wrong time and it cost him his life. I ended up guiding his family through a very difficult process in the aftermath of his murder, although no one was ever charged, which I believe remains the case to this day.

Not long afterwards, I was called in to work with the family of Moors Murders victim Lesley Ann Downey. Lesley's brother, Tommy West, and his eight-year-old daughter Kimberley had been killed in a house fire started by Caz Telfer – a woman who became obsessed with the 1960s crimes of Ian Brady and Myra Hindley. Telfer ended up serving eleven years of an eighteen-year prison sentence as a result of the blaze on New Year's Eve, 2001. Following her trial and subsequent conviction, and, along with a colleague, I managed to obtain a holiday to Disneyland for Tommy's wife and young son, who had survived the blaze that had killed his dad. It felt good to be able to make a difference in the lives of people who had already suffered so much and this was thanks to an amazing charity called

Child Victims of Crime, who I approached often and asked them to help children who had lived through sometimes the most horrific incidents.

*

I found myself dealing with serious crime on a daily basis. It was exciting, challenging and it kept me on my toes. I felt totally alive – and I knew I was making a difference. Again, life was heading in a whole new direction for me. Fired up by my new line of work and a growing sense of confidence, I started working towards exams to become a detective. I'd decided I wanted to be right in the thick of these types of investigations. Then, one afternoon, I was sitting inside the CID office in Moss Side when the phone next to me rang. Our eldest son Steve had been helping his dad out with a bit of labouring to supplement his student lifestyle, so when I heard his voice on the other end of the line, I wondered what he wanted.

'Mum,' said Steve urgently, 'Dad's had an accident.'

I felt my stomach lurch. They'd been working on a loft conversion, Steve explained, when a delivery had arrived and Norman had climbed down the scaffolding to accept it, leaving Steve and Neil, Norman's friend and fellow builder, working in the roof space with the radio blaring. Norman loaded his hod with bricks and began to climb back up the scaffold with the heavy load. However, as he reached the top, he let go of the scaffold to grab hold of the cat ladder, which led into the roof opening. As he did so, he somehow lost his grasp. With lightning reflexes, Norman threw the hod aside and launched himself onto the side roof, which was at an angle to the main roof. He knew he was in trouble, but hoped he could grip the gutters and try to hold on for dear life until help arrived. But he just couldn't hold on. The guttering broke and Norman plunged another twenty feet below, landing heavily on the hard ground. As he lay there, he knew he'd been seriously injured and had probably broken his spine, but the boys didn't hear his cries for help.

'We just didn't hear him, Mum, because the radio was too loud,' Steve explained to me in tears. 'It was the delivery man who eventually heard him. They're taking Dad to Macclesfield General, but they've strapped him to a body board. They say they can't tell yet what damage he's done.'

Without warning, my whole body began to shake. Then the tears came until soon I was sobbing uncontrollably; I just couldn't stop, I'd gone into complete shock. I thought about the possible consequences: that Norman might be paralysed. I'm not a religious person, but as I ran to my car parked outside, all I could do was repeat a prayer inside my head.

Please, God, please don't let Norman be paralysed. Please, God, please just let him be okay….

Prior to his accident, Norman and I had been going through another rough patch. The stress of work, home life, responsibilities and not enough hours in the day had slowly ground us down and had caused arguments and resentment between us. Suddenly, everything was put into perspective. All I cared about now was him. Nothing else mattered, not anymore. As I drove, I realised this was the wake-up call we both needed, not to take life for granted.

Arriving at A&E, I parked up and ran inside to find

Steve and Neil both waiting for me, ashen-faced. I hugged Steve tightly. Moments later, a nurse approached and took me into a side room, where I saw Norman strapped to a body board and in excruciating pain. The shock of seeing my husband in such a state made me burst into tears again.

I wanted to hug him properly, but I was frightened in case I did him any further damage. As I held his hand in mine, I looked into his eyes.

'What have the doctors said?' I asked.

He winced as he tried to speak.

'They don't know. I've not had my scans yet.'

My stomach somersaulted with fear, but I knew I must remain strong and find strength for us both. I had to spur him on and keep him positive, so that's exactly what I did. Sitting inside the hospital cubicle, I realised just how much this incredible man meant to me. Work, family and football had been his life. He'd always been so capable – a safe pair of hands – but now there was a strange vulnerability in his eyes and, for the first time in his life, he was scared.

'We'll get through this,' I insisted, wiping my tears away.

We seemed to wait for ages in that hospital room; every second felt like a minute and every minute an hour. I must have aged ten years waiting for the scan but, eventually, a nurse and a hospital porter came in to collect Norman.

'I love you,' I whispered, letting go of his hand.

After what seemed a lifetime, Norman was finally brought back up. Steve and I sat with him, waiting for a doctor to bring in the results. When he finally approached, I held my breath because I knew his words could change everything.

'Mr Oliver,' he began, 'I've had a look at your scans and

I'm pleased to tell you that you haven't broken your spine.'

The anxious breath I'd been holding inside came rushing out as overwhelming relief.

'You mean, he'll be able to walk again?' I asked.

The consultant nodded as I turned to Norman and smothered his face with relieved kisses. However, he still wasn't out of the woods and the serious injuries he'd sustained meant he'd have to take months off work. Not only had he punctured both lungs, Norman had managed to break all his ribs and his left arm had been shattered in the fall.

Our utter relief that he wouldn't be confined to a wheelchair was palpable. In fact, it was so intense that I burst into tears again, only this time they were tears of happiness. As I hugged him close, I also gave him a good telling-off.

'Don't you ever scare me like that again, Norman Oliver!' I scolded, my face breaking into a relieved smile.

'Got to shake things up a bit now and then,' he winced, trying to make a joke of it.

*

Norman remained in hospital for about three weeks. He was eventually discharged in February 2002, although he wasn't at all mobile and was still in a lot of pain. We'd already booked a holiday to Florida with the kids and my parents before the accident and were due to fly out less than two months later.

Norman was absolutely determined to be fit enough to fly and at our insistence, and because we were flying to America, the consultant agreed to do a scan. Unbeknown to us, the doctors decided they'd only scan him from the waist up rather than do a full body scan. We didn't know it then, but that fateful decision ultimately had far-reaching consequences. Instead, they told us everything was fine, so we looked forward to a holiday in the sun.

In April, we touched down in the Florida Keys, where we rented a house. Although he still wasn't back to his former fitness, Norman tried his best to make the most of the time away. After family and football, fishing was his other passion and as there was a private jetty at the back of the house, he was in his element. Still struggling to walk and unable to drive, he spent hours trying to catch one of the rumoured sharks that patrolled the surrounding waters, although none of us actually believed he'd ever catch one. A week into our holiday, Danny was out the back, helping his dad fish, when there was an almighty yell.

We all ran to the water's edge to find Danny jumping up and down in excitement as his dad tried to wrestle an enormous shark onto the riverbank. He'd only gone and bloody done it! He'd hooked a seven-foot shark, but was struggling to land it because of his injuries. None of us really knew what to do, but one of the neighbours, on hearing the commotion, jumped over the fence to help. Holding an enormous metal hook in his hand, he proceeded to pull the shark into the shore. The look on Norman's face was priceless as he held the shark up for the obligatory photo before we released it back into the river to fight another day.

All too soon the holiday was over. Back home, Norman continued to recuperate while I tried to sort out our finances. As he was self-employed and unable to work, we realised we were in a total mess as we had absolutely no insurance cover to help us through a situation like this. Norman's accident had been a wake-up call in more ways than one. We decided not only to put the house in my name, but also to take out a critical illness and a life insurance policy just in case, God forbid, something like this should ever happen again.

While Norman lay in hospital trying to recover, I'd returned to work but money was still extremely tight, living on just one wage, so by the end of May, he decided to return to work to ease the financial pressure.

'Don't worry,' he said, 'I'll not take on too much. I'll only do what I can.'

The fall had been a massive wake-up call in what had previously seemed an ordinary life. We both realised things could change in a split second and that changed us. Even though we'd already been away that year, we decided to put our financial worries to the back of our minds and take the kids to see our old stomping ground in Gran Canaria, where we'd once lived the hippy life. However, this time we decided to live for the moment, re-mortgage our family home and use the money to buy a holiday property in Gran Canaria.

One morning, I decided to go for a walk on my own. Not thinking about anything in particular, I suddenly spotted a huge 'for sale' sign at the side of an apartment. The place seemed deserted, but the property was in the exact location we'd been looking, so I decided to be cheeky and knock on the door. I was just about to walk away when the door was answered by a middle-aged Englishwoman.

'Excuse me, I'm sorry to bother you, but I just saw the

71

"for sale" sign and I wondered if I might be able to come in and have a look round?'

She was naturally suspicious but, using my powers of persuasion, I was eventually able to win her over and she invited me inside.

'I'm afraid it's a bit of a mess,' she apologised.

I waved a hand away as though it really didn't matter. However, as soon as I walked inside, I was shocked because the whole place was an absolute shithole. It also stank to high heaven! I was just starting to doubt myself when she led me outside.

'And this is the balcony...' she said, gesturing with an outstretched hand.

I was momentarily speechless. The apartment had been disgusting inside, but I knew that was just cosmetic and nothing Norman and I couldn't fix. However, the view from the balcony was something else – it was completely breathtaking. Later, I discovered the property had been languishing on the market for over six months. I hoped this would mean we'd get it for a good price.

'Can I bring my husband back? It's just I'd like his opinion,' I asked, trying to hide my excitement so she didn't hike the price up further.

As soon as he saw the place, Norman's eyes lit up and he fell in love with it too. As a builder, he knew the property had huge potential and, after the year we'd had, this felt like the beginning of an exciting new chapter in our lives, one we were determined to grab with both hands.

'I love it!' he whispered as we stood together on the balcony after the owner had gone back inside.

We agreed to buy it there and then and promised to go

back over in October to complete the sale. We were on cloud nine: the apartment was ours, life seemed good and we were excited about our future. Although Norman was still in some pain, we returned in October as promised to complete the purchase. We literally tore the place apart – knocking down walls and painting every square inch. We shopped for furniture, curtains and cushions, and worked around the clock to turn it into our dream home. We were excited and so were the kids, who were busy planning scuba diving lessons and deep-sea fishing trips.

Back at work the following week, I was busy trying to focus on my CID exams. I was working every hour God sent. We still had three kids at home and Steve at uni, but there never seemed to be enough hours in the day. The extra studying meant I never had a second to myself, so when Norman said he didn't feel well, I pushed it to the back of my mind, assuming it was natural because he was still recovering from his horrific accident. I was so busy that I left him to go to the doctor on his own.

Looking back, if there is one thing I feel guilty about to this day, it's those few weeks I took my eye off the ball. I just let him get on with it, but Norman was a man and men don't typically complain, even when things aren't right. Selfishly, I just wanted to move forward and look ahead, so I didn't tune in to what was happening – a regret I will carry with me to my grave. Norman went back to the GP, who told him he'd suffered a trauma so it was natural his injuries would take time to heal, but he never seemed to fully recover.

'What is it?' I asked again one night as he winced with pain.

'I just don't feel right... I'm not sure why, but I just don't.'

'Well, go back to the doctor again.'

The second time, the doctor told Norman he must be suffering from Irritable Bowel Syndrome and he should eat more fibre and pay more attention to his diet. Then he suggested a possible prostate problem, then a urinary problem, but it was all guesswork. We naively followed his advice to the letter, but nothing changed. Soon, I began to notice something else, too. Norman, my previously healthy husband – a young man of forty-six – would come home from a day's work and take himself upstairs to the toilet, where he'd remain for an hour or more. He'd come back downstairs, but rather than sit and watch TV, he'd lean on the back of the sofa for the rest of the night.

'Sit down,' I told him time and time again, but he always refused.

'No,' he said, shaking his head, 'it's too uncomfortable.'

Then Christmas was upon us and we had a big get-together to celebrate. It had always been a busy but happy time of year for us, but this year something was different: Norman seemed much quieter. Normally, he'd be at the centre of things and although not loud or a dancer, he was always sociable. But this year he seemed withdrawn and preoccupied, as though all the stuffing had been knocked clean from him.

Finally, after months of studying hard, the day of my CID exams arrived and off I went, Norman's words of encouragement ringing in my ears.

'Good luck, love. I know you can do it.'

'Thanks, I think I'll need it,' I chirped.

The nerves gnawed away at my insides. I knew that

if I didn't pass the exams then my dream of working in the Major Incident Team and the Serious Crime Division would be doomed. Although I felt scared, I knew my husband was always there in the background, driving me on and willing me to succeed. That morning, I sat down in the big hall surrounded by other prospective detectives to answer questions about all sorts of different laws, legislation, acts and rules. I left not knowing if I'd passed or failed, but I knew I'd given it my best shot.

I returned home and put the exams out of mind. I'd have to wait six weeks for my results anyway, so there was nothing more I could do. Norman had bought two tickets to watch his beloved Manchester United play Liverpool in the 2003 Football League Cup Final. He'd been looking forward to going down to Cardiff with our son Danny for ages, but a week after my exams, and to my utter astonishment, he gave the tickets away to a mate.

I was totally gobsmacked. Football was, and always would be, an important part of my husband's life. The fact he'd just given up the chance to see his own team play in the final was the jolt I needed to realise just how ill he must be.

'Right, that's it! I'm going to the doctor's with you and this time I'll make him listen.'

Norman was visibly relieved that I was going to fight his corner. He didn't say anything, but we were always a team and he needed me now as he was just too frightened to admit the unthinkable even to himself. By now, Norman seemed to be spending most of the night in the loo. I suspected something sinister and was determined I wouldn't rest until we found out what was wrong. But the

GP leaned back in his chair, put his pen down on the desk, considered me for a moment and then said, calmly and slowly, with the authority of a doctor:

'Mrs Oliver, your husband is far too young to get bowel cancer.'

Norman looked at the doctor and then at me. He didn't want me to make a fuss and believed that the doctor always knew best. But I didn't care what the GP thought of me – he could think I was a troublemaker, cheeky or whatever he wanted, I wasn't there to make friends. The fact was my husband was in daily pain. He'd worked all his life since he was fifteen, contributed his National Insurance payments every single month and now I felt he was entitled to a proper diagnosis, not guesswork to save the practice money.

'I know my husband,' I said. 'He's just given away his cup final tickets and for him to do that means things must be very bad. He's just not right and he hasn't been since he had his fall, a year ago.'

'Okay,' the GP said reluctantly, 'I'll refer him.'

Norman had remained pretty much silent throughout. It was because he didn't want to be a bother, but I didn't care. My young husband seemed to be deteriorating before my very eyes and I wanted someone to do something about it now, before it was too late.

'At last,' I said, as we stepped out of the doctor's surgery. 'I think we're finally getting somewhere.'

Only we weren't. When the appointment finally came through it was six weeks away, so I called the GP immediately.

'My husband can't wait six weeks,' I told him. 'He's in so much pain that he can't even sit down.' But again, the doctor wasn't much help. What I didn't realise then was the GP had referred Norman as a non-urgent case. Even though we'd stressed the pain had been there for months and explained the symptoms, the GP had decided that at forty-six, Norman couldn't possibly be at risk of bowel cancer. Had he referred him as an urgent case then the rules state he would have been seen within two weeks. I was upset that he hadn't been referred earlier.

The doctor had suggested it could be a urinary problem, so in desperation we went to see a consultant in Urology as a private patient. He sent Norman for a full X-ray and then called us in for the results. As we sat down, I noticed that he was grim-faced.

'Mr Oliver, this is definitely not your waterworks. I believe this is something to do with your bowel and you will need further investigation. I will write a report for you, which should speed things up.'

A few days later, on a Sunday afternoon, I stood by helplessly as Norman lay in bed, crying like a baby because he was in such horrific pain. It broke my heart to see him in that state, but something snapped. I finally took control and did what I should have done weeks before.

'This is bloody ridiculous!' I said, grabbing the phone. 'I'm calling 999.'

Norman had wanted to argue with me and if he'd had more strength, I suspect he might have, but all the fight had left him. My strong, capable husband had become a shell of his former self and now he was fading before my very eyes. The ambulance took us to A&E, where we explained everything that had been happening.

'We're sending you for a scan,' the consultant decided.

A short while later, the radiographer came in, holding images from Norman's scan.

'Do you know what it is?' I asked.

'It's something to do with his bowel,' he replied.

In spite of what I'd told them the private doctor had said, the hospital still transferred Norman to the Urology ward, where they gave him enemas.

'But it's not a urinary problem,' I tried to tell them. 'If you'd only look at the report the last doctor has written. I'm telling you the Urology consultant said it definitely was not a urology problem, it's a bowel problem.'

But my voice fell on deaf ears and they refused to listen. However, they did say if I got the report, they would read it. From that point on, things moved quickly. I went to collect the report that day, and by the next day, Norman was undergoing a scan. Immediately afterwards, a phenomenal colorectal surgeon who, as luck would have it, just happened to be on cover that day, came to speak with us. It was a sheer fluke that he had been the one to look at Norman's scans. He looked serious as he approached my husband's bedside and drew the hospital curtains around us. I felt my stomach clench with fear as he stood before us: whatever he had to say, it wasn't going to be good.

'I'm sorry to be the one to have to tell you this,' he said, 'but it is bowel cancer and it has spread to your liver. Sadly, your bowel has also now perforated and so surgery will be very difficult.'

My mouth fell open as I gasped with shock. I took a slow, deep breath as the news began to sink in. Clutching Norman's hand in mine, I looked up at the consultant.

'How bad is it?' I asked.

I needed to know what it was we were dealing with.

'I'm afraid it's Stage 4 cancer.'

I turned to Norman. The fear in his eyes – the exact same fear I'd witnessed only a year before, following his accident – was back again. It broke my heart. I thought back to the accident and how frightened we'd been, but now this. I desperately needed to ask the consultant more, but I didn't want to frighten Norman. My husband was the strong and silent type – he wasn't one to complain, yet now, because he never made a fuss, he'd been overlooked. In fact, his instincts and mine had been right all along. But none of that mattered right now. All that mattered was fighting this awful disease and focusing on getting Norman well again – and, by God, fight it we would.

Chapter Six

Operation Augusta

6 When the world says
'give up,' hope whispers,
'try it one more time.' 9
— Anon

After the consultant had delivered the earth-shattering news, I followed him outside into the corridor to ask what Stage 4 cancer actually meant.

He fiddled with the cuffs of his shirt and cleared his throat. 'There is no easy way to say this,' he said, 'but I'm sorry to have to tell you that Norman's condition is terminal.'

At that moment I felt the earth fall away from underneath me. I put a hand against the wall to steady myself.

'All we can offer now is palliative care and to make your husband as comfortable as possible,' the consultant added.

Up until that moment I'd remained positive; now, I felt anything but. Back in the hospital room, I cried, long and hard, and Norman cried with me. Left alone, I climbed onto the bed and we huddled against each other for dear life. We cried and couldn't stop. I looked into the future and all I felt was fear.

How on earth could I carry on without this man by my side?

Our life as we knew it had changed for ever and nothing would ever be the same again. He was just forty-six years old and we thought we had our whole future, our retirement and our grandchildren to look forward to. Now, all those dreams were gone, killed in an instant. The only thing we had left was hope and I clung to it like a lifeboat in a sea of uncertainty.

Believing it had been a superficial problem with his bowel caused by the fall, the hospital had given Norman enemas. Tragically, they'd perforated his bowel and this had released toxins and all the poison of the cancer into his body. Not only did he have terminal cancer, he now needed life-saving surgery to remove his bowel, with an operation scheduled for the next day. For the first time in my life, apart from the few nights at police training college, I returned home alone to an empty bed. That night I couldn't sleep. Instead, I lay there wondering what on earth I was going to say to the kids.

How could I tell them their dad wouldn't be there to see them grow up?

Maggie, you've got to hold this together, I told myself. *If you don't, then everything will fall apart.*

I had to tell the kids something, so I explained that their dad had to have an operation. 'We'll know more after that,' I said, trying not to alarm them.

*

The following morning, I sat in Norman's hospital room as he was wheeled down for an operation to save his life. As he disappeared from my side, I sat alone and didn't move. Instead, I waited in the dark and just sobbed, willing him to pull through, praying they'd made a mistake and pleading for a miracle. At one point a nurse came into the room although I was so distraught, I barely registered her.

'Shall I open the blinds for you?' she asked gently.

I looked up and shook my head.

'No, please leave them closed.'

I wanted to hide away in the darkness because I didn't want anyone to see my eyes – raw and blood red from crying. I couldn't bear to see the sunlight or the day outside, people going about their business without a care in the world, as I waited to see if my beloved husband would live or die.

Norman was eventually brought out of theatre and taken into Intensive Care, where the treatment he received was second to none. He had his own nurse by his side twenty-four hours a day, which only confirmed just how precarious his situation was. In order to save his life, the surgeons had removed his bowel and attached a colostomy bag. He was heavily sedated when he came back into the room and on a constant epidural for pain relief. It was a shock to see my once strong and athletic husband reduced to a shell of his former self. But my feelings didn't matter. It was vital to remain positive at all times, no matter how difficult things became. But I knew Norman, and I knew how devastated he'd be when he woke.

Overnight, he'd become a shadow of himself. Over the next few days he gradually began to come around, although he was being kept pain-free by high doses of morphine and an epidural that was constantly topped up. He didn't say much, but looking into his eyes all I saw was despair and a desire to just go to sleep and never wake up again. The sight of the colostomy bag permanently attached to his stomach was, for Norman, worse than the cancer diagnosis. He couldn't bear to look as nurses stripped his dignity further every time they changed it. Although the situation felt bleak, I did a lot of talking, trying to focus on every small positive to motivate him to start fighting.

'Come on, we're going to fight this, remember?' I said, clutching his hand in mine.

Norman turned his face away and stared out of the window. But I refused to give up.

'Listen, yes, it's awful and I wish it hadn't happened. But if this is the worst of it, then we'll deal with it. If we have to live the rest of our lives with that bloody colostomy bag, then we'll deal with it! It's not great, but at least you're alive.'

In spite of the consultant's words, I refused to believe that Norman would die. I refused to accept it. I would 'will' him to recover through 'mind over matter' and 'the power of positive thinking'.

We would win this battle because we had to.

*

That night, I went home to face the kids. I needed to be clear with them, but also to remain optimistic.

'Your dad has cancer,' I explained. 'But he's young and fit and he can beat it.'

I didn't know if it was the right or wrong thing to say,

but I refused to accept that Norman's condition was terminal. Instead, I learned to lock away negative thoughts in boxes at the back of my brain and became an expert in blocking them. Positive mental attitude was what was needed, not only for Norman but the kids too so they could carry on with their lives and enjoy their young years as much as possible.

All four kids were brilliant, but our daughter Vicki was phenomenal. She helped me care for Norman, fatten him up and get him back to a healthy weight. She'd always had her dad wrapped around her little finger, but now she jollied him along too. She also refused to take no for an answer when he said he didn't want to eat. Whenever his eyes were open we were virtually force-feeding him with full-fat cream, Fortijuice and Fortisip supplements (medical drinks which contained all the nutrients needed to rebuild a devastated body). We also put butter in everything. He was bullied mercilessly by the pair of us, but with the very best of intentions – we just wanted him well again.

I'd been so caught up in what had been happening that I'd completely forgotten about work – nothing seemed important any more, only Norman. It was only when I rang my sergeant two days after my husband had been admitted to hospital that I discovered I'd passed my CID exams: I was now a fully qualified detective constable. The news felt bittersweet: just as my career was soaring, my personal life was crumbling beneath me.

When Norman was eventually discharged from hospital after a month, I became his main carer. Our house was transformed into hospital and drug den, with his medication and morphine piled high in a cupboard. The consultant had showed me what to do and I did it. I did everything and anything to keep my young husband alive. During my absence from work, my colleagues were amazing. I was told to take as long as I needed.

*

In March 2003, the consultant told us Norman also had secondary cancer in his liver. Strangely, if the liver cancer had been in one big lump, then the surgeons would have been able to simply cut it out because the liver is the only organ that can rejuvenate itself. As it was, his only option was chemotherapy, which he started in April 2003. We met three amazing research nurses at The Christie NHS Foundation Trust in Manchester – Julie, Karen and Amanda – who soon became our best friends. Thankfully, the chemo not only killed off some of the cancer, it also dulled the pain. For the first time in ages, my husband wasn't in agony. After a while, he begun to feel a little better, so much so that he was able to drive himself to hospital. There, he'd undergo a scan every eight weeks and our hopes were raised when they showed the tumours had been reduced massively by the treatment. For the first time it felt as though we were winning.

'Maybe you should go back to work?' Norman suggested one day. 'I'm feeling much better now.'

Surely he needs me? I thought, taken aback. *Doesn't he?* Then I realised that him being a patient and me being his primary carer wasn't good for either of us, and to all intents and purposes, he was finally on the mend.

As it was, work turned out to be my salvation. As I said

earlier, my colleagues had been amazing and I returned to work in a new CID office as a proud and fully fledged detective. Home life settled down too. Despite all the odds, Norman seemed to make a miraculous recovery. In fact, he was on such good form that he took part in the first-ever Greater Manchester Run to raise money for Christies. He was the only patient at that time to have run while undergoing chemotherapy. It was a very proud moment and the whole family cheered him on to the finish line. The hospital was so impressed, it awarded Norman a medal, which was presented at a special ceremony.

*

In late 2003, I was called in by one of the bosses at work – Detective Chief Inspector Phil Owen – who'd been tasked with pulling a new job together.

'Maggie, we've got this job we'd like you to work on,' he said, inviting me to sit down. 'We think you'll be a good fit for this team.'

The DCI explained that a fifteen-year-old girl had died in September 2003 of a drugs overdose while in the care of Manchester social services. Her name was Victoria Agoglia and she had led a sad life. After losing her mum to cancer at just eight years old, and despite the family's fight to keep her with them, she'd been taken into care. A shy and intelligent girl, she'd become increasingly troubled and eventually was placed in a home in Rochdale, miles away from her remaining family. After that she'd begun to lose her way. I was told she'd been a regular missing child and had fallen in with the 'wrong crowd'.

A man had already been arrested and charged with

administering the drugs that had killed her but, according to the DCI, that wasn't what this operation was about.

'There's a letter,' he said.

'A letter?'

The DCI nodded and handed me a sheet of paper. I could sense him watching me closely as I read the words, in the handwriting of a young girl, on it.

> *Things I have done in the past.*
>
> *Things I have done in the past. I drank, smoked weed, took pills, had blown coke, had heroin – just for what? All you do is get a laugh out of it but it can also kill you. I am only 13. I got the rest of my life ahead of me. I have slept with people older than me, half of them I don't even know there [sic] names. I am a slag and that is nothing to be proud of. Now I think why I did it, just to impress the boys and they treated me like shit. Even one night when I was out I pilled up with some boy and Sam because they were out of their faces so much they crashed the car. Police looked all over Mosside Longsight [sic] but we never got caught and all the things I lost just for drugs. Boys, my family, and my family is supposed to mean a lot to people at the time it did, not for me. So I lost all of that. I just hope I knew that at the time but I did not. Next time you should think family before drink, drugs, sex, or money.*

'We believe this letter was written by Victoria,' said the DCI, as I looked at him in shock. 'We think she'd been groomed for sex and abused by many different men. I should tell you, Maggie, that all these men are believed to be of Asian origin.'

'How did we get hold of this?' I asked.

'We believe there'd been some kind of argument between Victoria and her social worker, which ended with her throwing the letter at her. After she died, it was handed to us.'

I shuddered. Victoria was dead at fifteen – the same age as my daughter Vicki. The similarities struck me immediately, even down to the two of them having the same name. As a mum, I couldn't comprehend how it must feel to lose a child, but it seemed unthinkable.

'We think there may be more victims out there,' the DCI went on, 'more girls being sexually abused. We need you to work on a scoping exercise. Find out what's going on, if anything.'

I had a proven track record of interviewing victims and working with children. My reputation for being able to gain the trust of vulnerable victims and witnesses was well known and exactly what this job needed. I also had four kids, so I hoped I understood what made teenagers tick. Up until that moment I'd been working shifts, including nights, but this new job offered me more flexible hours – time I could spend with Norman.

'I'll do it, boss,' I said. 'When do you want me to start?'

*

The team involved in Operation Augusta, as it became known, was initially made up of the DCI (as the sponsor with an overview), a detective inspector, Mark Willdigg (in daily charge of the job), me and two other detectives, DC Jerry Pointon and DC Micky Kelly. Our remit would be to look at potential sexual exploitation of children in the Greater Manchester Police's 'A' and 'C' divisions, which covered the city centre and areas a couple of miles south of Manchester, including Whalley Range, Longsight and the area around Rusholme known locally as the 'Curry Mile' due to the large number of Indian restaurants and takeaways. This was an edgy, run-down red-light area, populated by a mix of prostitutes, drug dealers, gang members and students (the university is very close by). The girls working the streets weren't bad people and I never saw them as criminals; they were people who'd been dealt a rough hand in life and were just trying to survive. I felt protective over the students in that area too. They reminded me of my own kids; away from home for the first time in an unfamiliar city, learning how to spread their wings – not always successfully. (I remember dealing with one student who'd been in a pub fight. It was six of one and half a dozen of the other, and I could have locked him up, but that would have destroyed his life. I let him go with a warning.) Finally, there were the homeless of the area, who slept in doorways right the way along the Curry Mile and down Oxford Road. Again, they weren't bad people – they were just lost in a society that didn't care.

Our brief for Operation Augusta was to talk to social workers, identify vulnerable children and eventually speak to them directly about any abuse they'd been involved in. We would also be consulting other forces to see if they were facing similar problems and, if they were, how they were tackling them.

Very quickly, it appeared that dozens of children were being abused. Social workers in central Manchester gave us extensive lists of names, which were narrowed down to an initial list of between twenty to thirty. I was shocked to discover that for years social workers had been telling the police about this problem. They complained of being 'fobbed off' because the children were seen as 'making a lifestyle choice'; in other words, they were child prostitutes.

But they weren't prostitutes. They were under-age children, not the adult women we knew worked the streets of Whalley Range and Rusholme, day and night. I was outraged and horrified that people could even voice such opinions of children, let alone allow the abuse to continue unchecked. Shockingly, these same kids had slipped through every protective net. They didn't come under the remit of Child Protection Units because the abuse hadn't met the official definition of being carried out by anyone with 'care, custody or control' of the child, such as a parent, uncle or teacher. At the same time, CID didn't see this as their responsibility either. Finally, the children themselves didn't consider themselves to be victims: they saw these men not as abusers, but as their 'boyfriends', hence the crime was allowed to continue unchecked by agencies who knew it existed, but failed to act.

Our inquiries with social workers yielded mixed results. Some seemed indifferent, at best, to what was happening to children in their care. Others were desperately concerned about their plight and had been trying for years to get something done. It was these social workers we needed to engage; the ones who would help us locate vulnerable children and, by a process of gaining their trust, eventually speak to us about what was going on.

We were gently sowing these seeds and eventually they started to bear fruit. In the late summer of 2003, I was directed to the flat of a young girl who had spent a lifetime in care and, at eighteen, had just had her first baby. Now alone in the world, she was in accommodation that was beyond dilapidated. I was shocked that after everything she'd been through, including years of abuse, she'd been cast out of so-called 'care', still little more than a child herself, and simply left to her own devices. She was willing to talk and the information she gave us really helped to build up a picture of what was going on in the area regarding the abuse of children.

The fact that her abusers, and those of the other vulnerable children, were predominately Pakistani men didn't matter to me: their origin was of no personal interest. I wasn't racist then, nor am I now. My attitude was that, as a police officer, my job was to uphold the law and prosecute offenders. To my mind, a group of men – no matter their background or origins – who sexually abused vulnerable children should be arrested, charged and locked up, and in my opinion the key thrown away too. It was as simple as that.

At the time we were investigating this abuse, police forces across the UK were being subjected to 'PI', or Performance Indicators. Greater Manchester Police, along with all other police forces, were being judged and funded by the Government according to how well they dealt with so-called 'acquisitive crime' such as burglaries, robberies and theft from motor vehicles. So, for example, if your car had been broken into, it went to the top of the investigation queue, whereas a thirteen-year-old girl being raped and abused by a fifty-year-old man was a very low priority – if a priority at all. It was a national scandal and I was outraged.

'They're kids,' I fumed to Norman. 'They're little kids, having sex with men old enough to be their fathers and grandfathers. They need protecting, but they're lost in a system that isn't protecting them.'

He simply shook his head in horror.

It was an unbelievable situation and the more information we gathered, the more it became apparent we had a major problem within GMP and needed more resources.

The evidence was shocking: these kids were still little girls. The youngest was only eleven years old and had been living in a children's home. One of the older girls had 'taken her under her wing' but, in fact, had inadvertently exposed her to a group of men who had gone on to groom and abuse her too. A few of the girls had reported the rapes to the police, but there was no joined-up system in place. This whole attitude of institutional neglect and turning a blind eye reminded me of what I had seen during my uniform days in Moss Side – kids constantly being reported missing as though it didn't matter. There was no sense of urgency and a total lack of action. Thoughts of 'David' and his premature death haunted my dreams.

Attitudes towards these kids seemed to be ingrained and widespread. They were widely viewed by fellow officers, senior officers and politicians as 'white trash' or the 'underclass'. In this new millennium, they were seen as 'losers'. As a result, they were left to fend for themselves, which they clearly couldn't do. Out of their depth, they were trapped in a system that didn't care. They were silent victims, lost children thrown onto society's scrap heap, and to me that was wilful neglect. My opinion was unpopular, yet it didn't stop me from voicing it. I even had several run-ins with colleagues – including some of the typists – who felt these girls 'just weren't worth it' and we should 'just let them get on with it'.

'But they're children,' I protested, time and time again.

The abuse had been going on for so long it had almost become normalised between the children and some workers had almost become desensitised to it. Many sexual health workers would just dole out condoms to eleven- and twelve-year-old girls without a second thought, and without question. The whole situation was incomprehensible to me.

What on earth was going on in our country? A country that I had previously believed took child protection seriously.

I'd seen children dragged by social workers from homes where they faced far less danger than these children were facing on our streets on a daily basis, allegedly in the care of the protective agencies. If parents had allowed this to happen to their own children, they would have almost certainly faced prosecution for child neglect, so why were senior police and social workers appearing to turn a blind eye?

*

Although the scoping exercise was initially meant to last for six weeks, soon we were given more officers as the scale of the problem began to emerge. We then moved into phase two, which lasted a few months. Victoria Agoglia's letter had opened a can of worms. By this time the team had grown from three to ten officers and we were allocated a dedicated social worker. We began to compile lists of children we knew were being groomed and abused; names of men we believed to be abusers, telephone numbers, car registration numbers and details of locations where the abuse was happening. I had discussions with many senior officers about the scale of the problem, including the head of the force's Child Protection Unit at the time, Steve Heywood. To my relief, things seemed to be moving at a pace.

A decision was taken that even though we hadn't yet gone into full investigation mode, I'd be allowed to take initial statements from a couple of the children who had been abused (including the eighteen-year-old with the baby) to add weight to our report. Both girls were no longer being abused, but were willing to speak to me. Naturally, they found having to relive their abuse difficult. They felt shame, guilt and fear, and a lot of confusion about how they had been groomed and abused. Yet they did speak and what they told me was horrifying. Young white girls, all in care homes, were being approached initially by Pakistani males in their teens and twenties, who would befriend them, then become their 'boyfriends'. Gifts, flowers, alcohol and drugs would be offered to these vulnerable girls and after coercing them into sex, their younger abusers would pass them on to older men for sex via cash incentives or threats of violence, even both. Many of the abusers were employed in businesses along the Curry Mile and much of the abuse was taking place in flats and houses in and around this area. There were sex parties involving up to twenty Asian men and one white girl, who was expected to have sex with them all in return for a few quid.

The eighteen-year-old was willing to accompany me on a 'drive round' the 'C' division area so that she could show me where some of the abuse was taking place. It was a typical Manchester weekday, rain hammering down on greasy, deserted pavements outside the Curry Mile's takeaways. As we drove towards Whitworth Park, we approached a large old pub on the corner of a junction. A sleek black 4x4 was parked up and as we passed, a man got out of the driver's side. Suddenly the girl slid down the front seat and covered her face with her hands. I drove another ten yards or so, then pulled up.

'What happened there?' I said.

'That fella...the one who got out of that big car...did you see him?'

'Yes,' I replied. 'Why?'

'He's one of 'em, one of 'em who's been abusing us. I'd recognise him anywhere.'

I looked in my rear-view mirror. The man had disappeared, but his car was still there. I made a note of the registration number and later, back at the station, I did a PNC (Police National Computer) check on the vehicle. Within minutes of doing so, I had a phone call from a member of what we nicknamed the 'secret squirrel' squad – a shadowy band of officers who investigated internal matters, including police corruption.

'Can I ask why you've just run a PNC on that registration?' said a male voice.

I explained how I'd come by the vehicle on the drive around with the abused girl.

'Right, well, this is to let you know that we have this person under surveillance,' he said. 'He's a serving officer, so let us deal with him, okay?'

Shocked, I replaced the receiver. So, it wasn't just takeaway workers and taxi drivers involved. If this was an organised ring of abusers, its tentacles were perhaps spreading further than we thought. I never found out what happened to that line of enquiry.

*

My team travelled to speak to other police forces and we were stunned by the magnitude of that type of abuse – it seemed many forces had the same problem. Liverpool, for example, not only had a problem; it had been investigating for a long time and was much further down the line than us. West Yorkshire Police had also identified a similar problem of underage white girls being groomed for sex by Asian men. However, the problem was that this particular type of grooming had been allowed to grow because no one had taken hold of it – people were afraid of being labelled 'racist', it seemed. But it was a serious problem and Asian men, predominantly Pakistani men, were not only grooming but raping white girls in their droves.

And it wasn't just the police who were aware of the situation. As we continued our investigations around Manchester, over in Yorkshire a Channel 4 *Dispatches* team had been following and filming a Social Services team around Bradford and Keighley areas for a few months. One episode included a segment in which mothers told how their daughters had been groomed for sex by Asian men. This programme was part of a series of documentaries called 'Edge of the City' and in that episode, the mothers claimed Asian men had been targeting girls from the ages of eleven and twelve, taking them out in their cars and giving them alcohol and gifts. In some cases, the girls were said to have been given drugs and raped, both vaginally and anally. The then-MP for Keighley, Ann Cryer, had been trying to highlight this issue for a number of years previously after several mothers in her constituency told her what was happening to their daughters, but when she approached the police, Social Services, the local mosques and Parliament itself, she was completely stonewalled. The fear of appearing racist, it seemed, was apparently stronger than the desire to tackle out-and-out organised child abuse.

This particular episode of 'Edge of the City' was due to be broadcast in May 2004 but was pulled on the request of West Yorkshire Police, who argued that it might inflame community tensions in the run-up to local elections. At the time, the British National Party (BNP) was campaigning prominently across the UK and there were worries that in places like Bradford there could be violence. Channel 4 had also been flooded with requests from groups such as Unite Against Fascism, the 1990 Trust and The National Assembly Against Racism to delay the transmission. Yet at the heart of this film was a very inconvenient truth about the abuse of white girls by Asian men – one of which we were observing very clearly in South Manchester. I wonder now whether, having heard whispers about abuse from across the Pennines, senior Greater Manchester Police officers had ordered Operation Augusta as a kind of PR exercise so that when news of abuse in Yorkshire eventually broke, in whatever way, GMP would be able to say it was already doing something about it.

The film was eventually broadcast in August 2004, three months after the elections, and attracted a lot of comment.

By the spring of 2004, we had an initial list of almost 207 Asian men who we believed had been abusing at least 26 children. And that was in just two divisions. The youngest victim was just twelve years old. But we knew this was only the tip of the iceberg. The final report was written, and I and another officer attended Greater Manchester Police HQ at Chester House, where we presented it to the Head of Crime at that time, Detective Chief Superintendent Dave Thompson. We made our case that Operation Augusta needed to be staffed properly – the whole investigation needed to be logged onto the HOLMES (Home Office Large Major Enquiry System) computer as a major crime. HOLMES is a system set up to help cross-reference and join up multiple pieces of evidence arising from a large number of detectives working on a major inquiry. Our opinion of the information we'd received as a result of the scoping exercise was that it was too great to be dealt with in any other way. It needed to be dealt with as a major incident and resourced accordingly, we felt. This would mean analysts, typists, indexers, action allocators, readers, receivers, a HOLMES sergeant and more to ensure enough resources were available to tackle what we'd identified as a major problem. It would also mean any information gathered could then be accessed and shared nationally, if needed, to provide consistency between all UK police forces facing the same problem.

Although I'd written the report, including much of the detail our team had gathered over the months, I was supported in my wish to print Victoria Agoglia's photograph on the very first page, along with a photocopy of the handwritten letter that the DCI had shown me. I felt it was important to demonstrate that whatever people's perceptions and prejudices might be, Victoria had been a child – one who had been sexually abused, raped, drugged, and was dead by the age of fifteen. I wanted senior officers, including the chief constable, assistant chief constables and detective chief superintendents, to see her photograph. I wanted to send home the message loud and clear that if we failed in our duty to protect and uphold the law, many more children would have their lives destroyed and would die. These were the human consequences of failing to act now.

'At the moment there is no defined ownership of this problem,' the report stated. 'This is one of the main reasons why the problem has escalated to the extent that it now has. The lack of defined ownership leads to an unwillingness to address or accept responsibility for the issue.

'Our recommendation would be that Force Command address this issue as a matter of urgency, and a decision is made as to who carries the Portfolio for this important and highly sensitive subject.'

We couldn't make it any clearer and, sure enough, the report caused a stir. DCS Dave Thompson presented the report and our findings to the force tasking and coordinating group. This was the Gold Command – the highest decision-making body in Greater Manchester Police – made up of the most senior officers. When we were notified a few weeks later that they had accepted the findings of the report and had decided GMP would resource the investigation with a full Major Incident Team (MIT), I was over the moon. Although we'd identified the problem late on, something was finally going to be done about it. In short, we'd stop this abuse in its tracks.

I didn't doubt for a single second that now the extent of the crimes was known that they would be dealt with. GMP command had acknowledged it was a major incident and, as such, would secure the resources necessary to fight it. The situation would no longer be swept under the carpet and allowed to fester and grow.

'We're going to sort it out,' I told Norman, my voice full of conviction. 'We can help these girls, and we will.'

I'd never been prouder to be a police officer than I felt in that single moment. It was what I'd joined the force to do – to make a difference, to protect children, to bring the bad guys to justice – and I could hold my head up high.

With new gusto, I applied and was accepted to work in the Major Incident Team (MIT). Although I remained working on Operation Augusta, the decision was made that I would actually join the Wythenshawe MIT syndicate – the team allocated to work on Operation Augusta for the foreseeable future. A senior investigating officer (SIO) was appointed, along with a HOLMES sergeant and a team of indexers, typists and many detectives. Things were moving at a speed. We'd been working on the case for nine months when the information we'd gathered began to be loaded onto the HOLMES computer and 'back record converted'. By now, there were almost thirty of us in the team.

*

By late 2004 and going into 2005, Operation Augusta had become a full major incident, ready to start raising actions and progress to further victim interviews and arrests and prosecutions in due course. But then something happened that stopped me dead in my tracks: Norman had begun to feel more unwell. He'd gone for a scan and the results were devastating – his tumour had begun to grow again, the cancer was back. His consultant agreed to go to the finance committee at Christie's and make a bid for them to fund my husband's treatment on a new drug trial, even though he didn't strictly meet the criteria. Because he was still a young man with a young family, however, they ruled in his favour and he was given a third type of chemo. As a family, we crossed our fingers and hoped for a miracle. Norman did his best to hide the fear he undoubtedly felt and just had faith that I would fight his corner to the very best of my ability, along with his consultant, oncologist and the nurses. In all the time he was ill he never once complained or was demanding. He did what the doctors said or was led by the kids and I, and just tried to beat it. After the initial despair at his diagnosis, he gradually came to see that we had a life, and so we packed it full and never really looked ahead to the unthinkable...

Chapter Seven

Nowhere Left to Hide

❛To live in hearts of those we leave behind is not to die❜
— Thomas Campbell

Soon, Norman was confined to a wheelchair and although he was having chemotherapy, this time instead of feeling stronger, he seemed to become weaker. He became so ill that he was having regular blood transfusions. We had to have a hospital bed downstairs now and a hoist to help me lift him in and out of bed. I slept on the floor beside him in case he woke in the night and, in short, became virtually his full-time nurse. In March 2005, I took leave to help nurse him through.

I had been trying to juggle my work and domestic commitments ever since Norman's accident and subsequent diagnosis and now, enough was enough. Work had been my salvation and sanctuary, a place where I could put aside all the roller coaster emotions of our home life for a few hours and get on with my job. When I was at home, Norman's care was all-consuming. At work, however, I tried not to dwell on what was happening to us and rarely talked about it to my colleagues. Although taking a step back from work would be difficult, I knew that the juggling had to stop. Perhaps subconsciously, I was realising Norman's fight was coming to a close and he needed me one hundred per cent. Finally, if reluctantly, I walked away from work. I know now without a shadow of a doubt that had I not done this, I would have regretted it for the rest of my life.

Having made this decision, I knew that I was not neglecting my duties as a police officer. The work we had done had now been passed to a Major Incident Team and so I left work and the ongoing Operation Augusta with an easy heart, feeling my efforts and those of the team would bring about the arrest and conviction of the dozens of paedophiles we had identified. I never doubted this for one single second. Our team had done a tremendous job, producing a full and thorough report which contained details of the offender profile, the victim profiles, the modus operandi and our conclusions and recommendations to address this evil crime. This had been scrutinised and finally resourced by the Greater Manchester Police 'Gold' decision-making group, which included the chief constable and assistant chief constables. Now I could focus exclusively on my desperately sick husband and make whatever time he had left the very best it could be.

Norman's health began to fade quickly as the doctors threw everything they could at him to try and buy him more time. During the first couple of years his chemotherapy treatment had worked and he'd been put on a trial chemo called Avastin. We were told it built on the immune system and at the time was considered revolutionary. It gave us hope and he was granted an extra six months of life, but eventually it stopped working and soon he was in excruciating pain as the cancer spread to his bones.

I was topping up his Fentanyl painkilling patches with extra doses of morphine to try and keep him pain-free. One evening, I forgot and he woke in the middle of the night, eyes wide and wild. Like a man possessed, he was scratching his skin with his fingernails. Panicked, I injected him with morphine and within ten minutes he was calm and quiet again. It gave me an insight into the desperation of drug addiction, confirming my belief that it is an illness, not a crime. I know I'd have done whatever it took to find morphine for Norman in those dark days if it would have helped his pain.

Sadly, his pain steadily grew worse and in late 2004 we paid to see a private back specialist. Looking back, I know we were in denial that the cancer had spread to his bones. But it had, and time was fast running out. He had trouble passing water because, as the specialists explained, a tumour was now pushing on his urethra. It was suggested he was fitted with yet another bag, this time for his urine, instead of a stent, but because his diagnosis was terminal it was felt that fitting the latter was a waste of time.

Angrily, I challenged this opinion, demanding my husband be treated with dignity. The doctors accepted what I was saying and he was treated with a stent. He was dying, yes, but he resented the loss of his dignity and pride. For Norman, that was almost harder to deal with than the cancer itself.

The last really happy memory I have of Norman was

his birthday, 17 June 2005. It always fell in the same week as Father's Day and although he wasn't well enough to walk, we used the hoist to get him out of bed and into a wheelchair. All six of us went to a local pub, where we had a meal. We knew this would be the last birthday we celebrated with him, which was heartbreaking, but we did our best to make it a happy occasion. Later, we sat in the back garden and enjoyed the summer sunshine. Suddenly, Norman became very disorientated and the atmosphere changed in an instant. I knew then that this wasn't fair: we were fighting to keep him alive, but who were we doing it for, us or him? At that moment, I made peace with myself. I stood up, went inside and called an ambulance. The kids saw what was happening, and although slightly in denial as we all were, they knew he needed to be in hospital. This was their dad's birthday, and Norman was not very lucid when the ambulance came. This type of confusion is one of the effects of becoming very ill and, although I didn't know that at the time, it was as clear as day that he needed to be in hospital.

Norman was admitted and given a blood transfusion, plus liquids to help rehydrate him. His latest scan was due around that time and, as usual, he asked to leave the room before the consultant made his diagnosis. 'Tell the wife she's in charge,' he'd say. 'Anything she wants to do is alright by me.' And the consultants would smile and respect his wishes.

This time, however, the consultant, Dr Valle, was adamant that he wanted to speak to both of us at the same time. I knew then that this would be bad news and as I sat by Norman's bed, holding his hand, I steeled myself for the inevitable.

'I'm sorry,' the consultant said, 'but I'm afraid this treatment has stopped working. The cancer has begun to grow again and there really is nothing else we can give you.'

At that moment the life went out of Norman and he just closed down. He'd always known in the deepest recesses of his mind that this day would come: now it was here. I broke down in floods of tears, realising there was nowhere left to hide. Norman turned to me and whispered: 'I want to go home, love.'

I desperately wished I could put him in the car and do what he wanted, there and then, but because he was on intravenous antibiotics, he had to stay in hospital. He had a Hickman line permanently fitted to his chest and district nurses weren't licensed to administer the types of drugs he needed. With no other solution, I rang our GP, Dr Norris, who not only came to the hospital but signed an authority to give me permission to administer Norman his antibiotics. Without her, we wouldn't have been able to grant him his last wish, which was to die peacefully at home, surrounded by his family. For that, I will always be grateful to her.

Up until that moment Norman and I had never had the conversation with the kids that he might die. Instead, we'd agreed to make his last few years as happy as possible. But on the day he left hospital, 29 June, Matt had finished his GCSEs and Vicki had completed her last A-level that very morning. Deep down, I'm convinced that Norman had hung on until Vicki finished. I rang her school and arranged for her to come to the hospital, along with our other children.

As gently as he could, a doctor told our gathered family

there was nothing else anyone could do for their dad. He said that if we took him home there was a strong possibility he would go into cardiac arrest in the ambulance. We had to decide if we wanted him to be resuscitated or simply to slip away. I felt this was a family decision and despite many tears and heartbreak, we concluded, given his frailty, resuscitation would be a brutal option. So, around 5pm that day, the hospital staff organised an ambulance and the drugs we'd need, and we took Norman home for the last time.

The following day, there was a knocking on the door. Visitors, two close friends who wanted to see Norman. I went into the back room to tell him they were here. He turned to me with pleading eyes.

'Maggie,' he whispered, 'I've had enough.'

I knew exactly what he meant and with heartfelt apologies, I turned away his visitors. That night, I slept on the floor as usual so I could be next to him, before lying on his bed and cuddling him. He was frail and I was frightened. They say your life flashes before you at the point of death and as I lay next to him, I heard him reliving some of the best moments. He mumbled something about scoring a goal and then spoke of his happiness when the kids had been born. The next minute he was talking to my dad. Initially, the two of them hadn't got on, but over time they'd become firm friends. Norman had always called my dad 'Butty' as his surname was Butterworth.

'Go on, Butty, come on,' he chuckled to himself.

A moment later, he was back on the football pitch, training the lads and, as I lay there listening to him, I felt my heart break. His time here was coming to a close and I cried quietly in the darkness.

The following morning, Sue and Ann, our district nurses, arrived. Kind, considerate and, above all, caring, they came into the front room to speak with me.

'Maggie, we've got to say this to you. It's not fair to keep Norman alive. Now is the time.'

I knew what they meant. Now was the time to give him the painkilling, opiate-based drugs that would ease his passage from this world to the next – usual practice in palliative care. We did what we had to do and a few hours later, around tea time, the kids and I gathered around Norman's bed. His eyes were closed and slowly, slowly, he stopped breathing. It was the first time I'd watched anyone die and I found it a strangely calm and loving moment, all of us there in his presence for the very last time. Norman had fought longer than he needed to because he didn't want to leave us, but this moment felt like his release from all pain and suffering. It was a strangely peaceful and loving atmosphere in the room. We were all together and, for the kids, it was the last time they would hold their dad's hand and kiss him. It was very emotional but also comforting to know he was no longer in pain, but at rest and in our hearts forever.

We sat with him for a few hours until I called the undertaker's at around 10pm. Without fuss, they arrived and took him to the Chapel of Rest. Letting him go to a strange place was the hardest part for me. From my work as a police officer I knew that his body would be kept in a fridge and that I found very difficult to come to terms with – a case of knowing too much, I suppose.

*

Norman was a lifelong Manchester United fan and Darren Fletcher, a player at that time and the husband of my son Danny's friend, Hayley, brought over a signed United shirt. We were going to dress Norman in it for his funeral, but eventually decided to frame it and send him on his last journey in his own favourite United shirt. We wanted to make his funeral a celebration of his life and so, a week after he'd died, on 5 July 2005, we did him proud. A packed congregation heard our sons Danny and Steve give the most wonderfully moving speeches and we ended the ceremony with The Mamas & The Papas 'California Dreamin''. It was my choice, as it reminded me of our carefree Moroccan adventure on the old bus and of a time when we'd been newly engaged and still thought we'd have our entire lives left, not just twenty-five years.

Seeing Norman's coffin up at the front of the chapel brought everything home to me and, despite so many people wishing me well, I just couldn't stop crying. At the wake, we put up a board of photographs of Norman so we could all remember the good times. On the back of the service sheet, and on his plaque in the crematorium, we had inscribed: 'To live in the hearts of those we leave behind is not to die'. For me, Norman lives on in all our hearts and I thank my lucky stars that we lived life to the full and didn't put things on hold for another day. No one can take away all those wonderful memories.

Our children were blessed to have the dad they did. Their memories of him are strong and we talk of him all the time. He is also talked about constantly by our two little grandsons Jake and Charlie, who call him Grandad Normy-Norm, as though he is still here. We have a little stone with his name on and even on Christmas Day he comes into the room to join in our dinner and we talk to him and joke about him and remember our happy times together. It's made us all determined to live life to the full NOW, and not put anything on hold because we don't know when our lives may be cut short.

Our kids remember their dad with enormous love. The holidays, the funny moments, the time he always had for them, the football on Saturdays, the drives to school in his battered old van, giving them his last pound so they could buy dinner, catching his shark in Florida, or running the Manchester Run whilst on chemo...memories that will last for ever, which we keep alive even now. He was one in a million, a very special man.

Danny's twenty-first birthday fell a few days after the funeral so we decided to get away from everything and everyone, and spend some much-needed time alone together as a family. Norman was irreplaceable and I knew then, as I know now, that I would never love anyone as much as I loved him.

In the weeks following my husband's death I felt as though I was wading through thick treacle. In many ways I was in a state of total shock, numbed by the loss of my soulmate. I was angry too. Angry that in early 2003 his doctor hadn't listened to him and he had been fobbed off for months with guesswork rather than proper tests to diagnose his cancer. But now with him gone, I suddenly felt so very alone. There were many days when all I really wanted to do was give up on life and join my soulmate in heaven, but the kids needed me and in truth that is all that kept me here in those dark, early days.

Around a month after his death, I had time to sit and think. Yet I couldn't think straight. My best friend, confidant and the man I'd adored had been taken from me. Dazed and wondering where on earth I'd go from here, I sat by Norman's memorial plaque in the crematorium, a place I visited often, seeking some kind of contact with him even though he wasn't actually there physically. One afternoon I was sitting there, thinking, when my mobile phone rang: it was one of my supervisors from work.

'Hi, Maggie,' she chirped, 'hope you're alright? I'm calling to let you know that you've been off work for six months now. Anyway, it's just a call to let you know that you'll soon be going on half-pay.'

She sounded so glib and matter-of-fact, but the severity of what she was saying jolted me. Half-pay? I couldn't survive on that – I had four kids and a household to look after. I began to panic. My mouth went bone dry as my palms prickled with a nervous sweat. Even though I felt sick with fear, I didn't say a word: grief had rendered me numb. I put the phone down, petrified – petrified I'd lose both Norman and my job in one fell swoop.

What if I couldn't cope or pay my way?

Norman was gone and now it was up to me. The responsibility was a lead weight inside my chest. The unexpected telephone call and my supervisor's words hit me so hard that now I felt frightened of going back to work. From that point I began to fall apart at the seams as all the hurt and grief came spilling out of me.

I was approaching fifty, yet the life we had planned had been stolen away from us. Because my husband was self-employed, many years before we had decided to put our mortgage in my sole name as a sort of protection. The irony was that his death meant it wasn't paid off and I had to continue making the monthly payments on my own.

I focused on helping Matt, our youngest son, get back to school, my daughter Vicki into her first job. Steve, our eldest, was a rock and moved back home to help me through the months ahead, so the remaining five of us had each other to rely on but now, finally, I had to face up to my own feelings of loss.

As I pressed the 'call ended' button on my phone, I felt my stomach churn with anxiety and I started to cry. I sobbed and sobbed until I had no tears left. Eventually, I walked back to my car. Inside, I kept a book of poems – ones that expressed different feelings. As I read through them, I was able to identify with the words. A large part of me had died along with Norman and I'd not only lost myself, but my confidence too. Now I doubted everything. How could I even exist without him by my side? The world and the future filled me with terror.

My life is finished, I thought. *I'll just look after the kids and have a quiet life, live out my days alone. I've lost everything.*

And yet, even at the darkest hour there is always the prospect of a dawn. My guardian angel and my saviour arrived in the form of Amanda, my brilliant, kind and wise occupational health nurse. She not only arranged bereavement counselling for me, she guided me through a difficult process and my eventual return to work. Fate (or maybe Norman) had sent her to me in my hour of need. For me, Amanda was a godsend who saved not only my sanity but also my career. She completely understood what

I was going through – she had lost her first husband to terminal bowel cancer too. As soon as I told her about the phone call, she took control and told me not to accept another call from work.

'Every call goes through me from now on,' she insisted.

I breathed a sigh of relief and shed bucketloads of grateful tears. It was just what I needed to hear. From that day on, Amanda became my rock, friend and confidante, and I remain eternally grateful to her to this day for the love, respect and wise counsel she gave me during my darkest hour. Overnight, it was as though a weight had been lifted from me.

Shortly afterwards, I was sat at home when the doorbell rang. I opened it to find the same supervisor – the one who'd made the insensitive phone call to me – standing on my doorstep.

'Hi, Maggie, can I come in?' she said, stepping forward before I'd even had a chance to answer.

I watched as she pulled some papers from her bag.

'I'm just serving you with these papers,' she said, thrusting an envelope in my hand. Dumbstruck, I took them from her. I couldn't process what they were or why she was here.

'They're just to inform you that if you don't go back to work next week then you'll be put on half-pay. Alright?'

And with that, she turned tail and headed back to her car.

As soon as she'd left, I closed the door and fell to pieces – I collapsed to my knees right there and then in the hallway of my home, my so-called sanctuary. She'd come into my house, uninvited, and had served me with these papers – a threat to return to work, or else.

I studied the papers. They were official documents. She was right: they would dock my pay by half if I didn't return. It was just 'procedure', of course, and my supervisor was only doing her job. Although totally insensitive, she was not vindictive, simply oblivious to my feelings of panic.

With trembling hands, I picked up the phone and called Amanda to tell her what had happened. I could hear the rage in her voice.

'Listen, you do not open the door or speak to anyone,' she ordered. 'I'll deal with this. If they want to meet you, I'll hold your hand through the whole process. Maggie, I promise you that I won't let you go through this alone. This is my job, you'll always have me.'

But my confidence was shattered and I'd been dismantled by grief. I needed Amanda's strength to help me put myself together again, piece by piece.

*

Even now, as I remember those dark days, I can still feel the tears come to my eyes and the abject fear and panic I felt then. But what my supervisor had critically failed to tell me though was that because I had always paid my Police Federation fees from the day I joined Greater Manchester Police, if I went on to half-pay then the insurance policy I had paid for would step in to supplement my half-pay for another six months. Had she mentioned this, then it would have put a whole different light on this veiled threat to return now 'or else' and saved me many sleepless nights, fretting about how I could go and do my job in the fragile state I was in.

With Amanda's unending support, it was agreed my

return to work would be staggered and I was back at my desk by September 2005. Although I had officially been a member of the Major Incident Team for about a year by that point, I was actually joining my own MIT team for the first time. It was totally daunting and in my shattered condition I didn't know if I could do this high-pressure job. However, fate seemed to intervene again when a colleague on my new team stepped in to guide me and hold my hand, show me the ropes and fight my corner when needed. Her name was Joanne and I will never forget what she did for me and how she helped me to pick up the pieces of my broken life and start to rebuild a future without Norman. She has since become a close friend and someone to whom I owe a great deal.

It soon felt as though I'd never been away as I hit the ground running with an ongoing murder investigation. But uppermost in my mind was the big job, the one I'd left to nurse Norman: what had happened to Operation Augusta and all those vulnerable children whose lives had been torn apart by a network of determined paedophiles?

'Oh yeah, they've warned a couple of the younger lads under the Child Abduction Act,' a colleague told me, off-handedly, when I asked.

My mouth fell open. 'What? You can't be serious! Is that all? What about all the information we gathered? What about all the offenders we identified? What about all those girls being abused on a daily basis?'

But he just shrugged his shoulders. In my absence, the entire job had just died a death and been buried as though it had never existed. The abused girls were seemingly forgotten and simply left to their own devices to try to survive alone. Mark Willdigg, the DI running the job, had fought tooth and nail to try and prevent the investigation from being axed, but he had suffered for his persistence and was moved to another office.

I was totally devastated – all that work, and for what? It just didn't make sense. The crimes we had uncovered on Operation Augusta were not simply minor offences of teenage boys picking up children from outside children's homes. These were predatory paedophiles in organised gangs, targeting vulnerable young children, taking them to sex parties, getting them drunk, passing them round groups of much-older men, who would rape and abuse them repeatedly. And now it appeared that Greater Manchester Police were pretending this wasn't happening. I could not make any sense of what I was hearing.

Had I not gone off the job, and had my husband not recently died, I might have been in a stronger, more determined place to tackle this with those higher up the GMP food chain. But I had been totally out of the loop for about seven months and there was a large gap in my knowledge. In my heart I knew that, at the very least, something odd was going on, but I didn't know how to address it, or who to turn to. I tried to open conversations, to speak to bosses, but I hit a brick wall at every turn and was told there was insufficient evidence to even arrest any of the offenders. Despite the sleepless nights and sense of unease, I was unable to reverse the decision and eventually had to deal with my feelings and accept that the job was closed.

In hindsight, perhaps I should have looked a little more closely at the timeline of Operation Augusta. I'd gone off the job in March 2005. Norman died on 5 July. Two days later, a team of four homegrown terrorists had exploded bombs on the London Underground and on a double-decker bus in the cause of jihad, killing fifty-two people and injuring almost 800. The 7/7 bombings happened the day after it had been announced London had won its bid to host the 2012 Olympic Games. The spotlight of the world was now upon us and the fallout had been wide and far-reaching.

I'd returned to work in September 2005, soon after the HOLMES database on Operation Augusta had been completely shut down. Some years later, however, I discovered that the last entry placed on it was the evening of 6 July – the night before the 7/7 attack. Up until that point, information had been routinely placed upon it, with the Augusta team seemingly working towards arrests and successful prosecutions. Then after 7/7, nothing.

Coincidence? I think not. In my mind, I'm certain that an order was given at the very highest level that to reveal the extent of child grooming of white girls by Muslim men at that point would be akin to adding petrol to an already inflammatory situation. I believe the decision came from the top and was made so the police could avoid accusations of Islamophobia – to avoid being labelled racist. Undoubtedly, it was a very fractious time for race relations in the UK. Equally, it was political correctness gone mad. In short, they didn't want riots on the streets of Britain. In the light of what has happened since 2005, and what we now recognise as a national scandal surrounding this type of sexual abuse, I see no reason to change that opinion as nothing else makes any sense to me. Call me a conspiracy theorist, but to my mind it was more convenient for the Government to ignore the plight of a few so-called 'underclass' girls than to tackle this issue, even if it reared its head at a most inconvenient moment.

Such children were seen as prostitutes, choosing to be horrifically abused and not reporting their rapes to police. There were no parents fighting for these kids because on Operation Augusta, all the children we identified were in care anyway. Forgotten and neglected children, who'd somehow 'brought the situation on themselves'. The powers that be decided that these children didn't matter and that they were worth sacrificing to keep the peace. These girls, these victims, didn't have a voice, especially not now. Here, I felt, were all the signs of neglect of duty.

Chapter Eight

A Mountain to Climb

‘She believed she
could, so she did’
— R.S. Grey

Outside work, I felt as though my life had fallen apart. I didn't have many friends because Norman and I had always been such a team. With nothing else for it, I decided it was time to try to live my life again for the sake of our kids. Norman wasn't here and if his death had taught me anything, it was that life is far too precious to waste. At work, I'd always been seen as a bit of a trailblazer, a little bit different. I'd trained to become a police officer aged forty and with four young children. Then I'd gone into CID, where I'd worked hard to prove myself, and now I'd transferred into MIT. I'd just lost my husband and I knew some people were waiting for me to fall flat on my face.

One of my first jobs in MIT was a fatal stabbing in Partington. No one could get the main witness – a woman – to speak, so I went to see her to try and win her round.

It turned out the woman wasn't hostile, she was frightened because she was trapped in an abusive marriage.

'It's my husband,' she said as her hands trembled against her lap. 'He won't let me speak out.'

It took a lot of coaxing, but I helped her find the courage to speak out. Not only that, but I also helped her to restart her life and go into the witness protection programme. Her vital evidence not only helped, it later secured a conviction in court.

'Good job, Maggie,' a colleague said, giving me a pat on the back, and I felt my team saw what my strengths were, as I had succeeded here where far more experienced detectives had failed. It had been a hard slog, but I finally felt as though I was getting back on my feet.

Back at home, however, we were all struggling, particularly the kids. I missed Norman so much that my bones ached with grief. I was at such a loss that I found myself nipping back to Christie's to see the nurses – the ones who had held our hands through Norman's long and gruelling treatment. They knew what I was going through because they'd lived it with me every step of the way. A couple of months after I'd returned to work, I nipped in and as one of them filled the kettle to make me a brew, I began to open up about how lost I felt without him.

'I just don't know what to do with myself anymore...' I said.

Julie, one of the nurses, handed me a mug of tea and sat down in an opposite chair.

'Maybe you need something to channel all your energies into, Maggie. What about this charity trek we've been talking about?'

'What charity trek?' I was all ears.

'Hang on a minute,' she said, getting up and crossing the room to look for something. 'Ah, here it is,' she added, holding a flyer up in her hand. 'I knew I'd put it somewhere safe.'

She smiled, crossed the room and handed me the piece of paper. I scanned it quickly.

'A charity trek to Borneo?' I said.

She nodded. 'Yes, it's to raise money for bowel cancer. I thought it could be perfect for you.'

I began to read the pamphlet more carefully. As I did so, the starting date burned sharply into focus.

'I don't believe it! The 17th of June…'

'What about it?'

I looked across at her in shock.

'That would've been Norman's fiftieth birthday!'

If I did take part, it would mean setting off on his birthday and I'd be over there on the first anniversary of his death. I took it as a sign that this was meant to be.

'How do I go about registering?' I asked.

I'd never been to Asia and I'd never travelled on my own before. Travelling had always been something Norman and I had done together, but this had fallen right into my lap. It was as though he was watching over me, guiding me and helping me to find the right path. It was an intense feeling and one I've experienced many times since.

Julie explained that I'd have to raise £1,500 for the charity just to secure my place.

'You'll have to pay for your own flights, too,' she warned.

'No problem, it'll give me something positive to focus on,' I said. 'It'll also be a good distraction for me and the kids.'

So, I signed up. Then I spoke to everyone I could think of and decided to plan a night in Norman's honour to raise money for the charity and the Borneo trek.

'I just know it's what your dad would've wanted me to do,' I told the kids later that night.

They agreed and threw themselves into arranging 'Norman's Night', at Nicholson's pub in Altrincham, in his memory. A DJ gave his time for free, we sold raffle tickets and I begged people to donate prizes. I even raffled off my own prize: a week's holiday at the apartment we'd bought in the Canaries. It was an amazing evening with so many memories shared about times spent with Norman. Everyone had their own stories and the night was a roaring success. We raised thousands and remembered Norman and his spirit in a fun and positive way.

One friend of mine, Sarah, a beautician, gave her time for free to set up a beauty salon in my home one Sunday. A different treatment was available in each room with everyone paying for their treatment.

All the money went into the charity pot until soon it began to take on a life of its own. My workplace was very supportive. My colleagues sponsored me for my trip and really held my hand, giving me the confidence and self-belief to push on.

This made all the difference. Within six months, we'd managed to raise an astonishing £5,500. The whole fund-raising experience was such a positive experience, filled with kindness from everyone around us, *and* it helped us get through the painful months following Norman's death.

I didn't realise it then, but I was on the first steps of a journey to heal myself. Although I had friends, they were all mutual friends – other couples. But it was actually when I was standing with other couples that I felt at my loneliest. Although everyone was trying to shore me up, I always felt like the odd one out. It wasn't their fault, it was how I felt inside. However, my planned charity trek changed all that because now I had something to focus on.

Although I'd turned fifty in October 2005, I was fairly fit for my age, thanks largely to all the running I'd done to qualify for the police. I laughed as I recalled Norman, the bloody bleep test, the runs across the freezing-cold field and the Early Learning Centre tape player.

'You were right, Norman,' I whispered as I looked up to the sky and smiled. 'All that running did come in useful.'

I decided I needed to get fit for my Borneo trip, so I took myself off to Derbyshire each weekend to climb every mountain I could find. I'd drag a different victim with me each week to keep me company, from my kids to my friends – there was no way I was suffering alone!

I was due to catch a flight from Manchester to London, where I'd meet the other members of my trekking group – people, like me, who'd lost a loved one to bowel cancer. From London, we'd fly on to Kuala Lumpur in Malaysia, where we'd catch our final flight to Borneo. The day finally arrived. As I sat waiting in the departure lounge at Manchester Airport, I suddenly started to doubt myself.

What the hell are you doing, Maggie? I thought. *You're fifty years old, for Christ's sake, and you're travelling to the other side of the world to trek through a bloody jungle in Borneo, the land of the headhunting tribes and orangutans!*

The more I thought about it, the more anxious I became. *You hate rats, but the jungle will be full of them. How are you going to sleep on the floor with rats running all around you?*

Huge, fat tears began to slide down my face until soon my whole body was wracked with sobs. I'd gone into complete meltdown. It was pure panic.

What if something happens to me? What about my kids? They've lost Norman, they can't lose me as well.

Before I knew it, my hands were fumbling for my mobile phone as I frantically punched at the buttons and called my sister, Di.

'I can't do it, Di,' the words came blurting out of my mouth as soon as she answered the phone.

Thankfully, my sister is extremely level-headed and soon managed to calm me down.

'Get on the plane to Heathrow and meet everyone,' she advised. 'Once you've met them, then decide if you can, or can't do it.'

I thanked her for her advice and put the phone back in my bag. I was fiddling about with one of the pockets of my rucksack when I spotted something: an envelope that had been tucked neatly inside. I was baffled because I knew I hadn't packed it. I tugged it out and opened the envelope to find a letter from my daughter, Vicki. Inside were lots of photos of the kids, me, happy times spent together, and one of me and Norman. My heart ached as I began to read the letter.

'*Dad would be so proud of you...*' our beautiful daughter had written.

As always, her kindness and thoughtfulness had saved the day and, once again, she helped me when I needed it most. I wiped away some stubborn tears that had pricked inside my eyes. She was right: I had to do this, and I would, for Norman. I tucked the precious letter safely in my pocket, followed Di's advice and caught the plane to London, where I met the other thirteen people who'd be doing the trek with me. I was shocked when the organisers told us we'd be the very first non-Borneo people to undertake this gruelling trek.

The group was made up of people of all ages who were there for different reasons, most having suffered personal loss because of bowel cancer, plus an army doctor who would accompany us every step of the way – a sobering reminder of the very real dangers we would face. As soon as we met, I knew I'd made the right decision.

Many hours later, a little weary but determined, we arrived at our hotel in Kota Kinabalu, where we met our local trekkers, Maurice and June. The following day, they took us to the Padua, a fast-flowing river on the edge of the jungle. The plan had been to do white water rafting as part of a team-building exercise, but the rainfall had been so heavy that the river rapids had been assessed as a Level 4 (Level 5 meant rafting was forbidden because it would be life-threatening). I'm ashamed to say, I prayed for more rain so that it would be called off completely. We caught a rickety local train into the back of beyond and got off at a small station in the middle of nowhere, where I was handed a safety helmet, a small oar and was separated into a group with five of my co-travellers.

'This isn't so bad,' I said, pleasantly surprised as we floated merrily along. Suddenly, we hit the first seething rapid known as the 'Washing Machine'.

I screamed as we bounced along and dipped down into

a swirling mass of angry white foam. The raft bumped and spun around like a waltzer until everything blurred. I didn't know if we were facing forwards or backwards.

My arms were absolutely killing me and I actually thought the raft would capsize and throw us all in. But I felt completely alive. For the first time in five years, I'd done something for myself – ever since the fateful day that Norman had fallen from the roof. Totally exhausted but exhilarated, we returned to our hotel to sleep.

The next morning, at the crack of dawn, a jeep arrived to transport us to the edge of the jungle. We were herded together and briefed in a small wooden hut, where we were handed some strange-looking socks. I shook my head as they dangled from my hand. Why on earth would we need socks in a hot, humid jungle?

'Leech socks,' Maurice explained. 'They help keep them out.'

Although Maurice was a local man and an expert guide, I gulped as reality began to hit home. Our lives depended on his skills in the jungle. He knew about things like leeches – horrible creatures that latch on to your skin and suck your blood. They could only be removed with a cigarette lighter, or by wrapping your nails right around them to prise them off. They were everywhere, making me cringe in horror.

It was true – we really were in the middle of the jungle. No mobile phones, no cars, no hospitals, and no contact with the outside world for almost two weeks. The purified water tasted like washing-up liquid and there was no fine dining either. From that moment on, we'd eat food and drink water purely to survive, but our team spirit helped us through each twelve-hour daily trek, sleeping at night in another lonely hut. And there were no beds. Instead, we'd spread our sleeping bags on the open jungle floor.

By day, we'd wade through swollen rivers and swamps fully clothed and up to our necks in the swirling waters; we'd climb uphill through the jungle, our clothes soaked with humidity and sweat, shoulders aching with the pain of carrying a heavy pack for twelve hours a day. One day, Maurice tied a rope around his neck and began wading into the middle of the raging river. He was trying to place a guide rope for us to hold onto while crossing so the current didn't sweep us away, but the river had become swollen with all the recent rainfall.

'It's no good,' he said, climbing back onto dry land, 'the water's too deep.'

'But what will we do? Where will we cross?' someone at the back piped up.

Maurice studied us. We were all completely knackered because we'd been walking all day. He looked us straight in the eye as he delivered a devastating blow:

'The safest place to cross is further up the river, about five more hours' walk from here.'

A collective groan filled the air as the group contemplated five more hours of complete and utter torture. We set off, but soon it turned dark, so we switched on our head torches. Maurice radioed ahead to let some villagers know we were coming. After treading many more miles underfoot, he stopped suddenly and pointed over towards something: we had arrived. But the villagers hadn't even seen us because they were busy, standing in the middle of the river, trying to rescue something. I looked over as water splashed all around – it looked like a deer, our supper for the evening.

That night we slept on bamboo canes the locals had cut down to create a makeshift platform. I was glad of it because all too soon the inky night had come alive with fluorescent insects of different shapes and sizes flying and crawling past. Gathering up the hood of my sleeping bag in my hands, I covered my head – I didn't want anything getting in to bite me. The following morning, the river current pushed against my body, making me sway left and right as I gripped Maurice's rope tightly and crossed the water. I prayed the rope would hold firm because it was all that was stopping me from being swept down the furious river to a certain death.

Shortly afterwards, we walked along in the dark with our head torches glowing, trying to navigate our way around a ravine. We were high up in the jungle but could hear the fast-flowing river hundreds of feet below, when an almighty scream rang out. The girl in front of me had somehow missed her footing and slipped over the side of the ravine, almost falling to her death. Thankfully, Maurice had cat-like reflexes and jumped over, grabbed her wrist firmly and dragged her back up as we all screamed in horror. We took small baby steps the rest of the way, placing one uncertain foot in front of the other, but finally we made it.

Although Maurice had saved my co-trekker, she'd damaged her knee in the fall and couldn't walk any further. With nothing else for it, he radioed for a helicopter. The next morning, we all cleared a landing spot in the remote forest and she was airlifted to safety, her trek well and truly over.

The following day, we approached a rickety old rope

bridge strung across a gorge hundreds of feet below that Maurice said we had to cross. Sadly, one of the girls in our group suffered severe vertigo and was a total nervous wreck.

'I'm sorry, I just can't do it,' she said, looking down at the vast drop below us. 'You go on without me.'

But Maurice refused to leave anyone behind. Instead, we encouraged, coaxed and generally cajoled her until she made it over to the other side. Once she'd reached safety, she was elated.

'I can't believe I've just done that,' she said, shaking her head in disbelief.

'You were brilliant!' I told her.

The gruelling jungle trek had pushed us past what we believed we were capable of. The change in us all had been remarkable.

We were all so busy congratulating her and ourselves that we didn't notice a group of very young children as they approached. The kids couldn't have been any older than five or six years old and each and every one of them was beautifully turned out, with neatly pressed, immaculate clothes. There was no adult with them and my heart was in my mouth as we watched them hop onto the same bridge, one by one, and skip across.

'Where are they going?' I asked Maurice as they crossed without fear or even a backwards glance.

'School,' he smiled. 'They walk two hours through the jungle to school every day.'

I was astonished. 'What? And they do it on their own? Every day? Without an adult?'

He nodded as the children reached the other side, stepped off, smiled, waved and headed off into the dense jungle.

*

By day ten, we'd reached the end of the jungle part of our trek, but the following morning we had to climb Mount Kinabalu, which stands 4,095 metres above sea level and is the highest mountain in Southeast Asia. The higher we climbed, the more we were hit with torrential rain. Soon, the rain had given way to red-hot sunshine before reverting to rain once more. It was truly punishing. At 6pm, we stopped off at a hostel, complete with food and bunk beds, where we had the luxury of five hours' sleep before being dragged from our beds for the last climb to the summit.

Totally knackered, we finally set off in a long line, head torches glowing in the dark, like a long, fluorescent caterpillar winding its way upwards, as the mountain gave way to rockier terrain. There was a flimsy rope that snaked along a well-trodden path for us to hang onto to prevent us from tumbling to our deaths.

As the summit came into view, the sense of achievement I felt was totally overwhelming. We had climbed more than 4,000 metres to the very top, but we'd made it. As I stood there, high above the clouds, the view was breathtaking. Feeling proud of us all, my eyes watered and tears began to fall.

The sun was just beginning to rise and a golden hue peeked over the edge of the horizon. A spectacular dawn began to break right in front of my eyes as I felt my heart soar.

I did it, Norman, I only went and bloody did it! And I did it for you!

Barely able to see because my tears had blinded me, I pulled off a glove and dug a hand deep down inside my coat pocket for my treasured photograph of us both. The picture, wrapped in plastic, had been saturated by rain, sweat and my tears but, as I placed it at the summit, I felt my husband with me, by my side. I turned back and glanced down at the sheer vastness of the mountain and felt a rising sense of pride.

Look how far you've come, Maggie, the voice inside my head whispered. *You've climbed a mountain, both physically and mentally.*

The next few moments were spent in complete silence, taking it all in. I was, quite literally, on top of the world as adrenalin coursed through my veins, flooding me with happiness as I breathed in deeply. Standing there at the top, it felt good to be alive, symbolic somehow. The mountain was the mountain I'd had to climb in my life. I thought about where I'd come from and, with tears rolling down my cheeks, felt the pain of losing Norman again and the struggle of the past five years – of learning to let go of all our hopes and dreams. But standing there, I vowed to build a new life, focus on the future and fight my way out of the darkness. I was fifty years old, yet I'd overcome so much. Norman had been taken too soon, but now it was my job – no, it was my duty – to live life for the both of us. And that was exactly what I'd do.

Chapter Nine
Moving On

❝ Being brave isn't the absence of fear. Being brave is having that fear but finding a way through it ❞

— Bear Grylls

Following my trip to Borneo, my life changed in more ways than one. For the first time since Norman's death, I began to look ahead to what I could do rather than what I'd lost. It was 2006, and it became the year that my confidence started to grow again. After the trek, I stayed in Borneo and treated myself to five days alone in a five-star hotel before flying home. For the first time in years, I felt at peace with myself and slowly began to heal. The life I'd known had ended for ever and I had a choice to make. It was sink or swim, and I chose to live life again. I'd fought many battles for others before, but this time I was fighting for my own survival. I was still furious and horrified that the young victims who featured in Operation Augusta had been badly let down, but what could I do? I was a low-ranking officer and that job had been firmly shut down. I had no access to any paperwork or any computer-based records. I had to carry on with my usual duties and hope that, one day, these victims would get the justice they deserved.

Back in Manchester, I realised I'd come home a completely different person. I enrolled at a gym and started going out for drinks with a friend I made there. I began to build a social life; I was emerging from the darkness. The Take That song 'Relight My Fire' became my anthem and I was determined to grab life with both hands instead of hiding away.

Working in MIT meant I didn't have to do night shifts, which freed up some spare time. By now, Matt, my youngest, was seventeen years old and studying for his A-levels. Although all the kids had been devastated by Norman's death, they were slowly moving on. Danny had met his soulmate and wife-to-be, Julie, and gradually, they moved in together. Vicki was working as a learning mentor in a primary school and doing an Open University degree, while Steve was forging ahead with a career in art after graduating from university. I knew the kids were protective over me because not only was I vulnerable, I was naive too. I'd found myself single and alone for the first time in thirty years and it was a very different world to the one I'd left behind.

In November 2006, Glenn and Elaine, my fellow Borneo trekkers, asked me to join them on a dream trip to Saint Lucia. It was my first ever holiday to the Caribbean. After Borneo, my eyes had been opened to new and wonderful opportunities. Life didn't seem as frightening anymore. I'd been terrified of the sea for as long as I could remember, but now I was snorkelling in open water, facing my fears head on, and I loved every minute.

Elaine (not my trekking pal, but another Elaine from home and my partner in crime from the gym) began to plan our weekends together. I felt like a teenager again as we decided what to wear on our Saturday nights out. She was a few years younger than me, but she was great fun and just who I needed to show me the ropes. Although over fifty, I wasn't quite ready for cocoa and slippers just yet! Spurred on by my new-found confidence, I joined dance classes and then a group called SPICE – a friendship group for single people. I also joined a dating website and would find it flattering when I turned on my computer to find dozens of messages waiting for me. It was an ego boost, even if a lot of them were a little strange. One guy had just come out of his marriage, but as soon as we met, I knew it had been a bad decision because I felt I was being unfaithful to Norman just by sitting there. I was so worried that I spoke to my mother-in-law, who gave me her blessing.

'Norman wouldn't want you to be sat there on your own. What you need to find is an old man with a weak heart and plenty of money!' she smiled.

I knew she was right, but even though it had been two and a half years since his death, it still felt too soon.

One Sunday, Danny asked the whole family round to the home he shared with Julie and Gary, her son from a previous relationship. Julie smiled as she handed me an envelope as everyone looked on. I was puzzled – it wasn't my birthday or Mother's Day. Sliding a finger along the seal, I opened the envelope. Julie and Danny were grinning

137

at me, unable to contain their joy, as I pulled out a photograph – a hospital scan. I was going to be a nana for the very first time!

'Oh my God!' I said, my eyes filling with tears of joy as I hugged them both. 'That is fantastic!'

The whole family was ecstatic. It was exactly what we needed – a tiny new life and hope for the future after all the dark days.

On 15 February 2008, my beautiful granddaughter Macie entered the world. The name means 'gift from god' and that's exactly what she was. She had the face of an angel, beautiful thick golden-brown curls and enormous brown eyes just like her mum. Adored from the moment she entered the world, she was the apple of her mum and dad's eye. Together, they made a perfect little family unit. During those first months of Macie's life, we were all totally besotted. We would even fight about who would bath her and who would feed her. But from the word go, Macie found it difficult to sleep or settle. Julie tried everything, including changing her baby milk.

'I don't know,' she said, 'but I feel something's not right.'

Julie's instincts told her something was different, but she just couldn't put a finger on it. I even wondered whether Macie was just being a little monkey, simply wanting to be snuggled and spoiled.

With a growing family and knowing only too well that life doesn't stand still, I decided it was time to spread my wings a bit and explore opportunities. I took a three-month career break between May and August 2008 and, armed only with a backpack, headed off alone to explore Thailand, Vietnam and Cambodia on a tiny budget, but my spirit of adventure reignited. The future looked exciting, I felt alive again, and as I walked through the 'Killing Fields' of Cambodia, stood awestruck in front of Angkor Wat and journeyed down the Mekong Delta, I looked ahead with hope in my heart that life could be good again.

But before I had to return to work, at the end of my career break, I decided to book a big family holiday for us all with kids, partners and friends. I wasn't sure where to go until Vicki suggested Turkey. So, in July 2008, with Macie just five months old, we all jetted off for our two-week break. Still, Macie was unsettled and screamed non-stop throughout the flight. There was something else too. Once we'd arrived, whenever she went into water she'd stiffen up and scream continuously.

'Maybe it's because the water's cold,' I offered. I could tell Julie wasn't convinced. However, we were determined to make the most of this precious family time together. On our second evening, I went out for a drink with Vicki and her beautiful friend Emma, who took me to a bar she knew from a previous holiday. I became aware of a good-looking guy who wouldn't stop staring at me. Vicki's protective instincts kicked in and she glared over at the stranger to try and warn him off. It didn't work though and he eventually came over to speak to me.

'Would you like to go for a drink with me sometime?' the stranger asked.

I shook my head: 'No, sorry, I'm not interested. I'm here on a family holiday.'

If looks could kill, he would have been struck down stone dead with the look Vicki shot him as she dragged me out of the bar.

*

A few weeks later, and back at work at Greater Manchester Police, I was working on Operation Viola – the biggest gang trial ever mounted to catch the most wanted criminals in Manchester – Colin Joyce and Lee Amos, the top operators of the notorious Gooch gang. I was the Family Liaison Officer (FLO) and also one of the detectives investigating the case. I spent a total of two years on the job, including six months taking the families of the two murder victims – Ucal Chin and Tyrone Gilbert – to Liverpool Crown Court on a daily basis. Joyce, Amos and nine other gang members were later jailed for life in 2009 for the murders. The days were long and gruelling and it had been a very intense investigation but, in between, I'd fly to Turkey to recharge my batteries. After the trial, I also spent several months working with a television producer and director from an independent film company as they met the victims' families: they had wanted to make a factual drama about the case. Throughout all this time, Macie had still been unsettled. Then, in August 2008, when I was away, Danny rang to say that she had been unwell again.

'Mum, we nearly lost her,' he said, his voice shaking with emotion.

Danny explained that they'd been so concerned about Macie that they'd taken her to see the doctor several times that week. By the Saturday, the locum doctor had told them to take her home.

'He told us to put her in her cot and let her sleep. He said she was just overtired.'

They did as the doctor said, but Julie's instincts still told her something wasn't right. Without warning, Macie started to stiffen up and turn blue in her cot. Utterly distraught, Julie called NHS Direct and spoke to a nurse, who immediately dispatched paramedics to the house. They took one look at my granddaughter and realised she was having a seizure. She'd been having a seizure for hours since their visit to the doctor's earlier that day. With no time to lose, Macie was rushed by blue-light ambulance, sirens blazing, to Wythenshawe Hospital.

'We thought we'd lost her, Mum. She was in Resus (the resuscitation bay) for what seemed hours, but then the consultant came to see us to say they'd stabilised her,' Danny explained.

But that wasn't all. He said the consultant had almost been in tears as he explained serious mistakes had been made – that someone had accidentally connected the oxygen tank to the air valve and the air tank to the oxygen valve. As Macie's oxygen SATs had dropped, someone realised she'd been given air instead of oxygen for 'in excess of' six minutes.

'Mum, we thought we'd lost her, but she's going to be okay,' Danny insisted, his relief palpable.

Three minutes starved of oxygen would surely mean possible brain damage, but Macie had been starved for at least six minutes. A voice in my head taunted me, but I didn't say this aloud because I didn't want to frighten Danny or Julie. Instead, I decided to come home and booked myself on the next available flight.

By the time I'd reached the hospital, Macie had been transferred to Pendlebury Children's Hospital and was lying in a bed, eyes wide open. Her tiny frame was attached to life-support machines and a ventilator to help her breathe. As soon as I looked into her beautiful big brown eyes, I felt my heart rip apart inside my chest. I couldn't explain it, but there was emptiness where once there'd been a vitality of life. It was as though someone had flicked a light switch off. She was just six months old, yet my little granddaughter now faced the fight of her life.

How could life deal us another blow like this? How on earth would my son and daughter-in-law cope with yet another tragedy?

Despite Macie's grave condition, Danny and Julie were determined to remain upbeat and positive that she'd recover. They had to believe their daughter would get better because hope was all they had left. In spite of my own fears, I put them to one side and tried to support them in any way I could. The doctors said that although Macie's problems were the result of their mistakes, there was also something else going on which they didn't yet understand. Macie had been starved of oxygen and would need twenty-four-hour care. She'd not only become blind, but from that day on, she lost the instinct to suck so she couldn't have a bottle anymore. Instead, we had to feed her through a tube which ran from her nose down into her tummy. It was unbearable, watching my son's heart slowly break again as he witnessed his beautiful daughter fade before his very eyes. He'd had to deal with the heartbreak of losing his beloved dad and now he faced losing his baby daughter too. I wondered how he and Julie – how all of us – would cope in the weeks that followed.

Macie was stabilised and eventually returned home. Both Vicki and I would help out to give Danny and Julie a break. Julie was forced to give up work to care for Macie full time, while Danny worked from 4am until midday just to earn a wage. It was a constant battle as Macie had to be fed every two or three hours by flushing milk through the tube in her nose into her tummy. Most weekends, I sat downstairs at 3am on my own, checking the colour of the litmus paper tester, making sure the tube was in her stomach and not her lungs. She was also having seizures up to five times a day. One day, she suffered a particularly bad seizure and was rushed to Alder Hey Children's Hospital. One afternoon, as we all crowded round her bed, willing her to pull through, the consultant came in to speak with us.

'I'm afraid we now know Macie was born with a very rare form of mitochondrial disease called Leigh syndrome. It's a very rare condition,' he told us.

We asked him what the life expectancy for a child with this condition would be as the world fell away from under our feet.

'We can't really say, but it is a terminal condition.'

Another devastating blow. However, now we had a proper diagnosis at least the doctors could prescribe the right medication and make Macie as comfortable as possible.

I did all I could to help, sometimes spending a weekend with Macie at Francis House Children's Hospice to give Dan and Julie a breather. Francis House is a magical place and a lifeline to families in the same position we'd found ourselves in. Places are few and far between and many children with limited life expectancy aren't so lucky.

My only escape from yet another heartbreaking situation at home lay in my visits to Turkey. One night, I met a widow like me called Sandra. We hit it off immediately and sat up through the night, talking. Sandra has since become my best friend in the world, my plus-one, my companion on countless adventures. Virtually inseparable, we are a real-life Thelma and Louise, and the stories of our travels and escapades would fill a book of their own! But the joy and laughter our friendship has given us both is precious.

Back home, Macie was growing bigger by the day and she soon became really heavy to lift. We were unsure how long she would live, but we all prayed for more time. Dan and Julie needed an adapted home and because of Macie's severe needs and short life expectancy, she went to the top of the list. While they waited for a house to become available they moved in with me for a few months. We continued to pull together and tried not to think about the time when Macie would be taken from us.

*

Work continued to be my escape and salvation. I threw myself into investigating many brutal cases, including a mother who had smothered and murdered her own baby, and a father who'd set fire to his own home, killing three of his kids. There was a little boy who'd been kidnapped for ransom in Pakistan, another little boy butchered and buried by a school friend, gang shootings and sexual crime. No two jobs were ever the same, yet each one showed the depths humanity sometimes descends to. I'd had my head down, working on many cases, when I heard about a new job that was breaking in the background.

A foetus had been found in an exhibits freezer and a child of fifteen had been arrested on suspicion of being a 'madam'. It was the beginning of December 2010, and although I didn't realise it then, this would become the biggest and most notorious case to date that Greater Manchester Police would deal with.

Chapter Ten

Operation Span

❝ The time is always right
to do what is right **❞**
— Martin Luther King, Jnr.

It was now late 2010, and I was working in the Major Incident Team (MIT) when I was called to Nexus House to speak with Detective Superintendent Sam Haworth. Sam was the Senior Investigating Officer (SIO) on a new investigation called Operation Span and someone I knew pretty well. He had been the boss on an earlier gang murder I had worked on in Moss Side in 2007 and we had visited Jamaica together for a couple of weeks to meet the victim's family and return property.

Sam explained that 'Op Span' (as we abbreviated it) was being set up to investigate the serious sexual abuse and exploitation of vulnerable white children by Asian men over a long period of time. It had been started by Greater Manchester Police following the discovery of a foetus in the police property system during a routine exhibits review. The foetus had been preserved inside an exhibits bag and held inside a freezer since 2009, when it had been seized by police following a termination by one of the victims – a thirteen-year-old child called Ruby. The father in question was a man who had sexually abused her. The powers-that-be were very concerned because Ruby's baby had been taken without her knowledge or consent at a time when the investigation had been run by Rochdale CID.

In a period spanning 2008 and 2009, and during hours of extensive police interviews, two other girls told how they had also been groomed and sexually abused by predominantly Pakistani men, who had abused dozens, if not hundreds, of other girls, in and around Rochdale.

Detectives from Rochdale had made a few arrests, but despite powerful evidence from these girls, no one had been charged. This was partly because the children had been written off as 'unreliable witnesses' who the Crown Prosecution Service had decided had made 'lifestyle choices' and chosen to become 'prostitutes', and so they had been judged as not worth protecting. This in spite of the fact that every single one was a child and almost every one of them was also on the Child Protection Register as being at risk of serious sexual harm. There were echoes of Operation Augusta and some of the attitudes that prevailed back then.

'At the centre of this case are two sisters – Amber and Ruby – who were sexually abused and exploited by these same men,' the Super explained. 'Ruby fell pregnant two years ago, but had an abortion, and Rochdale CID retained the foetus. However, the family still don't know.

That's where you come in, Mags. We need you to tell the family that we have this foetus in our property system.'

My stomach lurched. As a Family Liaison Officer, I'd had many uncomfortable conversations with people over the years, but this, if and when it happened, would be in a different league. Surely it was unlawful to retain a foetus without consent? My thoughts turned to the Alder Hey organ scandal of a few years previously, where the hospital in Liverpool had retained body parts secretly, without the knowledge of relatives. There had been a huge public outcry when that had become known and I felt certain that there would be an identical reaction to this news if it got out. And if it were my child, I'd be suing the police, for sure.

It seemed almost unbelievable that a twelve-year-old girl, who by rights should still be playing with dolls, had been sexually abused, made pregnant and had undergone a termination when she was just thirteen. Not only that, but she had a statement of Special Educational Needs as well. Somewhere along the line, this girl had been very badly let down and it seemed that we as a police force had some culpability too.

If that wasn't bad enough, Ruby's sister, Amber – also a victim of the grooming gang – had been arrested in March 2009 when she was just fifteen on suspicion of Procuring a Child into Prostitution. It was said that through her friendship with other girls of a similar age, she'd brought victims into the kebab shops and thus introduced them to the abusers. She'd never been charged and no further action had been taken, but by arresting her, officers had managed to traumatise and alienate the entire family.

'These two girls are at the centre of this whole investigation,' the super said, 'but because of their previous
dealings with the police, the family is extremely hostile and
unlikely to engage.'

I shook my head in total disbelief. That poor kid – it was
hardly surprising.

'If anyone can gain the trust of this family, we know
it's you, Mags, which is why I've called you in,' the super
added. 'These two sisters are considered pivotal to a
successful prosecution. There's also another girl involved,
called Holly. She gave Rochdale CID a statement about her
abuse and there were a few arrests, but nothing happened
after that. She was friends with Amber, but they've since
fallen out big time.'

It seemed that Amber had been arrested on the basis of
what Holly told CID – that she'd been introduced to these
abusers by her former schoolfriend. *No wonder they've
fallen out*, I thought. I sensed there was more to this story
than met the eye, but the super said that Holly and her
family were being looked after by another officer. My
focus would be on Ruby and Amber.

'So, what is it you want me to do?' I asked, sitting up in
my chair.

'First of all, we need you to tell them we have the foetus
and gain Ruby and her mum's consent for us to use DNA
to establish paternity,' the super said. 'We can then use
that as irrefutable evidence in a prosecution. It's the most
powerful evidence we have. Secondly, we need you to
persuade Amber to tell us about her abuse and reassure her
that this time she will be treated as the victim we all know
she was and she doesn't need to fear otherwise.'

It was obvious to me that I'd been drafted in to clear up someone else's mess. I immediately thought of Operation Augusta and how a decision had been made at a high level to pull that job. Five years on, and it seemed we were back in a very similar place – vulnerable young white girls being groomed and abused by older Asian men. Like déjà vu, it brought back vivid memories of all the anger, frustration and bewilderment I'd felt back then.

'Thanks, but no thanks,' I said, standing up abruptly.

The super looked at me in astonishment.

'I've been here before,' I said. 'Remember Operation Augusta? I've been there, got the T-shirt, and I'm not going to get these kids on board for it to all be dropped again. If GMP had done its job five years ago, maybe this wouldn't have even happened to these kids, Sam.'

I was in no doubt. I was not prepared to gain the trust of yet more vulnerable girls only for them to be messed around and let down again. But as I got up to leave, the super told me to sit back down again.

'I give you my word that will not happen this time,' he said. 'I know it's a massive challenge, but we need these girls, Maggie. They are our best chance of putting these men away and you are our best chance of doing that.' He shuffled through some files on the top of his desk and handed me several policy documents. I flicked through until I came to a paragraph written in bold type. It said:

With careful, considerate, and conjoined victim and witness management the subjects of this operation are attainable and justice can be delivered.

Of Amber, this was said:

> She is/has been both a victim, witness, and a suspect at various stages of this operation, in the preceding years leading to its commencement, and undoubtedly presents some investigative interviewing challenges.

And:

> There is a compelling school of thought that [Amber] is as she is as a result of her abuse as a child, that she is clearly a victim of sexual abuse and grooming when a child, that she was corrupted by the offenders and 'used' to supply child victims to sexual abusers.
>
> Whilst by no means unique, [Amber's] situation and status merits careful consideration, no less the engagement with her until that status is determined – undoubtedly a difficult decision and one which sits with the SIO to resolve (most likely in conjunction with the CPS).

Also this:

> Were she to become a Crown witness there is little doubt her evidence would be both vital and compelling.

Of Ruby, it was said:

> She has undoubtedly been corrupted as a child, let down by a 'system', and is unsurprisingly mistrusting

of authority. She will present a challenge to any interviewer.

These were very clear statements of intent. I read on. There was talk of re-establishing rapport with victims who had already been let down by the authorities. Another document said this:

> It is an investigation which may lead to some laying the blame on the victims. These children have become victims because of their vulnerability, and have been targeted specifically because of this.

Another document stated:

> The over-arching priority is that of safeguarding the victim.

and

> The second priority is to engage/reengage with all the victims and commence to build or reestablish rapport with the individual. Many of them have already been let down by the authorities so this is likely to be a most challenging phase of the investigation.

I was still sceptical, but I appreciated the clarity of these statements. There they were, in black and white – written guarantees that these children would be treated as victims and in a very careful manner. My job would be to persuade these girls to give evidence about their abuse and then hold their hands throughout the entire process until after the court case.

'There'll be no repeat of Operation Augusta,' Sam insisted.

I wanted to believe him, and these detailed documents in my hands told me I should, but I still felt uneasy.

'What about the girl who was arrested for getting other kids involved?' I said. 'She's a child herself. What's going to happen with her? She's a victim, not a criminal. We all know it.'

This was true and was official policy right from the very start of Operation Span. Greater Manchester Police and the Crown Prosecution Service had decided that, far from being a 'madam', Amber was one hundred per cent purely a victim of these men in exactly the same way as her sister, Ruby, Holly and all the other girls. There was no doubt about this at all. But there was a complication: the fact of her being arrested in the first place required a legally watertight explanation as to why she was being treated as a victim now, so that her evidence as a victim could be used in court to assist the prosecution.

Although the CPS recognised from the start that she was a victim, they now had to scrutinise very carefully what had happened to Amber. If they concluded that there was any possible way she could be viewed as an offender, we would have to deal with her differently and would then have to follow the guidelines set out under the Serious Organised Crime and Police Act 2005 (SOCPA), which detailed how we could still use Amber as a witness, while also recognising that she had actually done wrong.

This complex decision-making process had been handed to John Lord, the Head of the CPS's Complex Case Unit, their most senior lawyer qualified to make such decisions.

'The CPS are still thinking about it,' Sam said. 'They'll look at everything she's said, and what's been said about her. The truth is, we need her. We need both these girls. And to bring them on board, you need to read up on the whole thing. And then talk to Mum. There are some serious bridges need building here.'

'Okay,' I said finally. 'I'll go away and think about it.'

In truth, I didn't need long to decide. All the talk was of this operation and the resources being devoted to it, and this time it truly seemed that GMP was putting its money where its mouth was. Perhaps they had little choice – a foetus in a freezer wasn't just going to go away of its own accord. Operation Span was seen as such an important job that the HOLMES system was already up and running. Not only that, they'd devoted an entire floor of Nexus House to it. In fact, it was the biggest job GMP had running at that point in time.

In a subsequent phone call, I was assured that child protection was right at the top of the agenda. The more I thought about it, the more convinced I was that I couldn't just walk away. Every fibre of my being told me I had to get involved and bring these men to justice. They were dangerous paedophiles and they needed locking up and taking off the streets so they couldn't hurt or damage another child ever again. But could I trust GMP not to repeat what I considered the neglect of Operation Augusta? For the moment I had to put these concerns aside and read up on everything that had happened to these girls before I could make that daunting knock on the door. And I needed to do it quickly, because GMP were about to arrest several suspects who would be questioned before being bailed.

After reading the documents, the situation as I understood it was this: In the summer of 2008, a fifteen-year-old girl called Holly had been arrested for criminal damage at a kebab shop, The Balti House in Heywood, a couple of miles from Rochdale. This was a typical Indian takeaway shop, grubby, greasy and smelling of spices. The back of the shop was full of boxes and bottles, and a filthy staircase led to a few rooms above the shop, with stained mattresses on the floors and a wall-mounted TV playing a mixture of Bollywood movies or porn, depending on what time of day it was.

During her interview, Holly told officers she was there with her friend, Amber, also fifteen. At some point during the evening, one of the shop workers had tried to put his hand down Holly's trousers and she'd punched him before smashing a window. During the police interview she mentioned an upstairs room 'where they've got the mattress, where they sleep with under-age girls'. Pressed on this later, she began to tell a story of persistent sexual abuse going back several months, involving a dozen or so young girls, including Ruby and Amber, being preyed upon by numerous Pakistani men. These girls were being passed round like pieces of meat and repeatedly raped. One abuser, who seemed to have taken an obsessive interest in Holly and was the first of the men to rape her, was known as 'Daddy'.

This situation was complicated by the fact that Holly's family situation had fallen apart before she'd even arrived at the Balti House. She'd left the family home and moved into a dysfunctional and chaotic house where her boyfriend lived. This house was owned by a man known for his sexual interest in young girls. Amber and Ruby were both born in Rochdale and had grown up in the same road as this man. Following a temporary move to Nottingham, they'd returned to the Rochdale area, but had been housed by the council some distance from their old home. Bored and missing their old friends and cousins, the sisters had taken to staying over at this house at weekends, which is where they first met and befriended Holly.

Somewhere along the line, Amber and Ruby started to frequent the Balti House. At some stage, Holly accompanied them, and others, but who actually made the suggestion is (at the time of writing this book) a matter of contention. The sisters both agree it was Ruby, not Amber. Holly says otherwise. In the scheme of things it doesn't really matter – they were all children trying to escape from boredom, dysfunction and lives of unremitting poverty, and the kebab shops seemed something new and exciting – but of course it does, because Amber was implicated in coercing others into child prostitution. In the course of these interviews Holly described Amber as 'The Honey Monster', a childish reference to her size. It was a nickname that would come to haunt her as time went on.

I read Holly's account and her descriptions of what she and the other kids had been forced to do by these men was stomach-turning. There were long nights in scruffy rooms above takeaways and sordid sessions in taxis on the tops of pitch-black and lonely moors. There were accounts of multiple penetration while other men watched. Girls were taken on their own to squalid flats, where up to twenty men would pass them round and have sex with them, one after the other. Copious amounts of vodka were involved and girls would be given the occasional tenner for their troubles. Amber, of course, was arrested and interviewed by CID and kept in a cell for seven hours. She refused to comment and instead gave a prepared statement via her solicitor in which she denied any suggestion she was a fifteen-year-old 'madam' and was released and 'NFA'd' – meaning no further action was taken.

As a result of their inquiries Rochdale police arrested the takeaway worker nicknamed 'Daddy' (a man called Shabir Ahmed) on suspicion of rape. He denied raping Holly (despite forensic evidence indicating otherwise), but claimed falsely he'd had sex with Amber (which she always denied). He told police he thought it was consensual and that she was old enough to give that consent. Amazingly, crucial forensic evidence was lost, no further action was taken against him and, as time went on, Holly was considered to be an 'unreliable witness'. Then, in March 2009, Ruby went for a termination, having been made pregnant by one of her abusers, and it was then that the aborted foetus was seized and placed in a freezer awaiting permission to examine it for DNA evidence – permission that I now had to seek from the family, even though they were still unaware police had kept the foetus.

Undoubtedly, Rochdale CID had made mistakes – big ones. One minor incident in a takeaway had opened up a huge can of worms, too enormous for a local CID office to deal with. Yet, to their credit, Rochdale CID had done the one thing vital to any investigation of this potential size: every scrap of evidence had been written down and uploaded to the GMP Operational information System. This meant that as Operation Span got underway, we had a very clear picture of what was going on in Rochdale. A dedicated analyst had pieced together multiple and detailed 'Spider Charts' linking all the complicated strands between abusers and victims, including relationships, business links, cars used, locations visited, etc. I wondered if there might be any connections between this gang of abusers and those around the Curry Mile from Operation Augusta – the ones who were never arrested for anything. But while we had a lot of information, what we didn't have was the vital evidence that Ruby and Amber could provide.

It wasn't surprising that the family were hostile to the police. Amber and Ruby's mother, Lorna, had repeatedly told the authorities in multi-agency case conferences (which usually involved police, social services, sexual health, council and education representatives) that her girls were involved with Pakistani men and were being abused. Unfortunately, this woman came up against a wall of wringing hands and mutterings about girls who made 'lifestyle choices' – the very same attitudes I'd encountered while working on Operation Augusta. It seemed the authorities' emphasis on political correctness and a high-handed attitude to the so-called 'underclass' was again enabling child abusers to operate freely and without fear of investigation, arrest and prosecution. Yet up until Amber's arrest on suspicion of being a 'madam', the poor girl had never been in trouble with the police, which was very unusual among victims of the grooming gangs, who normally led troubled lives. There was an absolute belief among us on Operation Span, however, that she'd been a victim of child abuse and as such should not have been arrested at the age of fifteen and treated as a criminal.

In short, and despite misgivings stemming from what happened on Operation Augusta, I didn't have to spend too long deciding. A day or so later, I called Sam and told him I was willing to help. I trusted him and knew he was committed to this: 'I'll do try my best to get the family on board,' I told him, 'and get justice for these kids.'

'That's brilliant news, Maggie,' he said, 'and it's great to have you with us.'

But as I suspected, getting this family to cooperate with us would be easier said than done. Time was of the essence, so a few days after I'd agreed to join the job I found myself standing outside a run-down council house with a male colleague. It was a freezing cold December morning and I patted my gloved hands, rubbing them together to try and keep out the cold. The male officer standing beside me shifted from one foot to the other, trying to do the same. I tapped on the door. We waited for an answer. The muffled sound of dogs barking broke the silence, then movement and voices coming from inside as we waited patiently on the doorstep. After what had seemed like ages, a lock turned and the door creaked open, revealing a small, dark-haired, middle-aged woman.

'Yeah?' she said, wrapping her arms around herself. I wasn't sure if it was a sign of defence or to try and keep herself warm.

'Hello,' I said, smiling at her. 'Are you Lorna?'

But she didn't respond. She seemed guarded and on high

alert as she looked me up and down as though trying to suss me out.

'Who wants to know?' she finally responded.

'Hi, Lorna. My name is Maggie. I am a detective with Greater Manchester Police...'

I'd barely got the words out of my mouth when Lorna's mood clouded over and turned to anger. 'Fuck off! Whatever it is, just fuck off! I'm not interested,' she said, grabbing hold of the door to shut it.

My colleague stepped forward a little too defensively.

'Listen,' he said in a patronising voice, holding up his hands as if trying to deflect the fallout from an unexploded bomb. 'I know you don't want to speak to us, but we've got to go through the motions...'

He'd managed to sound both condescending and dismissive – I could have thumped him. Lorna obviously felt the same because she slammed the door right in our faces.

I turned to my colleague and glared.

'What?' he said, as though he didn't have a clue what he'd done wrong. Yet it was obvious to me and it had been obvious to Lorna. The way he'd spoken to her and the 'can't be bothered with this or you' attitude were the last thing needed if we were to win this family over.

Back at the office, I called in to see the boss: 'If you want this family to come on board, Boss, then you've got to let me do this on my own to begin with. I need to build bridges with Lorna, but in order to do that, I need to do it my own way – mum to mum. Without her support, I'm on a hiding to nothing.'

He thought for a long minute, turning it over in his mind, then leaned back in his chair and looked at me.

'Right, whatever you need, you have my support. If that's the way you want to work it, then that's okay by me.'

Now I had the green light to operate in the way I'd always done in these situations: with tact, discretion and relying on instinct rather than hard-nosed procedure. To begin, I telephoned the girls' social worker to ask for some background and was sent some notes.

The notes made for difficult reading – a mum was trying to hold a family of seven children together in circumstances best described as 'chaotic'. She'd lost one son to an overdose. The young boy had spent time in Knowl View, a local children's home that has since become notorious as a place that former local MP Cyril Smith, with other paedophiles, regularly visited to sexually prey upon the poor children living there. Lorna's son had been abused and had never recovered. For me, his tragic death highlighted the damage that child sexual abuse can do to any victim of it.

Both Amber and Ruby were on the Child Protection Register. The social worker knew both were being abused by local Pakistani men and although she had told police, it was still Amber who was arrested. Lorna attended case conferences involving Social Services and police but was told repeatedly that 'they couldn't do anything'. If she protested loudly, which she regularly did, she was told to either stay quiet or be thrown out of the meeting. Then she dealt with the horrendous circumstances surrounding Ruby's abortion and all the fallout over that. Despite everything, it seemed she was trying her best to be a protective mum and I very much wanted to meet her to form my own opinion of her – not one based on case notes.

I couldn't hang around. Eight suspects had now been brought in and told why they'd been arrested. Many of us were shocked – it seemed the cart was being put in front of the horse and that we'd not even done one interview to uncover fresh evidence when the men were brought in for questioning. Our opinion was that arresting them at this stage was making them aware we were on to them to tip off any other men involved with child sex offences and not yet arrested, who could dispose of evidence and get their stories straight. But it happened anyway.

The day after I'd read the report about the family, I dialled a Rochdale number and waited for an answer.

'Hello,' a gruff voice answered after the fifth ring.

'Hello, Lorna, it's Maggie here, from the police. I came to visit you the other day. How are you?'

There was a stunned silence on the other end of the line.

'I've told yer, I don't want to speak to yer,' she said bluntly.

'Listen, that's fine,' I said. 'I just wanted to wish you and your family a Happy Christmas.'

'I said, leave me alone.'

'Okay, I won't bother you before Christmas, Lorna, because I'm sure you're really busy with all your tribe,' I said. 'But I'd like to pop in on my own in the New Year, so would it be okay if I gave you a call then? Would you mind?'

Another silence. I crossed my fingers, hoping she'd say 'yes'.

'No, I don't mind,' she said. 'Right, I've gorra go.'

And that's when I saw it – a small chink of light at the end of a very long and dark tunnel. 'Great! That's great, Lorna. Thank you.'

It had been the breakthrough we'd been waiting for.

'Well,' I continued breezily, 'you have yourself a lovely Christmas and I'll call you in the New Year.'

I felt absolutely elated when I put down the phone. There was still a long way to go, but at least now she was willing to speak to me.

*

Just after Christmas I picked up the phone again. I didn't want to harass Lorna, but neither did I want to lose the small amount of rapport we'd established. Back in the 1960s there was a police-themed drama on TV called *Softly, Softly*. This, in a nutshell, was the way I was approaching Lorna.

I rang and she picked up the phone.

'Hi, Lorna,' I said, 'it's Maggie. I said I'd call. How was Christmas? Did the kids have a good time?'

There was a pause. My stomach turned over. How would she respond? Would she just put the phone down?

'It were alright,' she replied. 'Nice enough. How were yours?'

And with that, I began to build up a relationship, calling her most days. I realised from the outset that Lorna was a good mum – she'd just been dragged down by life. By the beginning of January 2011 we'd spoken a few times. It was clear she had a lot on her plate and the last thing I wanted to do was add to that. But I also wanted to help her, even though I totally understood why she didn't want to help the police.

'I'll tell you what,' I said one day during one of our chats, 'let's go for a brew tomorrow. I'll come and pick you

Left: Me, aged 5, with a home-knitted cardigan and crooked fringe.

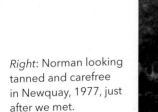

Above: My wedding day, April 1981 and three months pregnant with Steve.

Left: Me and my beautiful kids, with my 80s mullet. A very happy stay-at-home mum.

Right: Norman looking tanned and carefree in Newquay, 1977, just after we met.

Left: My graduation in BA (Hons) Humanities, July 1997. A very proud day I'd waited over twenty years for.

Right: My swearing in, 23rd October, 1997. I swore that day to honour every word of the Oath of Attestation.

Left: Danny and Norman on holiday in Florida, 2002. Catching that shark was a lifetime highlight for them both.

Right: Norman after completing The Great Manchester Run in 2004 – one year into chemotherapy.

Left: I carried this photo with me in my battle to reach the summit of Mount Kinabalu. I left a copy there in Norman's memory.

Above: With Amanda, my special nurse from occupational health and her daughter. Without her, I wouldn't still be standing today.

Below left: Me and my best mate & partner in crime, San.

Left: At the top of Mount Kinabalu... totally overcome with emotion, after a gruelling climb to the summit.

Right: White water rafting on the Padua River in Borneo. Terrifying but exhilarating!

Left: Setting off on my travels around spiritual India just before my first public disclosure on *File on Four*.

Margaret conquers Borneo for Norman

by Julia Taylor

MARGARET Oliver, a widow from Broadheath, will be whitewater rafting down the Padas River in Borneo on June 17 - the day her late husband, Norman, would have celebrated his 50th birthday.

Norman died from bowel cancer last July.

She will also be trekking through the jungle and climbing Mount Kinabalu, the highest mountain in south east Asia, for the charity, 'Beating Bowel Cancer'.

It aims to raise awareness of early warning signs such as a change in bowel habits or passing blood. Early diagnosis often leads to a complete cure.

Norman first suffered symptoms in January 2003 but they were put down to piles or irritable bowel symptom.

It wasn't until March 2003 that he was diagnosed with

Margaret Oliver is looking forward to whitewater rafting in Borneo

bowel cancer but, although he received surgery and chemotherapy treatment, the condition had already spread to his liver.

The spur for Margaret was

the gratitude she felt to Christie Hospital for allowing Norman to use the drug Cetuximab when he didn't strictly meet the criteria, and the support given by district nurses at the end.

"The drug allowed us to have another seven months of happiness together," said Margaret.

"After eight weeks there had been a 60 per cent reduction in the tumours in his liver.

"He was so much better that we went on holiday to the Canaries. He even built a conservatory when he was on chemo.

"He was always laughing and joking."

After the cancer entered his spine, Norman spent his last months at home.

"Me and the four children (now aged 17-24) were with him when he died. He just fell asleep.

"Home was the best place for him to be," said Margaret.

Before she even contemplates fitness training, Margaret, who has already raised £1,200 at a beauty evening run by 'Peaches and Cream' from Timperley Village, is planning 'Norman's Night', a huge fundraising evening for 250 people, to be held at Nicholson's in Altrincham on Sunday.

Tickets, priced £5, are available from 0161 928 7732.

Below right: Me in the *Sale and Altrincham Messenger*.

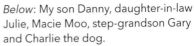
Below: My son Danny, daughter-in-law Julie, Macie Moo, step-grandson Gary and Charlie the dog.

Above: Making the most of my precious time with our little Macie Moo.

Left: Family time with my precious daughter Vicki, gorgeous grandsons Jake & Charlie, son-in-law Mike and step-granddaughter Aimee in Turkey.

Below right: My three gorgeous sons... Danny, Matt and Steve. (Clockwise)

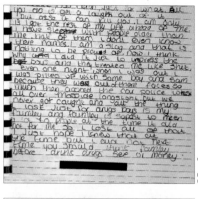

Above: Victoria Agoglia and her letter...

Middle right: Thank goodness for Andrew Norfolk and his brave reporting for *The Times*.

Below: Heywood, Rochdale. The place many of these men sought out their victims.

THE TIMES

Move over Carla Meet France's new first lady

A nation's shame

Nine men are found guilty of sex grooming crimes against vulnerable young girls after a trial that has exposed the shocking scandal in Britain's children's homes

Left: Three Girls. L-R: Ruby (Liv Hill), Holly (Molly Windsor), Amber (Ria Zmitrowitcz).

© BBC

Right: Lesley Sharp playing yours truly!

© BBC

© PA Images

Above left and right: Cleaning up at the BAFTAs with the cast and crew.

Top: Memories from *Celebrity Big Brother* – I still can't believe I went on!

Above left: With the *Loose Women* team and Sammy Woodhouse, to promote our campaign *Never Too Late To Tell*.

Right: At a charity event for Fresh Start – new beginnings with (L-R) Jo Grant, Patsy Johnson-Cisse, me, Kieron Dyer, Minnie Molls, and Diana Porter MBE.

up, then we can go somewhere we can talk in private – give you a bit of a break, eh?'

'Erm, okay, go on then,' Lorna replied.

The following day, I called round as arranged, but this time when I knocked on the door she didn't slam it in my face.

'I'll just be a mo,' she grinned, grabbing her coat.

I drove over to the nearby supermarket, where we sat in the café and chatted about everything and nothing in particular. It had taken an enormous amount of work just to reach this stage and I didn't want to go and sabotage it by moving things along too quickly. I walked over to the counter, where I bought us tea and two slices of cake. It was obvious from the look on her face that this trip out was a rare treat. I sat back down as we both began to natter away.

'I've got a few kids too,' I told her in a bid to break the ice. 'Four of them.'

Lorna looked surprised as she sat back in her chair. 'Four?'

'Yes, we didn't have a TV in my day either!' I joked. 'I also have a beautiful granddaughter, Macie. But it's not been easy for her...'

The more we talked, the more I opened up, until soon I was telling her all about Macie and the difficulties she'd faced.

'Poor little lamb,' Lorna said, shaking her head sadly.

I'd opened up to Lorna, because I wanted her to trust me. How could I expect her or her girls to confide their darkest secrets in me, unless I was prepared to share some of my own troubles with them? If Lorna saw me as a

165

mother too, as a human being rather than just a detective, then it would be easier for her to speak to me – it seemed like the natural thing to do. That day, she and I connected properly for the first time. It was obvious to me that she loved all her kids – she was just exhausted, trying to juggle a hundred balls in the air at once, and as she confided in me, it became very clear that she had suffered a lot in her own life too, from the moment she had been born. In many ways I admired the fact she was still standing.

'Same again on Tuesday?' I asked as we stood up to leave.

For the first time, Lorna's face broke into a smile.

'Yeah, I'd like that, Maggie,' she said.

Talking to me soon became a form of respite for Lorna, even if I was a copper. However, first and foremost, I was a mother and I understood her loyalty to her girls. After that day, she seemed to look forward to our cuppas. Back at home, her life and house were chaotic, with people coming and going, and four dogs taking up every available space. So, a couple of hours out, even if it was only in a supermarket cafe, was a bit of respite away from the madness.

There is a lovely reservoir outside Rochdale, called Hollingworth Lake, so, one day, I picked up Lorna in the car and we drove over there. With her youngest child in a pushchair, we fed the ducks and walked around the lake together. By now, I realised that Lorna saw me as a person rather than a police officer. After our walk, we stopped off to buy a bag of chips and sat down on a bench to eat them.

'Those men, they pulled out a gun and threatened to kill Amber, yer know,' she said suddenly.

It was the first time she'd touched on the abuse of her girls.

'Did they? And what did you do?' I asked her gently.

She turned and laughed out loud. 'That's bloody ironic,' she said, a note of bitterness in her voice.

'Why?' I asked.

'Because you're a copper, Maggie,' she said, 'and I've tried for years to get the police to listen to me. I told them all, yer know. I told them in different meetings, but no one wanted to know, not the police, not Social Services, no one.'

'So, what did you do? About the man who'd threatened to shoot Amber, I mean?'

Lorna sighed and rolled her eyes.

'That was it, yer see. I didn't know who to turn to. I kept banging on doors, telling them, but no one would listen, so I spoke to me son. He's in prison, you see, so I knew he'd know someone who'd have a quiet word, if yer know what I mean.'

A shudder ran through me. I knew exactly what she meant – she'd been forced to take the law into her own hands just to try and protect her girls. Then she told me about her other son, who'd been abused as a child in the now notorious Knowl View Children's Home in Rochdale (where Cyril Smith had operated) and had eventually died of an overdose at a very young age.

'It broke me heart, Maggie,' she said quietly, her voice cracking with emotion, as she rubbed an imaginary mark from her trousers. 'And to make it even worse, it was our Amber who found him on our couch the morning he died. She's never really got over it.'

The more she spoke, the more she opened up to me. I listened to her and became someone she could finally talk to. I didn't judge her, I tried to understand her, and over the weeks that followed, as her trust in me grew, she began to tell me what had happened to her family. I'd already read a very one-sided account in a social services report, but I wanted to hear it from her – in her own words. I didn't need somebody else's 'version' of the truth.

'Look, Lorna,' I said, 'I'm not going to lie. You know there's a big investigation going on and I want your girls to tell me what they've been through. If they agree to do that, they'll be supported right the way through. We *all* want to see these men prosecuted and put in prison. Your Amber and Ruby are the best people to help us do that. And they'll help stop other kids being abused too.'

Lorna suddenly grew angry as she recalled what police had done to her eldest daughter. Her kind, exhausted face turned into an irritated snarl.

'I've been asking for help for years, but no one wanted to know. Then, just when I thought it couldn't get any worse, they arrested Amber.'

At this I nodded. I understood where she was coming from because, in her position, I would have felt exactly the same.

'I just don't trust them – the police, I mean,' she said, before holding up her hand. 'Sorry, no offence, Maggie.'

'Don't worry, none taken,' I said, hugging her close and feeling her anger mixed up with her despair and fear.

Lorna smiled briefly, then her face clouded over as she recalled what had happened.

'They put her in a police cell for seven hours. Seven

fucking hours! She was fifteen years old and terrified out of her wits. She'd done nothing wrong, Maggie. She was a victim, just like my Ruby and all the other kids. Why would they do that? Why would they punish her like that, and only her?'

Of course we now know that countless other children throughout the UK have been failed in the same way too. I had no answers, I just felt shame at what the police and the authorities had done to this family and how they had been failed.

'What do you think they'll say if you ask them to talk to us?' I said.

Lorna looked down at her hands, then impatiently wiped away the tears that streamed down her face.

'I know it's going to be so very hard for them to talk about the abuse,' I continued as gently as I could. 'My bosses all know what's happened before, but this time it will be very different, Lorna. They've given their word.'

She sat in silence as the enormity of what I was asking her sank in. Her poor abused girls would have to put themselves through hours and hours of interviews to remember and describe in the most minute detail the worst times of their lives, times they had now left behind them, and which they had spent almost two years trying to forget. And for what? To ensure these men were stopped from abusing other children in the same way. They stood to gain absolutely nothing themselves, except pain as they relived their worst nightmares. Why should they help us when we had failed them repeatedly in the past?

'The police wouldn't even allow me to go with her, did you know that?' she said. 'They treated us all like criminals.'

I shook my head.

'It left her scarred, up here,' she said, tapping a finger against the side of her head. 'Messes a kid up, something like that. She was bloody terrified – still is. Gave her a phobia of police stations. She's scared stiff because she thinks they're gonna throw her in a cell again and never let her out.'

'Lorna, that isn't going to happen,' I said, taking hold of her hand. 'Amber is a victim, the same as all the other children. We know she should never have been arrested before, but this time it is different, I promise. We will support you all right through this process. Trust me.'

In response, Lorna began to tell me about her girls' lives now. Amber had eventually found the strength to break away from the grooming gang and had settled down with a boyfriend, when she found herself pregnant. She'd given birth, but because of Ruby's 'anger issues', Social Services decreed she wasn't allowed to live at home with her mum. Even worse, because Holly had also had a baby at almost the same time and was put into the mother and baby unit, Amber was not allowed to go there either because the two girls had fallen out after the police became involved. So pretty much abandoned by the state, this lonely girl had been forced to live in a room on the top floor of a hostel for the homeless – hardly the ideal place to bring up a baby.

Aside from the abuse and subsequent abortion, Ruby had other challenges. She had a Statement of Educational Needs, attended a special school and had been diagnosed as having a younger age than her chronological age. The poor kid had been vulnerable in more ways than one. But unlike her elder sister, Lorna told me that Ruby was very vocal. She had been in lots of trouble and already had a minor criminal record. And yet, Amber alone seemed to be the one who'd been demonised, painted as a 'bad girl' – a label that now seemed to be permanently attached to her. I just couldn't understand it.

'Amber hates it in that hostel,' Lorna told me. 'It breaks my heart, Maggie, because she's such a good mum, if only they'd give her a chance.'

She explained that Amber was now eighteen and her baby just a few weeks old.

'I'd like to meet her and her baby,' I said.

Lorna's eyes filled with stubborn tears but she used the back of her hand to wipe them away before they had a chance to fall. This poor woman had been banging on doors, trying to ask for help for years. In return, those who were supposed to protect her children had effectively punished her and still were. They'd destroyed her family and had almost broken her spirit. She was down, but she wasn't out – not by a long chalk. There and then, I vowed to do my utmost to help them all as much as I could and give them the strength to tell me about their abuse so the monsters who had destroyed their childhoods went to prison for what they had done.

I was lost in my thoughts when Lorna turned to me.

'Our Amber, well, she's a great little mum, Maggie. She really is, but it'll break your heart when you see her in that homeless place.'

'So, do you think she'll see me?' I asked tentatively.

She nodded. 'I'll have to ask her,' she said, 'but yeah, I think she will.'

At this I smiled. I couldn't have hoped for better.

Chapter Eleven
Two Children

> ❛Children need your presence far more than your presents❜
> — Jesse Jackson.

What first hit me when Lorna and I walked inside the homeless unit was the smell – a mixture of chemicals trying, but failing, to mask the underlying stench of piss. I shuddered. Lorna was right: it was no place to bring a child, never mind house a three-month-old baby.

'She's up on the top floor,' Lorna muttered as she began to tackle the stairs.

'What about the lift?' I asked, pointing over towards it.

She looked over her shoulder and waved a hand dismissively.

'Oh that, it's always buggered.'

I was stunned. 'But the pram? How does she get it up all these flights of stairs?'

'Carries it.'

I felt breathless just climbing the stairs, so I couldn't

begin to imagine how Amber did it, day in, day out, with a small baby and pram in tow. Once we'd reached the top, Lorna paused to catch her breath, then she pointed down a long corridor towards a cheap brown door right at the end.

'She's down there.'

The hallway was dimly lit – a flickering light bulb was all we had to try and navigate our way along it towards her door. Outside, Lorna knocked loudly.

'Amber, it's me, it's yer mum.'

I heard footsteps on the other side and the sound of metal scraping against wood as a key turned, undoing what sounded like a substantial, solid lock. The door creaked open a fraction and a nervous eye peered through, studying us both.

'Who's that?' a voice asked suspiciously.

The single eye quickly darted over towards me.

'This is Maggie,' Lorna explained. 'She's the one I've been telling you about. She's alright, Amber, I promise.'

The sound of a metal chain being uncoupled followed and as Amber removed the latch hesitantly, I caught my first glimpse of the young girl who had been locked up on suspicion of being a 'madam' more than two years previously. Still just a child now, I saw her frightened eyes as she looked at me through the gap in the half-open doorway.

'Come in,' she said in a voice that sounded as if it had been numbed by exhaustion. As the door opened further, it revealed a meagre and sparse bedsit that was miserable to say the least. The depressingly cramped room was empty apart from a cot, pram and other bits of baby paraphernalia. Amber's little boy seemed clean and happy, and he was surrounded by toys. It was clear, even given her dire circumstances, that she was trying her very best.

'Can I have a hold?' I asked, gesturing over at her baby.

She eyed me warily and looked over at her mum, who nodded as though giving her permission. Reluctantly, Amber picked up her little boy and handed him to me. His face momentarily scrunched up as he stretched both arms above his head, his body arching and stiffening slightly, as he yawned silently. I felt my heart melt: he was absolutely gorgeous.

'He's just had a feed,' Amber explained quickly, as though I was there to judge her. She stepped forward, stroked his cheek lovingly with her fingertips and looked down at him adoringly.

'I think he's tired,' she added.

'What a little cutie,' I replied.

I pressed my face up against the mass of dark hair on the top of his head and inhaled the sweet, buttery smell – the one that only newborn babies have. His tired eyes already closed, I rocked him gently to sleep. With him slumbering in my arms, I glanced around the grim surroundings. The small room felt as oppressive and claustrophobic as a prison cell, which was exactly what it was to Amber. She was stuck inside her solitary bedsit, too frightened to leave in broad daylight for fear of bumping into the men who had abused her. The whole set-up felt thoroughly unfair and depressing.

'Well, he's absolutely beautiful,' I said, trying to lift the sombre mood, 'and it's quite clear to me that you're doing a fantastic job.'

Amber sighed as her face broke into a proud and relieved smile. It was clear she wasn't used to receiving compliments. I felt for her. She was the same age as Matt, my youngest child. I couldn't begin to comprehend my children in that situation. Also, her baby boy was just two years younger than Macie. It broke my heart to see them existing in such squalor when Amber was still just a kid herself. Lorna was trying her level best to support her, but she had enough on her plate with her other children.

'Would it be alright if I came to visit you again, Amber?' I asked gently.

She looked at me and shrugged her shoulders. 'Yeah, if you want.'

I knew she was suspicious even though her mum had told her I was trustworthy and I didn't blame her. Amber was nothing like the 'madam' she'd been painted out to be. In fact, I couldn't square it inside my head – how this young, frightened girl had been treated the same as the vile men who'd abused her, her sister and countless other children, but unlike all the other girls, Amber alone had been punished and was still paying the price. It seemed both morally wrong and inhumane, and I felt every protective instinct within me rise with the injustice and cruelty of her situation.

Afterwards, I visited her most days, with the encouragement and full support of the Senior Investigating Officer (SIO). Not only was I concerned for her wellbeing, I felt responsible because, in my opinion, but more importantly in the opinion of the SIO and every senior officer on Operation Span, she'd been badly treated by Rochdale CID. Instead of interrogations and accusations,

I offered support, encouragement and compassion. I also treated her as a human being.

I took her out for a brew, baby in tow, just as I'd done with her mum. Whereas I'd built bridges with Lorna as one mum to another, now it was time to do the same with Amber. But my relationship with Amber was more like mother and daughter as she reminded me so much of my Vicki. I managed to borrow a baby seat for the car so we could take Amber's precious cargo with us wherever we went. We never once spoke about the ongoing investigation because I followed my orders to the letter. We were all waiting impatiently for the top lawyer in charge of the Complex Case Unit in the Crown Prosecution Service to deliver his decision on the way to proceed with interviewing Amber – should she agree to tell us of her abuse, of course.

Lorna soon began to open up even more to me. She told me that around the time of her daughter's arrest, she'd spoken to Amber, who had told her the police had wanted to talk to her about people 'she'd been hanging around with'. Lorna had been away nursing a terminally ill family member, but when she returned to Rochdale, Social Services came to see her and put her children on the Child Protection Register. Soon after that, Amber was arrested.

No charges were ever brought because this girl had been a child victim of abuse, not a sex offender. But now, more than two years later, she was still paying the price for that arrest and being punished. A year after her arrest she was attending a training course locally and, by all accounts, doing well. But after she'd had the baby Social Services had forbidden her from attending a new mums and tots group simply because she had been arrested in connection with an alleged sexual offence. She was also banned from going into a drop-in centre at a young mothers' hostel.

Lorna said: 'She turned around to me and said, "Mum, why can't I go anywhere there are young people? Why do I have to be with old people all the time?" It broke my heart. I argued with the police and every other agency, and made it very clear what was going on at every case conference, but they just said they couldn't do anything. I felt like I was going mad.'

She shook her head in despair as she recalled: 'I asked them why they were chasing my girls when they were doing nothing about these taxi drivers who are licensed by the council. They're supposed to be safe, but these men take young kids to school and they're doing nothing.'

I shook my head along with her. *What on earth was going on?*

'They used to threaten to chuck me out of the case conferences if I didn't shut up, but they were punishing my kids, putting them on a Child Protection Register even though it was my girls who were being sexually abused,' she said.

It soon began to emerge that the girls who had been victims of these men had been failed in more ways than one, and by all the different agencies that were meant to protect them. It made me even more determined to get justice for them. Then I discovered something else: I'd been reading Social Services notes that had mentioned something about an organisation called the Crisis Intervention Team (CIT) – a sexual health service that provided condoms and confidential contraception advice to the children who dropped in there. I felt this organisation might be useful so I called them and spoke to a woman who worked there called Beth. She'd been Ruby's support worker and the person she would go to for contraception. Up until this point, no one in Operation Span was aware that CIT even existed, so I decided to just drop in there one afternoon.

I introduced myself to Beth and told her why I'd called in. She was keen to help, and as Ruby's sexual health worker, Beth had actually driven Ruby for her termination. As we talked, she pulled out an enormous file containing more than 900 pages of notes, which she personally had gathered about Ruby, and we began to go through it.

Beth told me that Amber was also a regular at CIT and had dealt with another lady, Tanya. Beth and Tanya had soon begun to see a pattern of behaviour between the girls. They were so concerned that they'd started to keep notes on all the children they'd dealt with and informed the CIT manager, Sara Rowbotham. It was Sara's job to write reports, attend case conferences and pass on information gathered by Beth, Tanya and other support workers. Amber and Ruby's files were thick with information on men the girls had told them they'd had sex with. It was not only dynamite evidence collected by two professionals who would add a level of credibility to the investigation, it backed up everything the girls had already told us.

Naturally, I asked Beth if I could take copies of the files to take away, but she said she would have to speak to her boss. After a few moments Beth re-entered the room with Sara, and she and I circled each other like lions stalking their prey. I think we both considered the other to represent 'the enemy' in a way. My opinion was that handing out condoms like sweets to vulnerable kids, some as young as eleven or twelve, without having a conversation with their parents seemed somehow questionable to me, a mum of four. Sara saw me as part of a police force which had failed to investigate or act on the information shared with us at numerous case conferences. Perhaps this was the reason why, as CIT manager, she refused point-blank to let me copy any of the twenty-six files and instead told me I would have to go through official Data Protection/ Subject Access channels. I felt this wasn't the most helpful approach, though I did understand her refusal to hand over documents to a police service which, to say the least, had been late dealing with the problem.

Mindful that I didn't want to make enemies of these people because they held so much evidence, I didn't argue with Sara's refusal. Instead, I returned to the office to speak to Sam, my super.

'Oh my God,' I said, barely able to contain my excitement, 'we've got the key to this case! There are files with names, places, even car registration number plates.'

The boss raised an eyebrow. 'Then go and get those files, Maggie,' he said.

Fired up, I spent hours filling out the necessary forms. It was frustrating because I knew it would take weeks for them to come through but, in the meantime, I focused my efforts on continuing to get to know Amber.

*

Back at home, Macie's health continued to fail and juggling work and family responsibilities was a daily pressure, but one I was very well used to. In fact, in many ways my work became a way to cope with the uncertainty surrounding Macie's life expectancy. I insisted we all tried to balance her needs with some kind of life too. At times we took a little step back to recharge our batteries so that we didn't all burn out at the same time. In January 2011, I was away for a few days visiting friends in Turkey when my phone rang. It was San, my best friend from back home.

'Mags, your Danny's been on the phone,' she said, urgency in her voice. 'Macie's taken a turn for the worse. They've rushed her to Manchester Children's Hospital.'

My heart began to pound. I put down the phone and immediately rang Danny. He'd been trying my phone but it had been night-time and it was turned off. He confirmed my greatest fear: Macie was very poorly and had been admitted to Intensive Care. My head was buzzing as I desperately booked the first flight home. Waiting at the airport, I said a silent prayer inside my head:

Please don't let Macie die. Please let me make it in time.

On the plane, I switched off my mobile and checked my watch constantly, willing my granddaughter to live long enough to allow me to say goodbye. A few hours later, the plane touched down in Germany, where I needed to catch my connecting flight. As soon as the cabin crew turned off the warning lights, I turned my mobile phone back on. As it fired back into life it bleeped loudly as a flurry of text messages came through from the kids, asking what time I'd land. There was another message – a voicemail – from Danny. I felt sick to my stomach as I pressed play, held the phone against my ear and listened. I'd expected the worst, so I was dreading what he was about to say, but to my utter astonishment his voice sounded almost buoyant.

'Mum, it's me. The specialist says her heart is weak, but he thinks she will live a few more weeks.'

The anxious breath I'd been holding in came rushing out as a sigh of relief. A small glimmer of hope rose inside me as I dared to hope my prayers had been answered. I wiped tears from my eyes as I glanced up at the TV screen for news of my connecting flight. Puffing and panting as I ran along the airport corridor, I called Danny, who repeated the good news.

'Thank God,' I sighed. 'I'll be there as soon as I can.'

Once I'd boarded the aircraft, I reluctantly turned off my mobile again – my lifeline to what was happening back home. I told myself to stay calm because the situation wasn't as bad as I'd first thought: we still had hope. However, by the time we landed at Manchester Airport, things had taken another turn for the worse.

'Mum, it's me.' It was a new voicemail from Danny. This time his voice sounded panicked and urgent. 'Mum... we don't think she'll last the night,' he said, his voice shaking with emotion.

Oh my God, I thought as panic set in, *I need to get to the hospital fast!*

I ran outside, where I flagged down a taxi.

'Manchester Children's Hospital!' I shouted as I climbed inside, asking the driver to put his foot down.

As we drove, memories of a recent child murder I'd worked on came into my head and I recalled taking the distraught father to identify his baby daughter at the very same hospital I was now racing to. I tried to shake these negative thoughts from my head as the hospital loomed into view. Vicki, Steve and Matt were waiting there for me. As soon as I saw them, I knew things were desperate.

'Mum, thank God you're here!' Vicki sobbed as she threw her arms around me.

Everyone was frantic as they led me to Macie's hospital room. Danny and Julie were sat at her bedside, along with Julie's older son, Gary.

I wrapped my arms around my precious son and daughter-in-law, holding them both tightly as we all cried together. I wanted to comfort them both, but it was impossible to know what to say or do. Their faces were etched with exhaustion and fear that they would lose their precious daughter at any moment. I looked over at Macie lying in her hospital bed and felt my legs give way. My baby granddaughter was surrounded by various monitors, all flashing and bleeping, tracking her vital organs. A complicated network of tubes led out from her tiny body to the machines that were keeping her alive.

'Oh, my little Macie noodle,' I sobbed as I looked down at her.

She looked perfect, as though she was just sleeping peacefully, when in fact she was barely clinging to life. We were utterly devastated, but spent the next few hours sitting with her, willing her to live. I'd just left the room when the consultant went in to speak to Julie and Danny. Moments later, they came out into the corridor.

'They say she's not going to improve,' Danny began. 'We've asked if we can take her back to Francis House Hospice, but they say she's not well enough.' My strong and usually invincible daughter-in-law Julie wept by his side.

Now it was just a matter of hours. Dan and Ju asked the doctors to remove all the tubes and medical paraphernalia that covered her little body and, shortly afterwards, surrounded by her loved ones, our beautiful Macie took her final breath. It was 28 January 2011 and she had died just a few weeks before her third birthday.

Danny and Julie asked the doctors to take Macie back to Francis House Hospice, where they stayed with her in the Rainbow Room until her funeral, a week later. She was dressed in a beautiful angel dress and snuggled up with her little Tinkerbell for her final journey. The funeral was a celebration of her short, but precious, life and her big brother Gary's speech brought the congregation of many hundreds to tears, so powerful and magical were his words. I felt utterly broken in two.

How could life be so cruel? How would Danny ever survive this? First, his dad and now his beloved daughter. Life just wasn't fair.

*

Although we tried to deal with our grief privately, I'd already told Lorna and Amber about Macie and how ill she'd been. So, when I eventually called them the day after she passed away, the first thing they did was to ask after her.

'She died,' I said, my voice crumbling with emotion.

'Oh my God, Maggie! I'm so sorry,' Lorna said. She was a decent woman and I knew she meant every single word; after all, she'd lost her own son to an overdose.

'I'm sorry, too,' Amber added in tears.

Lorna's family showed me nothing but love and kindness

and the beautiful texts they would send me each day helped me in my grief. I took a week off to support my family and help plan Macie's funeral for Friday, 4 February, but I returned to work on the Monday. I'd kept the Senior Investigating Officer (SIO) fully informed, but I didn't ask for, nor was I given, any special treatment. I could have taken more time off work with the full support of my doctor but, at the request of the SIO, I agreed not to. This was because I felt a great sense of responsibility towards Lorna and her girls. They'd just started to trust me, and for me to suddenly disappear would have hindered the ongoing investigation and the trust we'd built up over the previous two months was special. I also felt it would have been unprofessional and unfair to expect them to have to get used to yet another officer, so I put my personal life to one side and focused on my absolute commitment to my job. I wanted to bring these serial paedophiles to justice, which would never happen without the cooperation and help of Amber, Ruby and other victims.

The girls were considered pivotal to this investigation. Whatever it took, we needed them to tell us of their horrific abuse and it was my job to ensure that happened. So, at a time when I should have been grieving for my granddaughter, I spent time with Lorna and Amber. When I wasn't with them, I made up extra hours so that I could spend time with my family. It was an extremely stressful period. This job had quite literally split me in half. My responsibility to those I loved had been pitched against the girls I desperately needed to protect. In spite of her previous arrest, and her fear and suspicion towards the police, I slowly began to win over Amber's trust and I was determined not to let her down – it was the very least I could do. But there was a sticking point: the more I spoke to Lorna, the more I realised how difficult it would be to try and get Ruby on board.

'She'll not speak to you,' Lorna insisted time and time again, 'Ruby is the difficult one.'

Ruby, still only a child of fifteen at this time, didn't want to speak or cooperate with police because she didn't view herself as a victim. She still didn't see these men as her abusers, but as her friends. One in particular – the father of her aborted baby – she actually considered to be her boyfriend. Ruby was hostile towards the police, to say the least. The hardest part of my job wouldn't be to try to win her over, it would be to tell her the police had her unborn baby in an exhibits bag inside a freezer back at the station. Neither she nor Lorna knew – no one did, only us. Retaining the foetus without Ruby's consent or knowledge hadn't just been illegal, it was highly questionable and immoral, and I was shocked to my core that anyone could ever have considered it ethical to do this without even speaking to the family.

Chapter Twelve

Amber Tells All

> ❛Respect is earned.
> Honesty is appreciated.
> Trust is gained. Loyalty
> is returned❜
> — Gackt

I returned to work on Monday, 7 February 2011, just three days after Macie's funeral. Ironically, I was told I could no longer operate in my role as a family liaison officer (FLO) due to my own bereavement. Management considered such a person-centred role would be detrimental to my own welfare. It seemed an illogical decision, especially when the pressure on me to 'deliver' Amber and Ruby to the Span investigation continued unabated, and so I challenged the decision, arguing that Operation Span was the most stressful investigation I'd ever worked on – far more stressful than working as a FLO. I questioned why I'd be able to work on Operation Span, but be prevented from carrying out my FLO duties. However, the decision was upheld, subject to review later in the year, and I decided to follow the order. Looking back, I don't think I'd have been able to take on another FLO job anyway due to the sheer workload of the ongoing investigation, so perhaps it was the right decision.

Instead, I continued my work with Lorna and her family. I was just starting to feel like I'd hit a brick wall when the long-awaited news came through on my first day back that the Crown Prosecution Service had reached a decision: they had finally given the green light for me to interview Amber and, furthermore, after taking more than two months evaluating all the facts, John Lord of the CPS had decided that Amber was just a victim, exactly the same as all the other girls. There had been no need to use the guidelines set out under the Serious Organised Crime and Police Act 2005 that dealt with offenders-turned-witnesses. She was never an offender in the first place, always a victim, and had now been legally classified as such and could be treated in the same way as any other victim.

My job was to guide Amber gently towards a taped interview, this time as a victim. She would have the chance to explain how she was groomed into this situation and to identify those who had abused her and the other girls. There would be no one accusing her of being a 'madam' or coercing others into doing what she was doing. She would tell her story as a victim, pure and simple, and she would appear in court to give evidence against her abusers.

I was elated. At last, Amber would be able to help put these men away for what they'd done not only to her, but to her younger sister and dozens of other children too. There was no time to waste, yet I was still very wary of exerting any pressure on Amber to talk 'on the record'. The trauma of her time being interviewed as a 'criminal' in a police station was still very evident and I had to tread so, so carefully. For me, the big hurdle was getting her to see me as friend, not an enemy. That was how I was different. I reassured her, told her she had done nothing wrong. I had to work to overcome her fear, anxiety and mistrust of the police. Why should Amber assist an organisation that had virtually destroyed her? This was the mountain we needed to climb.

The day after the CPS sent its directive I called round at the hostel and took Amber and the baby out into the fresh air. For the first time I began to talk about her abuse. It was very emotional and, as I talked, I saw Amber retreat back into her protective shell and close down as she began to remember those dark days, three years before, that she had tried so hard to forget. She tried hard not to show her feelings, but those raw and painful memories were etched into her face. I could see the fear in her eyes, along with the mistrust and suspicion. The shame and guilt she felt about having been arrested was self-evident and, even at this stage, I knew the shame would last a lifetime. Amber knew there would always be people who would say there is no smoke without fire. She had been treated appallingly and there was no undoing that.

I let her talk, gently probing where necessary and holding back when she wanted to go off on a tangent. Finally, I felt the moment was right to ask her the question both of us knew was coming – the one we had skirted around for several weeks.

'Amber, how would you feel about telling me properly

what happened to you and the other girls?' I said. 'When I say "properly", I mean in a police interview. As a victim and a witness.'

Her face darkened. 'I dunno,' she said. 'I dunno if I can go back there. To a police station. I think I'd freak out the minute I got near the place. They didn't do owt for me back then, why should I go back over it all now?'

It was a fair point. 'I don't really have much of an answer for that, Amber,' I replied. 'All I'd say is that if you speak out, and give evidence in court, you might be able to prevent other kids from going through the same nightmare as you.'

Amber shook her head. 'It's really scary just thinking about it,' she said.

'It won't be in a police station, Amber,' I said, trying to reassure her, 'we've got special interview suites for victims and witnesses now. It's nothing like being taken down to the station, like the old days. You can even have your mum and your baby in a nearby room.'

'But how do I know I can trust you?' she said. 'Look what the police did to me before.'

I looked her directly in the eye.

'Amber, you know me now and I give you my promise that you can trust me. We need you to help put these men away so they won't be able to abuse other children in the future, children like your own baby.'

Although she had every reason to be suspicious of the police and our motives, she promised me she'd think about it despite her fear, so I took her home to her lonely room. There, I left her to decide if she was prepared to churn up all that pain again when all she really wanted was to put it behind her, move on with her life and try to forget it had ever happened.

*

Up until this point I'd had absolutely no contact with Ruby. Lorna had told me in no uncertain terms that her youngest daughter would never speak to me: 'She's the difficult one,' was all she would say.

I didn't want to push my luck because I knew Ruby had anger issues. Also, I didn't want to make a potentially explosive situation worse before I'd even begun. After all, I'd already spent the best part of two months trying to win Lorna and Amber over as we had waited for the CPS to decide the way forward.

Each morning, in our Operation Span briefing, I'd give an update of my contact with the family to a roomful of forty or fifty people involved in every aspect of the operation. Such meetings are a crucial part of any major police operation as they give the chance for every member of the team to update on what they've been doing and how their work is fitting in with each twist and turn in the investigation. At the meeting following the conversation with Amber, the team was delighted that she'd at least agreed to 'think about' a formal interview.

The senior investigating officer then asked me about Ruby.

'It's still a no-no at this stage,' I said, 'but I'm working on it. I'm banking on the fact that she might be curious enough to wonder what's going on between me, her mother and her sister. That might be the only way she agrees to meet me.'

'Keep at it, Maggie,' said the SIO, taking a sip of his coffee. 'We need both those girls to tell us what's been going on.'

*

The senior detectives in charge of Operation Span were particularly keen to place Ruby's account on the record. At only fifteen years old, she was still a child in every respect. She'd been abused by this gang since the age of twelve and had fallen pregnant just after her thirteenth birthday. Our team had hoped we could prove she'd been pregnant at just twelve, because the legislation is slightly different and would have given us more power. This is because the law presumes a girl under the age of thirteen isn't mature enough to consent to sex, even if she has done so 'willingly'. It's similar to the age of criminal intent, which assumes children under the age of ten cannot commit a crime because they do not understand what crime is. Therefore, anyone who has sex with a girl under the age of thirteen would commit 'statutory rape', of which there is no defence and a maximum sentence of life.

I thought back to Victoria Agoglia's letter – written when she was thirteen – the same age Ruby had been when she'd fallen pregnant. Victoria's letter spoke of repeated sexual abuse and I didn't want to replicate that or another damaged girl's possible death. And I still had the very difficult and unpleasant job of telling Ruby and her family that not only had Greater Manchester Police kept her aborted baby, we needed consent for Ruby to provide her DNA so that we could determine the parentage of her dead child. It was a conversation I wasn't looking forward to having, but something that would be imperative to the investigation.

My chance came sooner than I'd anticipated.

A few days later, Lorna and I were walking around the frozen lake at Hollingworth when I decided to broach the subject. Lorna pushed her youngest child along in a pushchair as we pulled our coats around us and buttoned them up against the cold. The whole place was deserted, remote and peaceful – the perfect spot to have a private conversation. I gestured with my hand towards a bench and asked her to take a seat.

'Lorna,' I said, my mind scrambling to try and find the right words, 'we've got to know each other now and I hope you trust me.'

She smiled and nodded warmly. It gave me the green light I needed to go on.

'I know how much you've fought for your kids,' I added, 'but there's something you need to know...'

She turned to face me; her expression had changed from relaxed to one of worry.

'What is it, Maggie?'

I took a deep breath and continued.

'You know in 2009, when Amber was arrested? Well, the team at Rochdale CID were told that Ruby was pregnant.'

Lorna nodded – she already knew that part.

'The thing is,' I said, looking her directly in the eye, 'Rochdale Police attended the termination so they could seize the aborted foetus.'

Her worried expression melted into one of complete horror.

'What?!' She clamped a hand over her mouth in shock. 'You're kidding me, right?'

Even though she was mortified, I knew I couldn't leave it there: I had to give her the full facts.

'The authorities all collaborated,' I said, 'and the foetus was taken away after the termination and booked into the police exhibits system.'

'Hang on, hang on!' she said, waving a hand to slow me down for a moment. It was clear she was still trying to process the information. 'So, hang on, you're telling me they kept Ruby's baby as...as an exhibit?'

I nodded. She gasped and looked back over towards the lake. A deafening silence followed as she considered what I'd just told her.

'I...I can't believe what I'm hearing here,' she said, still shaking her head in disbelief. 'I really can't.'

I knew I was at risk of undermining her already low opinion of the police, but both she and Ruby had a right to know the truth and it was my job to tell them. I thought for a moment before deciding to try a different tack.

'Listen, you want the men who did this terrible thing to your daughters to go to prison, don't you?'

'Course I fucking do,' she said vehemently.

'Right, so do I, and what we have with the baby is proof that one of the men who abused Ruby got her pregnant.'

But Lorna was still shaking with shock. 'I just can't believe it. I can't believe you've got Ruby's dead baby,' she repeated as she stared out at the half-frozen lake.

I knew I was dealing with a fragile person, but I also knew she was determined. Up until that point, she'd fought like a she-devil to try and protect her children.

'Lorna, look at me,' I said, trying to bring her back into the moment. 'We need to put these men away and this will help us do it.'

She shifted uneasily on the bench, thought for a moment and then turned to me.

'Jesus, Maggie,' she said, 'that's some information you've just given me! But I trust you. Whatever you think is right, whatever's the best thing to do, I'll do it.'

I gripped her hand in mine and gave it a comforting squeeze.

'Thank you,' I said and hugged her close as relief surged through me. Now I had her on our side and it felt like the breakthrough we'd been waiting for.

A few days later, I picked up the phone, rang her and arranged to meet for tea and cake in the supermarket.

'Listen, I know it's a shock, what I told you the other day,' I said. 'It's a shock because you've just found out your grandchild is in police custody. But, Lorna, I promised I'd never lie or try and mislead you, and I won't. You have my word.'

And I meant it because Lorna had no incentive to help us with the investigation: her girls were older now and were no longer being abused.

Lorna lifted her mug of red-hot tea and blew across the top of it in an attempt to cool it down. She tipped the mug towards her mouth, took a cautious sip and swallowed.

'Whatever you think, Maggie. I want exactly the same as you, but I don't think Ruby will talk to you. You'll have a real problem with her. I'll help you, no problem, because I want these men put away for what they did to my girls. But as for Ruby, well...' Her voice trailed off and she shrugged her shoulders and held out her upturned palms as though she had no answers.

*

While we wondered how we'd get Ruby onside, there was the matter of Amber's first formal interview to contend with. She'd agreed to do it and we'd arranged a date for mid February 2011. I would also be taking her baby, and Lorna, so that Amber would feel safe and reassured. But on the appointed day, as we approached the interview suite located next to the main police station in Bury, Amber went into complete meltdown.

'There's no way I'm going in there!' she shouted as she looked at the smart new red-brick building. 'No way at all!'

I explained that we wouldn't be going into the station itself, but through a separate door into the purpose-built victims' and witnesses' interview suite. It was fine to bring her mum and the baby into the suite and they would only be next door. In all honesty, our only aim at this point was to at least get her through the door and see the room, which we hoped would help to quell her anxiety and make her understand that we weren't trying to trick her in any way. We didn't expect her to talk about anything on this first occasion, we just wanted her to feel secure so that when the time came and she felt ready, she would speak with confidence.

We sat in the car park for a good few minutes until Amber settled down and told us she felt ready to take a look around. As she stepped through the door she looked terrified, but when she saw the waiting room full of toys and books, and the interview suite itself decorated in a comfortable, homely way, she settled down somewhat.

'Alright,' she said, 'let's do this. Let's just talk.'

I won't deny that first interview was difficult, but I understood she was very much testing the waters, testing me too to see whether I would abandon her like others had in the past if she said anything untoward. She was incredibly wary, skirting around the main issues and constantly on her guard in case a uniformed officer walked in to lock her up. That was what she was frightened of.

From the beginning, and completely as directed by the big bosses and lead lawyer in the CPS, I reassured her that she was being treated as a victim/witness, would not be arrested as a suspect and shouldn't be frightened to talk about what happened to her. At first, she seemed angry with one of the other girls involved in the abuse – the result, I suspected, of the friendship breaking down. But, as the minutes passed, she began to open up.

'It was Ruby and her friend who took me to Tasty Bites and Balti House for the first time,' she said. 'We'd go upstairs in the shop and drink two bottles of vodka.

'The first "Paki" I had sex with was Pino and I was really drunk. I'd been drinking Jack Daniels that he'd bought me. I was fifteen and I felt sick and dirty afterwards because I'd shagged a "Paki".'

There was more, much more. She talked about a stream of men who called her up, men she only knew by their 'street names' – Car Zero, Cassie Cars, Tiger, Taz, Tariq, Pino, Saj, Billy, Daddy...the list went on and on. There were trips to Nelson, Halifax, Bradford, Rossendale, the local moors.

At one point Amber said, 'They just used me because I was a white girl. When I was having sex with men nothing was going through my mind because I was pissed. They always gave me loads of alcohol.'

Amber also mentioned another guy known by the name 'Google', who had threatened her at gunpoint.

She confirmed that a list she'd compiled of all the 'Pakis' (as she called them) she knew, plus their phone numbers, was in her own handwriting and had been passed to her social worker in early 2010. This contained the names of some of the men we'd already arrested and bailed, plus many more, and was a vital piece of evidence in the case. It became known as 'Document 29'.

I felt elated that she was even talking about them by name, bearing in mind she was riddled with anxiety. This was a monumental breakthrough in itself and, what's more, it was her very first interview. I was in total awe of this young girl who had put aside her own fears and suspicions of the police just to help others.

She said that after what had happened she 'didn't have friends anymore and didn't want any'. She 'didn't socialise any more' but just 'sat in the hostel now with her baby on her own or with her mum, but wasn't lonely because she had the internet' and I saw the sad life she had retreated into because of the way she had been demonised.

She explained that when she had first been taken along to the 'kebab houses', and introduced to the men, Ruby and another thirteen-year-old child had already been going there for a while. At first it was fun and they would be given somewhere warm to sit, where they would eat food, watch videos and drink alcohol. But as she began to talk about some of the other abused children, including Ruby and Holly, I watched as her face changed to reveal the frightened child who had been treated so differently from the other victims. She clearly blamed Holly for her troubles in a way that only a child would and she went on the defensive, just as Holly had, when the police had questioned her the first time back in 2008.

The fall-out had obviously been nasty, each believing the other had landed them in trouble. So, Amber began by referring to Holly as 'Sweaty Betty' because Holly had called her the 'Honey Monster'. It was nothing but childish name calling, but these girls had been abused and damaged and their natural instinct to protect themselves kicked in. This was obvious to me when, during the interview, Amber denied she had been abused or groomed. Instead, she insisted she'd had sex with the men 'free willingly'.

'Free willingly?' I repeated.

She nodded.

'Yeah, free willingly.'

To acknowledge she had, in fact, been raped again and again was still one step too far for Amber to admit at that point and to pretend to me that she had been in control just made it easier for her to deal with her own pain. It demonstrated the child she still was in so many ways. In truth, it didn't actually matter whether she considered it 'free willingly' or not, because a jury would hear the evidence of these kids and make up their own minds. Had they 'consented' or had they simply been exploited by a gang of sexual predators targeting vulnerable children for their own selfish reasons?

After an hour, I decided enough was enough for that day and I told Amber she was now free to leave.

'Really?' she said, looking up at me in astonishment.

'Of course, you've done nothing wrong.'

She hadn't, but I had to prove to her that she could go home again and I wasn't trying to trick her. In many ways I felt quite exposed myself because I'd never interviewed anyone in relation to so many years of sexual abuse, including multiple victims and offenders. So, after the first interview, I spoke to the SIO, who agreed to involve another officer and I introduced a female detective constable to the family so that she could also build trust up with them.

*

Amber's second interview came around quickly and this one was almost four hours long. This time there was a total change in her demeanour and attitude. She hadn't been arrested this time and she'd had time to process what she'd said. The childish anger in the first interview disappeared, and never reappeared. This time, she began to reveal the most gruesome details of the events that had destroyed her life, unburdening her soul to tell me of the first man who had raped her at the age of fifteen at the Balti House in Heywood while a thirteen-year-old child was being raped by another man in an upstairs room – the same place where Holly had been raped the first time by 'Daddy'. She said that afterwards she had felt 'sick and dirty' and threatened to tell her mum, but he had threatened her at knife point and told of what would happen if she did that. She said this man, known as 'Pino', had fled to Pakistan when he found out about Operation Span and to this day he has never been arrested.

There was more, much more. Men who picked up young girls in their cars and raped them up on the moors, far from view. Vodka, beer, cigarettes and cannabis offered as incentives for sex. Heroin dealers who thought nothing of selling their wares to young people. Places where girls were taken, locked in behind a series of doors and raped.

Once she started to talk, she couldn't stop. The information poured out of her and the following week, I used my car to take Amber on a drive round so she could try to identify all the locations she'd talked about on tape and she corroborated everything she was saying by showing me these physical landmarks – flats, houses, where she and other kids had been taken to be abused.

In her next recorded interview, Amber acknowledged for the first time that she had been sexually exploited. She said the reason she'd done it at the time was for booze and money, and she thought that the more sex she had, the more drink and cash she'd get from her abusers. She hadn't realised she was being brutally and shamelessly used. But she was just a child. How could she have had the maturity to understand the true reason why older men would be so interested in being her 'friends'?

This whole process was unrelenting and draining for us both, but the SIO and the investigation team were over the moon at the progress being made with Amber. In reality, I don't think any of us had ever really believed she would open up so completely and the information and facts that she was disclosing were overwhelming.

With each new interview she became more relaxed, revealing the most intimate details of her rapes to me. She described the moment a man pulled a gun on her, just as Lorna had told me:

'"Google" [the abuser's nickname] wanted sex with me, but I said no. Ruby said no too. That made him mad, so he told me he'd kill me – shoot me. He had a gun in his car, which I saw, and then next time he said he'd kill me, I were really scared. I told my mum and she got my brother who was in prison to sort it, because the police wouldn't do anything.'

Amber described the night-time visits to the lonely moorland above Rochdale. As she was being abused by a man she called 'Car Zero', other girls who'd been taken up there in the man's car would get out of the back and wait around. 'We'd be up there for hours,' she said, 'even when it were freezing in winter. We'd be dead cold, but we'd just get pissed and put music on. I weren't so scared then cos I'd drunk loads of vodka.'

Amber was visibly uncomfortable talking about various sexual acts. 'I'd never kiss them,' she insisted. 'Not ever. That'd be disgusting.'

'Why was that?' I asked.

'Cos they stunk,' she replied. 'Their breath stunk of curry. They had food stuck in their teeth and they were greasy. It would've been harder to kiss them than have sex with them.'

She named a man who took girls back to an upstairs flat: 'To get in, you have to go through these big metal gates, then through another door like a garage, then upstairs. There is a room upstairs, you go straight ahead and there's a front room and then a bathroom.'

Amber paused, then closed her eyes as though reliving a particularly difficult episode.

'He used to lock all the doors behind him,' she said, shuddering. 'Every single door, and there was maybe six of them. I thought he might lock us in and not let us out.'

As she recounted her ordeal, in my mind's eye I could see a frightened fifteen-year-old feeling that if she didn't do what she was ordered to do inside that prison of a flat, something terrible might happen to her. By making her relive all this for the benefit of the tape, I felt as though I was abusing her all over again, but Amber understood why I had to do this and by this time, her trust in me was unbreakable. I actually think it became a sort of therapy for her to finally talk about things she had never spoken about to anyone before, knowing I didn't judge her. Despite the fact she knew she would eventually be questioned about all the grim details in a court of law, she still chose to continue, which was brave beyond belief.

During one interview she spoke about her younger sister.

'Ruby sees these men as her friends,' Amber told me. 'She was in love with one of them. She doesn't want to help the police because she doesn't want her friends to go to prison.'

Yet strangely, the more interviews Amber gave over the weeks and months that followed, and the more time she spent with me, the more jealous Ruby became. Soon, and true to the child that she still was, Ruby began to feel left out. Both Lorna and Amber had told her all about me and now, six weeks after my first meeting with her sister, Ruby was ready to talk.

'She wants to meet you,' Lorna announced unexpectedly one day.

It came like a bolt out of the blue, but I kept a lid on my excitement.

'Okay,' I said, remaining both measured and calm. 'Tell Ruby we'll be in supermarket on Tuesday afternoon, if she wants to come along?'

I wasn't sure what I'd find with Ruby. Already I'd been warned by both her mum and sister that she could be unpredictable, and she was.

*

On Tuesday, as arranged, Lorna and I were sat having our usual brew and cake in the supermarket when, out of the corner of my eye, I spotted a young girl bounding over towards us. Although she was only fifteen, she was big, loud and extremely intimidating.

'Hiya,' I smiled as she approached the table.

I knew without a doubt that this must be Ruby, but she refused to make eye contact or return my smile. Instead, and in typical teenage fashion, she flopped down on the seat opposite me, but next to her mum. Like a naughty schoolgirl, she rolled her eyes, huffed loudly and fidgeted as though she was already bored just being there. She made the plastic chair squeak as she continued to shift about, looking everywhere but at me, reminding me very much of the teenage TV characters, Kevin and Perry.

'Mum says you wanna speak to me,' she grunted in a voice that told me she really couldn't be bothered.

It was obvious she was in a mood, so I tried to change the subject.

'Do you want a drink?' I asked, rising to my feet.

Ruby put her elbow on the table, perched her chin on her

hand and huffed as though everything was a huge effort.

'Yeah, I'll have a Coke…and some cake,' she added quickly, eyeing our slices on the table.

I walked over to the counter to order, knowing I needed to be careful how I handled this. We were in a public place, yet it was obvious Ruby was wound up like a bottle of pop that had been shaken – she seemed ready to explode at any moment. I paid for the cake and Coke, then headed back to the table with them on a tray.

'Well, it's lovely to meet you, Ruby,' I said, handing them to her. 'So, how's school?'

She grabbed the Coke off me and took an enormous bite of cake.

'School's s'alright, I suppose,' she said, shrugging her shoulders.

There was an awkward silence as Ruby continued to munch. Throughout the exchange, Lorna's eyes flitted nervously between the pair of us.

'Ruby,' I said gently, 'you know what your mum and sister have told you. Well, I work on Operation Span and we're trying to put a case together to put these men away.'

It was as though I'd flicked a switch. Without warning, Ruby threw what was left of her cake down on the table. She leaned over the table aggressively, her eyes burning with anger.

'I'm telling you,' she said, showering me with cake crumbs as she pointed a finger at me, 'I've told my mum and I'm telling you, these men are my friends…' Her voice became louder as her anger grew until soon she'd reached boiling point. 'These men are my friends, so you can just fuck off!'

205

The chair almost flipped over backwards as she stood up abruptly, her face purple with rage, and she continued her tirade.

'I'm not helping you, understand?!' she shouted as though I was deaf. She was standing, but leaning over the table towards me aggressively. 'It was a mint time,' she said, 'and I loved it. It was the best time of my life!'

I felt everyone's eyes upon us as Ruby turned on her heels and stormed out of the cafe. Her cake lay on the table, half-eaten, her Coke barely sipped. Other shoppers looked across. I knew what they were thinking – that we were a dysfunctional family. But we weren't. The family wasn't the problem, they'd just been caught up in a highly dysfunctional situation and one that was beyond their control. I glanced around to see who was looking, but as soon as I caught them, the shoppers either politely looked down or away. Instead, cups of tea were stirred as they glanced at one another and muttered quietly underneath their breath, trying to second-guess what Ruby's rant had been about. I sighed. My first meeting with her had been a complete disaster. That said, I was used to teenagers and how to pick your battles with them. I understood she was really angry, but she was just a kid. My attitude was to let her have her say, soak it up and wait patiently for the volcano to settle down.

Suddenly, Lorna broke the silence.

'See what I mean?' she said, arching a knowing eyebrow as she sipped her tea.

I smiled, but said nothing. She was right: Ruby had been a force of nature alright, a tornado. I wasn't sure what to do, so I decided to let her calm down before I tried again.

However, I was well aware that the clock was ticking. The men we'd arrested before Christmas 2010 were out on bail and waiting to be released or charged. In order to do that, we needed Ruby. More importantly, I needed Ruby to understand that these men hadn't been her friends or even her boyfriend, they'd been her abusers and they would – and could – go on to be a very real threat to other vulnerable young girls.

Chapter Thirteen

Ruby Joins the Fight

> 6 I believe the root of all evil is the abuse of power 9
> — Patricia Cornwell

Although we still had to gain the cooperation of Ruby, there was no doubt that what had been gathered in the short few weeks since Operation Span started was compelling stuff. The case against the alleged abusers was building strongly and we hoped to pull in more than the initial list of suspects. Even at the start, we knew we had at least twenty-six victims and twenty-nine abusers. We were confident we could smash a network that seemed to have spread far and wide. Yet, as the weeks passed, I had a growing uncertainty about the way the operation was being conducted. Call it gut feeling, but it seemed to me that the bigger it grew, the more it was being contained. This wasn't an attitude among those at the coalface, but from people 'higher up'. Perhaps I'm saying this with hindsight, but even at the time it seemed that Greater Manchester

Police were getting rather more than the 'quick hit' they were perhaps seeking when they had suddenly pulled in a handful of suspects at the outset of Operation Span.

I knew, and so did my colleagues, that these arrests were only the tip of the iceberg. Amber's subsequent months of interviews had confirmed that. I felt we were in a great position to make many more arrests and expose the whole thing, but somehow there seemed to be a feeling among me and my colleagues that this might not be allowed to happen.

Only a month into the investigation we'd received the shocking news that the dedicated analyst assigned to Operation Span was now off the job and wouldn't be replaced. We were incredulous. The analyst had looked at all the information inputted from the original Rochdale CID investigation and, from it, had produced a series of very detailed 'spider charts' linking perpetrators and victims across a range of dates and locations. Amber's 'Document 29' – the list of abusers with their nicknames, places of employment and phone numbers – was an integral part of this. It was a great piece of work, but as more information poured in, it was obvious that these charts needed updating regularly. By taking the analyst off the job, GMP were stymying that process.

The removal of the analyst caused outrage among every officer working on the job. It made absolutely no sense at all. Even on a murder where there was only one victim and one offender, an analyst was always a permanent and integral part of the team. They had a standalone computer system that drew together all the evidence submitted to the room by dozens of detectives. This not only identified links, it produced a timeline. It seemed incomprehensible why the biggest job GMP were running, with more than two dozen victims and dozens of offenders identified at the outset, didn't have even one analyst. Ultimately, the decision led to heated stand-up rows between management and some officers who questioned the reasoning behind it. However, the decision was not overturned: she was being moved to another job, and that was that.

Shortly afterwards, in early March 2011, the female DC who'd been working with me and Lorna's girls left Operation Span and was sent back to her normal duties. She was followed in early April by the removal of Sam Haworth, the SIO, who was posted elsewhere in GMP. He was replaced by DCI Sharon Scotson. I knew Sharon well and liked her, but her background was in Child Protection. This was her first time on such a big investigation. I didn't think she had quite the same feel for it as Sam. Again, the removal of these two officers was, at the very least, extremely puzzling and, without really knowing why, a small voice inside me was saying that this wasn't how things should be on a job of this size and importance. I couldn't quite put my finger on it, but there seemed to be a feeling that as we already had a handful of suspects clearly in the frame, with enough to prosecute them, for GMP, that was enough. Yet all of us on the ground knew Operation Span was much bigger than that, with dozens of other offenders. So why didn't they get it too?

My concerns were heightened one evening almost three months into the job during a conversation with a Crown Prosecution Service junior lawyer who was attached to Operation Span. We were talking about Amber and at one point the lawyer mentioned that she wasn't a victim.

'What do you mean?' I said.

'Well, she's only a witness, isn't she?' the lawyer replied. 'She's not talking about herself as a victim or of any abuse she's suffered. She's only telling us what she's seen happen to other girls.'

'Have you heard her interviews?' I asked incredulously. 'Of course she's a victim!'

I was outraged. It seemed that no one had bothered to read this girl's evidence. Did they care or not that she was giving them exactly what they'd asked for – compelling evidence that would send a gang of predatory paedophiles to prison? In my bones I knew that this attitude had to have come from higher up, because it had been mentioned so casually, as though a fait accompli.

The lawyer shook her head. She hadn't heard the interviews, she said, because they weren't in the system. I couldn't believe what I was hearing. By this time I'd conducted three separate video interviews with Amber, all following procedure and over a period of more than a month, and it seemed that nobody had bothered to listen to, type up or upload these interviews from our key witness on to the HOLMES system.

Why was that? I was astonished, angry and incredulous.

The lawyer had, apparently, been given misinformation about Amber's status from someone else and that worried me. I copied all the printouts from the interviews and handed them to her, but was left feeling angry as well as very puzzled.

One day, not long afterwards, I was sat in the office when the phone rang and a colleague picked it up.

'No, you've come through to the wrong number, but

I'll put you through to the boss.' I heard him say before transferring the call.

'That's strange,' he said, looking over at me.

I was busy typing at my computer, so I didn't look up from the screen.

'What? What's strange?' I asked absentmindedly.

'That was someone from the Home Office.'

I stopped typing and sat up in my seat: now he had my full attention.

'The Home Office?'

'Yes, I'd heard they'd been ringing for regular updates, but I didn't believe it until I answered the phone to them myself.'

At that time, I felt pleased that the Home Office seemed to be paying close attention to what we were doing. I considered that, finally, the Government was taking the issue of child sexual abuse seriously. With hindsight, I question why the Home Office was so interested. Were they also hoping the job wouldn't grow and explode in everyone's faces? Memories of Operation Augusta disappearing without a trace flashed before my eyes. Surely this wasn't going to happen yet again?

Notwithstanding these concerns, there was still pressure being put on me to interview Ruby and get the consent we needed to take DNA from her and match it with any potential abuser. This difficult conversation loomed large over me but I couldn't rush into it, especially not after our first encounter. So, I was very surprised to take a phone call from Lorna in early April, letting me know that Ruby had agreed to talk. She still knew nothing about the seizure of her aborted child. Even so, just agreeing to speak at all was an achievement and Lorna must have worked hard to get her daughter to this point.

The plan had always been to interview Amber fully before interviewing her sister. Even though her mum now knew, I still had to have a conversation with Ruby about the foetus we'd retained and the investigation team needed her consent to examine it and to provide us with a DNA sample. First, though, I needed to gain her trust.

Quickly, I arranged to meet Ruby in the supermarket cafe again. This time she seemed less aggressive and angry. I soon realised that she liked to be in control – in stark contrast to Amber – and was a bit bossy, preferring to call the shots.

'Hi, Ruby,' I said as I placed the tray of drinks and cake down on the table.

She shifted uneasily in her seat as though she still wasn't convinced she should be there.

'You know Amber's doing some interviews with me, Ruby?' I began tentatively. 'Well, I'd like to interview you, if that would be alright?'

She looked sideways at Lorna, who nodded her head in encouragement.

'You see, what happened to you shouldn't have happened to you,' I continued. 'You've done nothing wrong, Ruby. People have let you down and they're going to do it to other kids. I'd like to speak to you so that they don't put other children through what you've been through. Would you be willing to speak to me?'

I sat back and waited for her answer. I'd purposely played it low-key because I didn't want to frighten her off.

Ruby took a gulp of her drink, put it down on the table

and sighed as though she was already bored by both me and the situation. I held my breath, half-expecting her to kick off again to the amusement of nearby diners, but instead she thought for a moment and then answered.

'Oh, alright, I'll come.'

It was music to my ears.

Her consent had arrived in the nick of time too, because the suspected offenders were coming back on bail. I was told by my supervisors to just 'steamroller ahead', so I did, even though I had serious misgivings about pushing things along too quickly. Shortly afterwards, Ruby came along to the video interview suite, where another colleague sat in on the interview and acted as a 'note-taker'. Again, I carried out an initial 'scoping interview'. By now it was almost mid-April; however, Ruby was completely different to how her sister had been during her first interview. Instead of being anxious and defensive, she went straight into a detailed account and named and described multiple offenders, including the identity of the father of her unborn baby, along with five men who had raped her between the ages of twelve and fourteen. Yet, like her sister in her first interviews, Ruby was unable to see that she was a victim of these men. She described them as 'nice people', none of whom would 'force' her into anything: 'They wouldn't ask me for sex when I was drunk,' she said in a monotone. 'They would say it when I was sober. They would always wait till I was sober, then ask me.'

How considerate of them then, to ask a twelve-year-old girl if they could rape her when she wasn't drunk...

And it wasn't just one or two men raping this child. Once her phone number was known, she was preyed upon by many offenders. 'Your number gets passed on,' she explained. 'One passes it to a friend and they pass it on to another and, before you know it, there's a massive circle and everyone's got your number.'

Her words chilled me to the bone. If this was happening to one young girl, in a small town in the north of England, how many others was it happening to right across the country? The scale of this abuse was unimaginable.

'There's a man who picked me up from school. I'd have sex with him,' she said. 'He took me to another house, where there were ten men sat in a circle.'

'And what did these men do?' I asked.

'They passed me around like a ball.'

'A ball?'

'Yeah,' she said, fiddling childishly with the sleeve of her hoodie. 'They passed me around like a ball and took it in turns to have sex with me. They'd put the white girl in the middle, but the men always knew each other.'

Even though I already knew how these gangs and abusers operated from my time on Op Augusta, I was still shocked. But I had to remain calm, encouraging and not so visibly distressed that Ruby wouldn't feel able to talk to me. I needed to retain a sense of normality but, inside, it just made me more determined than ever to bring these men to justice for what they were doing to generations of children.

Ruby was adamant that her abusers, and those who abused others, seemed to take a pride in picking up white girls. There was a lot of boasting from the abusers about 'chilling with white girls' and now, looking back, I believed strongly that we should have brought in a 'racially aggravated' element to our investigation. There was no doubt these girls were being targeted for their ethnicity and the perception that white girls are 'easy'. As it was, such charges were never brought, but maybe it would have been appropriate, because in law an offence is deemed to be racially aggravated if 'the victim perceives it as such'.

My heart ached for Ruby. She not only had special educational needs, but her mental age was much younger than her chronological age. She'd been vulnerable in more ways than one.

'When you say "sex", Ruby, what do you mean? Can you explain to me, in your own words, what you think sex is?'

As soon as she'd finished telling me I had no doubt in my mind that Ruby had had sex with most of these men when she'd been only twelve and thirteen years old. Not only that, but within her very first interview, she had named five of her abusers – men also named on the handwritten list known as 'Document 29' provided by her sister. Amber had also told me she'd been abused by these same men, along with many others. I was in shock at how much information Ruby had disclosed in her first interview. She'd not only named the men but identified different locations, again matching the locations Amber had already taken me to.

'They took me to one address in Falinge, where there was a list on the back of the door. It had about twenty names on it.'

'A list?'

Ruby nodded again and explained all the men using the house for sex on any particular night would tick a box to say they'd been there. Usually, they'd only take one 'white girl' back to the house, where they'd pass her around and all the men would have sex with her. Then they'd put a tick against their name and at the end of every week or month they'd be 'charged' money for the use of house – a kind of paedophile 'honesty' box.

Shocked to the core, I felt my stomach churn, but detail was exactly what we needed. In all my years as a copper I'd seen and heard most things, but this was on a whole different level. Ruby talked about a suspect the girls had called 'Daddy', the delivery driver for The Balti House takeaway restaurant – the man Holly had previously accused of raping her.

'But I didn't have sex with Daddy, neither did Amber. But Holly had sex with him. He's my friend.'

Just as her sister had done in her first interview, Ruby insisted she'd had sex 'free willingly', not realising that at just twelve years old, it would have been classed as statutory rape. The expression 'free willingly' was one that Ruby and Amber used right from the beginning. It isn't quite the right phrase, as we know, but it made me realise the extent of their naivety and also that they had been completely brainwashed by their abusers – almost as if the men had used the same phrase to justify their despicable actions.

It was heartbreaking to sit there and listen to a child try and defend the actions of a gang of paedophiles. Never had loyalty been so misplaced.

'And what about the man you think was the father of your baby?'

'What about him?' she shrugged.

'Well, you said you were in a relationship with him.'

Ruby nodded.

'Yeah, we were. We were going out for about six months…' Her voice began to trail off. 'Then I had the abortion.'

I sat forward slightly in my chair and looked at her. 'Ruby, can you tell me about the abortion, and the man who got you pregnant?'

Again, she rubbed her face against the sleeve of her hoodie like an infant seeking comfort from a blanket.

'I told my mum. She was upset.'

'What about the man, did you tell him?'

She nodded.

'And what did he say?'

'He said, do what you want to do.'

Ruby explained how it soon became clear to her that he didn't want the baby, so she'd gone along with her mum and Beth, the worker from the Crisis Intervention Team (CIT), to have the abortion. At this stage I was still awaiting files on the girls from CIT.

'And what happened to you and the man after that? Did you carry on seeing him?'

Ruby shrugged her shoulders again.

'I only saw him three times after I'd told him I was pregnant.'

She explained how the man had a house on one of the estates, where he'd take her for sex, but he actually lived somewhere else in Rochdale with his wife and kids. It made me wonder what child protection measures had been put forward two years earlier at the time of the abortion to protect this man's own children. She also said she'd had sex with a man called 'Ray' – the one who kept a list of names on one of the inside doors of a house.

'Other Pakis (a word she used) who had plenty of money would pay Ray. They'd never take two white girls back to the house at the same time, only one. No one got raped. People had sex, but they wouldn't get raped. They'd say things like, "I've got a white girl to chill with".'

I realised from my previous interviews with Amber and now Ruby that 'chill' was the code name for sex. I also think that by only taking one girl back, there would be no others to corroborate the rapes, should the police become involved. Also, a lone child is more vulnerable, unlikely to cause a fuss and easier to control.

'I had sex with a man called Tiger and one called Raja,' Ruby continued. 'There was another one called Castleton, but I never had sex with him... I hated him,' she added, pulling a disgusted face. 'I once threw a can of Coke at his window,' she smiled as she recalled the incident.

'They'd pick me up in a car park outside Morrisons. They were my friends. If we had nowhere to chill, we'd chill in back alleyways. There were loads of them. They'd give me drink, I'd neck a bottle of vodka neat. Sometimes I'd be sick all over the car. I went to Oldham, Bradford, Preston, Bolton... They'd ring and ask if I wanted to chill. They'd buy me cigarettes and give me money, but sometimes I'd rob them because they were thick,' she said, suddenly beginning to laugh.

'What do you mean, rob them?'

Ruby continued to smile as she recounted these incidents. 'Well, they'd give me £40 to buy vodka, but I wouldn't give them the change and they wouldn't ask, because they're thick,' she grinned, pointing a finger towards the side of her head. 'But I was clever...'

'Clever in what way?'

Ruby chuckled to herself yet again. 'Well, they tried to give me an opened bottle of vodka but I wouldn't drink it because I'd ask for it sealed.'

'Sealed?'

She looked at me and rolled her eyes as though it should be obvious.

'Yeah, sealed, so that I knew it hadn't been spiked.'

I couldn't believe her naivety – in some small way Ruby had felt as though she'd won against these men. She told me that one man had pointed a gun at both her and Amber and threatened to kill them, which is when their mother had been shouting for help from both social workers and the police. Amazingly, none of these allegations had ever been logged onto the police computer. There wasn't even a written record of any of the offenders' details or what they were alleged to have done; it was as though poor Lorna had been screaming into the wind and this was quite apart from the danger these paedophiles presented to other kids – including their own – by not being assessed in relation to safeguarding and child protection issues.

Ruby named five men during her first interview and her sister had already named a total of thirty-three suspects in her first two interviews. It didn't matter if one or both said they'd had sex 'free willingly' because both had been children, so consent or no consent, it was irrelevant. Lorna had first become aware that her youngest daughter, Ruby, had been having sex with Asian men when she was just twelve years old. She'd spoken to a police officer over the phone to see if she could get anything done, but nothing had been done other than a case conference.

It was then that social workers decided Amber and Ruby should both be put on the Child Protection Register (Ruby was thirteen, Amber fourteen). Not long afterwards, Amber had been arrested. Frightened and alone, she'd been given a solicitor and, guided by him, she had answered 'no comment' to all police questions. As we know, she offered a prepared statement that stated she had never 'incited other children into prostitution'. However, even as far back as 2000, legislation and official guidelines had made it very clear that 'any child under the age of eighteen caught up in prostitution should be given the same help, support and protection as any child in need' and also that it was recognised that 'children do not voluntarily enter prostitution; they are coerced, enticed or are utterly desperate'. I personally have major issues with the word 'prostitute' ever being used when referring to child victims of abuse. In 2000 those were the words of government and lawmakers, so how had it even been possible that a fifteen-year-old vulnerable child had been treated this way and arrested, blamed and treated as a criminal?

In my opinion, what happened to Amber was inhumane. She had been arrested because she'd taken money from these men, but then, so had all the others. That is precisely what grooming is. Abusers draw the most vulnerable of kids into their net with gifts and bribes like kebabs, vodka, money, cheap jewellery, a warm room in winter, the chance to watch a DVD, a ride up to the moors in a car. Any police officer or lawyer who doesn't understand that is clearly in the wrong job.

Amber's only 'crime' had been that she was four months older than Holly. The arrest had impacted on her life in every conceivable way. Once she'd had her baby, she was not allowed to live at home due to Ruby's anger issues and had also been prevented from attending mum and toddler groups because she was seen by one professional as a 'danger to other children'. In my opinion, this was a clear violation of her human rights. A letter dating from January 2011 expressed concern that she was an 'unsuitable candidate' for a college course in Health and Social Care and that her accessing a Connexions young parents' group 'may also be inappropriate'. Although the Young Parents Support Team said there were no concerns, the author of the letter objected and a meeting was held at Middleton Police Station.

The letter stated: 'I clearly expressed all my objections in relation to what I believe to be the potential threat posed by this young woman specifically in relation to other vulnerable young people attending these courses.' However, other professionals at the meeting challenged this opinion, saying that Amber was not convicted of any offence, that she had specific needs which could be addressed by attending these courses and that she could feasibly bring legal action as 'her rights were being withheld'.

But because one person had written a report, expressing an opinion, like a game of Chinese Whispers, this eventually became the accepted truth about a child victim of gang sexual abuse. I firmly believe that a victim is a victim and there is no such thing as a good victim or a bad victim, particularly when we are talking about a child of fourteen or fifteen who is being raped on a daily basis by a gang of sophisticated paedophiles. She should not be punished for trying to survive, rather we have a duty to protect her.

Sadly, Amber was prevented from attending the Health and Social Care course.

The letter was signed 'Sara Rowbotham, Crisis Intervention Team Co-ordinator'.

Meanwhile, a lonely young mum sat in a shelter for homeless people, nursing her newborn baby and wondering when she could just get on with her life.

Chapter Fourteen

Doing the Right Thing

> *6* Always trust your gut.
> It knows things your
> head hasn't yet
> figured out *9*
>
> — Anon

Although we were now five months into the investigation, the only 'new' victims on board who hadn't been working with Rochdale CID in 2009 were Amber and Ruby, and this from an initial list of twenty-seven children. This seemed unbelievable to me, given the magnitude of what seemed to be going on in relation to grooming and child sexual exploitation on our patch and the potential for arrests of dozens upon dozens of men. Yet some of the girls on the list had officially been put 'on hold' and were never approached at all, others had supposedly refused to co-operate, or had 'disengaged'.

Although she'd now been interviewed, the subject of Ruby's aborted foetus still hadn't been broached and, with Easter approaching, she was planning to go away for a two-week break to visit relatives. I'd hoped to transcribe my notes from her first interview, but was told to do a second interview with Ruby before the notes from the first had even been evaluated. I was also told it was critical that I obtained Ruby's consent to take DNA before she went on holiday as it was needed before the suspects came back on bail. I felt I had no choice but to comply, even though it seemed to show a complete disregard for the needs of the victim. Also, I actually thought it'd be unlikely that Ruby would even attend another interview, but knowing this was crucial, I went to speak to her.

'There's just a couple of things I'd like to check on before you go off on your jollies, Ruby,' I said. 'Can we just do a quick interview?'

She was reluctant, but with Lorna's help she agreed on one condition – that I drive her over to her relatives in another part of the country afterwards, because by speaking to me it meant she would miss her bus. I said this would be fine.

The following morning, I picked up Ruby and Lorna from home and took them to the video interview suite. When you conduct a video interview you have to have two officers present. However, the officer who accompanied me clearly didn't want to be there and I felt this set the tone for the rest of the day. Within ten minutes, it became clear that Ruby didn't want to be there either, but instead on her way to her holidays. She huffed and sighed like the annoyed teenager she was; she just wasn't in the right frame of mind. Then the video equipment kept breaking down, which meant I had to keep stopping the interview.

Ruby sighed in annoyance. I was worried she'd go off like a rocket at any moment.

'I'll tell you what,' I said, suddenly straightening up, 'let's just leave this, shall we?'

'Can we?' Ruby asked. Her face lit up like a Christmas tree, excited at the prospect of starting her holiday a little earlier than expected.

It was clear that the other officer didn't agree with my decision but, in my professional opinion, I thought it would be better to keep Ruby on board *and* would also give me time to thoroughly assess her first interview. I was also beginning to question whether I, or any police officer, should even be interviewing Ruby, given that she had a Statement of Special Needs. I considered she'd perhaps be better speaking to a specialist interviewer or psychologist interviewer as we had used on other major jobs when it had been deemed necessary and so I decided to request a meeting to raise this with the force interview advisor and the Senior Investigating Officer (SIO).

We headed out to the car and climbed inside. My colleague decided to drive, so I sat next to him, while Lorna and Ruby got in the back. But before we set off, I knew I had something to say to her – something extremely uncomfortable and painful for her to hear.

'Ruby,' I began, 'before you go on holiday, there's something me and your mum have to tell you. We need your consent. We need you to sign a form because we need to do a DNA test.'

Lorna stared at me: she knew what was coming.

'Why?' Ruby asked suspiciously, her eyes darting from Lorna to me and back again.

'Ruby, your mum knows this. When you had your termination, well, the police took the baby away afterwards.'

Ruby's eyes widened and I wondered for a split second if she was going to kick off. But she didn't.

'What?! That's not right. Why did they do that?' She looked at me and then at Lorna in complete horror. 'Mum, how could they do that? It's terrible...'

I nodded in agreement.

'Ruby, it should never have happened,' I said. 'But it did. But it means that we can prove who got you pregnant and stop him from doing the same to other children. This is why we need to do this DNA test, so that we can prove who the father is. Do you understand?'

Ruby turned to face Lorna again. I could see that Lorna was upset, but she put on a brave face and nodded – my ally, as always. I knew Ruby was angry with me; I also knew she trusted me.

'So, I need you to sign a form, giving us permission, then I need to take a mouth swab from you,' I continued. 'Do you understand what I'm saying? I need you to help us so we can stop this from happening to other children.'

As ever, Ruby rubbed the sleeve of her hoodie against her face for comfort, then looked up at me.

'Have you gorra pen?' she said. 'Just show me where to sign.'

I was astounded by the maturity she had shown in that moment. I had enormous respect for her, Amber and Lorna, and was determined to fight their corner until the end. With the consent form signed, and the mouth swab taken and placed in the sealed evidence bag I'd brought along for this very purpose, we were all finally able to relax – everyone apart from my colleague, who made it very obvious that he wasn't happy at having to drive Ruby and her mum to their destination. By the time we left Bury it was almost lunchtime. I'd collected them early that morning, so I suggested we pull in for lunch somewhere on the way – it was the least we could do, I felt. But my colleague didn't seem keen. He told me he thought it was inappropriate to buy them lunch because I could be accused of 'giving them an incentive'. To me, that was nonsense – I was just treating them with respect. However, he refused to join us at the table and instead sat in the car eating his own sandwiches while we all went for something to eat.

I felt extremely uncomfortable because there was an obvious tension in the car when we climbed back in. In a bid to lighten the mood, I turned the radio on and tuned it to Key 103, which plays the sort of music a fifteen-year-old would listen to. Soon, Lorna, Ruby and I were laughing and singing along, but my colleague stabbed a finger against the radio and turned it back to Radio 2. The remainder of the three-hour journey felt tense, to say the least, and there was an atmosphere in the car you could cut a knife with.

*

That night, I couldn't sleep as I turned my colleague's comments over in my mind. I started to question myself and my abilities. The next day, I asked for a meeting with the SIO and the Force Interview Advisor. I was worried that my colleague had been critical of me, believing we'd missed 'our last opportunity to interview Ruby'. To my mind, that wasn't true. Interviewing vulnerable and key witnesses often takes months and the months of interviews with

Holly clearly showed this. I also said I felt Ruby would be better being interviewed by a specialist interviewer, given her needs. It wasn't because I didn't want to be involved, I just felt this approach would deliver better evidence. I still wanted to be there to support her as I was the officer she and her family trusted.

They listened to my comments and after discussing everything at length, it was agreed officially with the SIO that my suggested approach was the best way forward with Ruby. This wasn't about me or my ego, but about gaining the best possible evidence to secure a successful prosecution against the men who had abused these girls and gaining the very best possible evidence from Ruby was key to that.

At this point I was due for a period of leave and given all that had happened to my family in the last few months, I was determined to take the holiday we had booked. However, on the horizon was an identity parade that Amber had agreed to attend. The work had already been done and this had involved close liaison with the standalone 'Viper' unit (Video Identification Parade Electronic Recording), the specialists in that area who now just had to fix a date when they were fully prepared.

Instead of the old ID parade attended by real people, the modern-day 'parade' consists of images on a screen that the victim/witness looks at, which in my opinion is harder than physically seeing the person standing, walking, moving and perhaps talking in front of you, and I believe is yet another cost-cutting exercise.

I was delighted that Amber had agreed to take part in this, the first of several planned Vipers. They are exhausting and certainly no fun for the person looking at image after image after image. Amber's task would be to identify no less than the first ten suspects she had named as men involved in her abuse – an awful lot to ask of an eighteen-year-old with a baby and already traumatised by what had happened to her. In my absence, my colleague agreed to keep in contact with the family and arrange the date for the Viper that Amber had agreed to attend, so I went away with a happy heart, knowing all was going to plan.

Towards the end of the fortnight I received a text message from Amber. When I read it, I almost dropped my phone: she told me she didn't want to be involved in Operation Span anymore and wouldn't attend the Viper. Very concerned, I called her, to be told that there had been no contact with anyone from Greater Manchester Police other than one text informing her of the date for the Viper since I'd left to go on holiday. Evidently, she'd got cold feet.

'I'll come and see you when I get back in two days, I promise,' I told her.

I ended the call and put my head in my hands. It had taken six long, hard months to get to this point and many hours of interviews, where Amber had explained in the most gruesome detail the abuse she had suffered. She had described the rapists, named them, told me where they worked, their phone numbers and done everything she possibly could to help. Now we were at the point where she would physically identify them too. I knew that this young girl was nervous about the whole process, and of the police in general, and she just needed reassurance and support as she travelled this road, someone she trusted to hold her hand and believe in her. Being left alone for weeks to worry was what had led to this change of heart.

The day I returned, I went straight round to see Lorna and her girls. This critical Viper was scheduled for the next day but, as soon as I walked in, Amber told me she couldn't attend because she had a Social Services meeting on exactly the same day that weighed heavily on her mind. Evidently, there had been no discussion with her about a convenient date, no liaising about a suitable time, and a total lack of communication that had risked our key victim walking away. I was furious, but not really surprised. Concerned that she wouldn't attend the Viper, I called Social Services and had her meeting shifted.

The next day, after liaising with the senior investigating officer, I collected Amber, her baby and Lorna, and took them to the Viper ID suite at Bury. Amber needed to identify the first ten offenders she'd named and described in her interviews. As the officer in charge I wasn't allowed into the Viper and so I waited impatiently with Lorna and the baby in another building while Amber went in alone. About two hours later, I got a call from the Viper officers telling me that Amber had successfully identified three offenders but had then broken down and said she no longer wished to continue. Steeling myself, I went to see her.

She was shaking like a leaf, big tears rolling down her cheeks and visibly upset when I saw her, so I told her to take a breather and have a cigarette to try and calm her nerves.

'I can't do it, Maggie,' she sobbed, once we were outside.

'Amber, I truly believe that you can do this,' I said as I squeezed her close. 'You've come so far, love – look what you've done over the last five months. I know you can do this and you owe it to yourself and to the other girls out there to do it.'

She took a long drag on her cigarette as she contemplated the huge task ahead. I was aware that by doing this I was making her relive the very abuse that had almost broken her first time round. But she needed to identify these men if we had any hope of convicting them of raping her.

'You need to be brave, Amber,' I said. 'We need to put these men away for the terrible things they have done to you, your sister and countless other kids. I believe in you and I know you can do this.'

She looked off into the far distance and considered what I'd just said. After a brief pause she turned to me, threw her cigarette to the floor and ground it out with the heel of her shoe.

'Okay, I'm ready.'

'You're okay to continue?'

Amber took a deep breath, composed herself and nodded. I wrapped my arms around her tightly, hugging her in an attempt to send her all my positive energy to help her through this ordeal.

'Let's do this,' she said, turning to go back inside.

Despite her obvious fear, that brave girl went on to identify eight out of a possible ten suspects. It was better than anything we could have hoped for and this was only the beginning. We planned further Vipers to identify every single offender Amber had spoken of in her hours of interviews.

'You've done brilliantly!' I told her afterwards.

Amber gave me a weak smile. I could tell she was thoroughly exhausted. One Viper is hard enough, ten is a marathon, and we had been there almost the whole day. But now, with Amber and Ruby's statements, the foetus, the files we'd successfully received from the Crisis Intervention Team and the men she'd just picked out from the Viper, we were almost ready to submit the case to the Crown Prosecution Service (CPS). I was certain we had enough to charge the male suspects and hopefully take them off the streets for a very long time.

So why was it then, that when I delivered this spectacular news to the bosses, I sensed something wasn't right? They should have been ecstatic at this result, but instead it felt like someone had died. This just added to the sense of disquiet that I had been feeling for some time and I wondered again what was actually going on here.

There didn't seem to be as much interest in Amber and Ruby's testimonies as there had been previously. They weren't being discussed as fully at briefings and even my regular updates seemed to be treated differently – as though the sisters were somehow less important now. A growing voice inside me was telling me that their needs as victims were being disregarded. All that seemed to matter was certain boxes were being been ticked. There'd also been a few snide comments made on various occasions. I overheard one officer say we needed to 'take more control of victims', insisting they were just 'lazy'. Some senior officers now seemed disinterested whether Ruby came on board or not.

'If she does, then she does. If not, she can always come forward in future,' one remarked.

I was utterly bewildered because his attitude seemed directly at odds with everything that had previously been said, so I challenged him. His response totally disgusted and outraged me. He dismissed my comments as though I'd said something stupid. Then he waved his hands around.

'Maggie, let's be honest about this. What are these kids ever going to contribute to society?' he said. 'In my opinion, they should have just been drowned at birth!'

For once in my life I was rendered totally and utterly speechless, so horrific were his comments. I turned away and sat down at my desk in utter despair that someone with such despicable views was working on an important investigation like this and held some influence in how things would progress. It was an attitude sadly shared by many in positions of power, which may account for much of what we see today.

*

In the weeks that followed, as well as working on Operation Span, I also had to attend Manchester Crown Court as a Family Liaison Officer on a murder trial. I had been FLO on this job since the end of 2010, so I was juggling lots of different balls. One afternoon in May 2011, I was standing outside the court with the family of the deceased when I was contacted by an officer I will call 'The Supervisor', who wanted me to re-interview both Amber and Ruby that week. I explained I was in court for the rest of the week and so was unable to comply, but he insisted it be done. It was a ludicrous order. Embarking on hastily arranged interviews with our two key witnesses without any proper planning or preparation was, quite frankly, ridiculous and a recipe for disaster.

I told him politely it wasn't possible. I also explained

that two weeks earlier, when he'd been away, there had been a meeting with Sharon Scotson, the SIO, where it had been agreed that a specialist interviewer was to be brought in to carry out further interviews with Ruby and therefore she was not to be interviewed again by any police officer, including me. At that point he began to scream at me down the phone, in the full hearing of the family outside court, insisting he was my supervisor and I would do as he said.

I said he should speak with the SIO, who would confirm that decision, but I felt another agenda was at play here. This was further reinforced when the supervisor said that Amber's next witness interview was to be held in Middleton police station, not Bury Witness Suite. I couldn't comprehend what I was hearing. This one action alone would destroy every single thing we had done since the start of Operation Span to reassure Amber that she was a victim, not a criminal, and could trust us after her previous arrest. Carting her off to a police station where suspects were interviewed would destroy all the months of hard work we had put into gaining her trust and take her straight back into panic mode as she would be reminded of her arrest in 2009.

By now I felt Amber's case in particular was being sidelined and even steered towards failure. It seemed there was some sort of agenda. I'd spent months successfully gaining the trust of Lorna and her girls, as I had been directed to do, but now my input wasn't sought, or even seemingly needed. I worried about what I perceived as a lack of witness care, particularly when dealing with such damaged children, and so I contacted the SIO and explained my concerns. She agreed and overruled the supervisor so for the moment the crisis seemed to have been averted.

Ironically, on the very next day I was scheduled to attend my annual one-day Advanced Victim Interview refresher course at Sedgley Park training school. Walking into the conference hall, I just froze on the spot. There, in front of me, plastered on every wall, were copies of Greater Manchester Police's monthly magazine – *Brief* – and staring out from the front cover was the smiling face of our chief constable, Peter Fahy, alongside the heading 'Doing The Right Thing'.

In the article he said every police officer, whatever their rank, was encouraged to 'challenge established policies where they hindered our service to the public'. He said we should 'rely on our gut instincts', that sometimes 'force policy conflicts with our values', but where that happens, we should 'challenge those policies if we think they are wrong'.

He went on to say that 'behind every incident there is a real person and we should do the right thing by them and not just by the process'. Furthermore, he added that police were 'the agency of last resort and often had to step forward when others are not there' and had an overriding 'responsibility to protect the vulnerable'.

It seemed like fate, or perhaps God, was stepping in to guide me in this hour of need. I read the article and it felt as though he was talking directly to me, giving me strength to speak out about what I was witnessing. I saw clear parallels between what our chief constable was telling us to do and the approach being taken towards our victims on Operation Span.

I left the conference hall and, totally inspired by our chief constable's words, I finally found the strength to put pen to paper for the very first time and emailed the SIO – Sharon Scotson – requesting a meeting to discuss my serious concerns. She agreed to see me and so the very next day, I went into her office and explained that I had been ordered to interview Amber in a normal police station, where we would take suspects under arrest. Sharon immediately overruled the supervisor, so for that moment at least the crisis seemed to have been averted and I hoped that the SIO would now step in and take control.

Tired, and unable to sleep, I felt stressed, exhausted, confused and isolated, but still totally committed to fighting for the rights of these girls, who I felt were again being treated disgracefully by the police. I feared these many serial sexual predators would once again be allowed to escape justice, as the only way they would be prosecuted is if we had victims prepared to testify against them in court. My instincts made me think they were being pushed away and, ridiculous as that sounds, the facts were that of the original twenty-seven on our initial list at the start of Operation Span, we were now down to just the two pre-existing victims from 2009, plus Amber and Ruby. In fact, I was so disgusted with the way things were moving that I felt ashamed to be part of what was evolving.

My colleague then started to assemble a statement from all the detailed ROVIs (Record of Video Interview) I had worked so hard to compile. This same officer, who wouldn't give the time of day to these girls, or even sit at a table to eat lunch with them, was now compiling this critical statement from my hours and hours of interviews and, as I read his draft, there were so many details omitted that the alarm bells rang louder in my head.

*

Amber was re-interviewed on 24 and 25 May, and although she didn't have to go to Middleton police station, neither was she taken to Bury Witness Suite. Instead, on the insistence of a senior officer, for no good reason she was interviewed in her own home. As she tried to remember details of her abuse, her six-month-old baby was crawling around her legs, clamouring for attention. It went totally against every scrap of training ever given, where it is stressed that we should remove any barriers for any victim/witness so they would feel relaxed and comfortable and talk freely, not be distracted or rushed. It's really just common sense, but here we were with our key witness being forced to talk about the most horrendous abuse with her baby crying for a bottle. It just beggared belief, but in spite of this she still did her best to help and disclosed further detail in relation to the offenders.

Now I believed for sure that Amber was being driven away, alienated and that she would withdraw from the case. But why? Here we had a girl that the police had identified as a key witness, pursuing her relentlessly, and who had helped us in every way she could, turning her life upside down for seven months and yet she was now being treated in this way. It made no sense at all, but I knew that was what was happening.

A few days later, at Nexus House, there was the very first meeting held between the barrister appointed to prosecute the case and officers from Operation Span. This lasted the entire day and as the officer dealing with Amber and Ruby, our central victims on this case, I would have expected to be invited into that meeting alongside the officers dealing with Holly and another victim.

But I wasn't.

After many hours the meeting finished and the officer responsible for Holly came straight over to my desk. She had been invited to attend, but as she approached there was a look of disbelief on her face.

'What? What is it?' I asked.

'I can't believe it, Maggie,' she said, looking at me in total shock. 'They're saying they're not going to "use" Amber anymore.'

'WHAT?' I looked at her with astonishment.

'They're saying she could undermine other witnesses,' she said. 'I honestly can't believe it…'

It was clear to me this was just a ploy to exclude her and also clearly showed me that they had not listened to Amber's hours of interviews. No two victims gave identical accounts, but the variations were minor and a jury would surely see that. To my mind it was another way of doing what Greater Manchester Police did to Holly in 2009; another way to say Amber was an 'unreliable witness', a convenient way to limit the trial, stop the job growing bigger and the can of worms spilling ever wider, and of course without Amber's interviews having been put onto the system, the only version of her abuse put to the meeting was the one delivered by the very person who had made it clear to me that he felt these children were worthless.

I was raging. After all the months of work, after pursuing this girl with a vengeance on the direct orders of senior officers, after all the assurances we had given this family that they would be supported if they trusted us, after all the guarantees made to me that there would never be a repeat of the failures of Operation Augusta, here we were again. Only this time, GMP had thrown poor Amber under a bus for the second time in her young life.

Amber had opened up this investigation beyond our wildest dreams, but now that she had done that, the top brass had decided they didn't want that at all: they wanted a quick and easy case, based on what Rochdale CID had uncovered, and no more. Amber's evidence made it impossible to pretend that this case wasn't an epidemic of abuse in Rochdale and quite probably in other places too. That is the truth and for me, it is the only explanation that makes any sense.

Now I totally understood what had been going on over the previous weeks and why I had been excluded from that crucial meeting with the barrister. Had I been in that room, there is no doubt whatsoever that I would have told the truth about what Amber had said in her hours of interviews. Had this been listened to and acted upon, I firmly believe it would have changed the course of the trial, Amber's journey and my own life too. But it wasn't to be. Instead, the supervisor came over to speak with me. Incandescent with rage and heartbroken for what Amber had endured, only to be tossed aside now as if she didn't matter, I couldn't contain my anger.

'I don't believe what I'm hearing!' I shouted. 'After the CPS decision, then six months of putting her through hell, reliving the abuse, months of interviews, drive-arounds, Vipers and now this? I just can't believe this is happening again!'

I was outraged. They had effectively done to Amber

exactly what they'd done to Holly, two years before. And exactly what they had done to the Augusta victims, eight years before – they'd abandoned them.

The supervisor listened, but it was clear what his thoughts were.

'Maggie! Calm down, calm down,' he said, patronisingly. 'Remember, this is all just a game.'

As I looked up at him in total disbelief, I could feel the tears pricking at my eyes. I'm not a 'crier' naturally, but at this moment I felt completely overwhelmed by the injustice of what I was hearing.

'A game?'

He nodded and explained the justice system was just a game.

'Look, maybe we are not going to use Amber, but we're still going to use Ruby,' he added, as though that made everything alright.

'Well, let me tell you that I'm not going to "use" anybody,' I said in disgust. It took every ounce of my self-control not to flatten him right there and then. Instead, and with the whole office looking on in silent disbelief, I grabbed my coat and bag and made for the door. You could have heard a pin drop and as a couple of colleagues approached me to try to intervene, I realised I needed to get out of there that very moment before I did something I would later live to regret.

One thing was for sure: I felt such a great sense of responsibility to Lorna and her girls that even if others let them down, I sure as hell wouldn't.

Chapter Fifteen

In the Pursuit of Justice

> ❝Every step toward the goal of justice requires sacrifice, suffering and struggle❞
> — Martin Luther King, Jr.

I was due some leave around the time I walked off Operation Span and now was the moment to take it. My head was spinning with everything that had happened from the time I was brought on to the job to the moment I was told Amber's critical evidence was no longer going to be 'used'. I couldn't believe that all her efforts would go to waste and no one had given anything approaching a proper explanation of the reasoning behind this.

One thing was clear, though. I felt a great responsibility towards Lorna and her girls. Not only had I given them my word, they had no voice in the process happening around them even though they'd done nothing but help us in every way they could despite the fact it had caused them immense pain and distress. It seemed to me that limiting the case in the way we were meant the jury wouldn't hear the testimony of the many victims. I truly believed that the more victims we took to trial naming the same offenders and giving similar accounts, the better chance we had the offenders would plead guilty, which meant the children would be spared the ordeal of having to give evidence in court.

I talked to close friends and colleagues about the situation and they were all as shocked as I was. I had to do something – but what? I knew for sure that this time I couldn't just walk away and see a repeat of the failures of Operation Augusta.

I was being made ill by the whole situation and my doctor signed me off work for a few weeks. This gave me a little time to try to decide what to do. I was expressly forbidden from contacting Lorna, Amber or Ruby, and although it was never explicitly stated, I felt immense pressure to toe the party line. Many police officers feel that whatever your personal thoughts are about an investigation, you put these aside and stick together as a team.

Although we were undoubtedly failing this one family, we were also failing hundreds of other victims by not bringing these serial paedophiles to trial. Yet constantly running through my mind were the chief's powerful words, telling us we must 'do the right thing', giving me hope that if all else failed, I could approach him, reassured he felt exactly the same way as I did about our duty to protect the vulnerable.

At this point, I still felt overwhelming loyalty to the new SIO, Sharon Scotson, who I believed had been put into a role she was unprepared for and I was very aware that if I went over her head to report what was going on, it would cause her problems, something I wanted to avoid at all cost.

I continued to receive phone calls from both Lorna and Amber, which was totally understandable, because after months of almost daily contact and assurances that I would support them throughout the whole process, suddenly, in their eyes, I had disappeared off the face of the earth. I didn't know what they were thinking, but I guessed they thought I too had let them down, the same as everyone else who had let them down before. What they didn't know was that I had been ordered not to contact them and no one else had seen fit to visit them or explain that Amber was no longer to be 'used' in the case.

I didn't discuss the investigation but just reassured them even though I knew what was happening behind the scenes.

Then one day, Amber rang me in a panic to say she'd been threatened by a friend of one of the offenders, who had heard she was helping the police. She was frightened, vulnerable and living alone with a small baby. Concerned, I immediately passed the information on to the inquiry and a Home Link Alarm was installed for her. Incredibly, she was still unaware of the real situation.

'You can call me anytime, Amber. I mean it. If there's anything worrying you then pick up the phone.' I couldn't just abandon them. I never called them because I couldn't discuss the job at all, or the evidence, but I could still pass on messages to Operation Span.

'Thanks, Maggie,' she said, though I sensed she was confused about what was going on, her trust in me wavering, and wondering why I had suddenly left her high and dry without even a conversation, let alone an explanation.

*

In late June 2011, about three weeks later, Amber called me again – this time with critical information. She told me that she believed one of the main suspects on Operation Span was living in a flat above a taxi company. At that time, he'd not been arrested because the police couldn't find him, but his details had been circulated on the police national computer as 'wanted' for allegedly raping a child at knifepoint and we considered him extremely dangerous.

'Maggie, he's talking about fleeing the country,' Amber warned.

Though fearful for her own safety, she was so desperate to help the police convict these men that she'd put herself at risk so that he wouldn't escape prosecution.

'He's talking about going to Brazil, so you'll need to catch him quickly,' she added. 'But he's not there during the daytime, only at night.'

'Amber, that's great news,' I replied. 'Thanks for letting me know. I'll pass it straight on, as soon as I put the phone down.'

And I did. I immediately sent a text to the senior investigating officer, who replied to say she was on leave but she had passed the information to a detective sergeant. I felt relieved that Amber had had the courage to pass the details on so quickly and I expected someone to go round straight away, speak to Amber, get all the details and arrest him. You can imagine my horror when she called me again on 3 July, twelve days after her previous call.

'Maggie, why hasn't anyone been round to speak to me? Why haven't they arrested him?'

I was completely dumbstruck.

'He's still there,' she added. 'He's still there, living above the taxi rank.' She sounded scared.

'Are you sure?'

I was flabbergasted that he hadn't been arrested, but perhaps even more thrown that no one from Operation Span had seen fit to even visit this girl to find out more about what she was telling us.

'Yeah, I've seen him. Maggie, he's still out there, walking the streets. He could do this to another girl. Why haven't they taken him in?'

I shook my head. I wanted to answer her, but no words would come – I was as shocked as she was.

*

Once again I sent a text to the SIO, but she was still on holiday so again she passed the information on to a detective sergeant. I crossed my fingers and hoped to God that someone would have the presence of mind to arrest this man before he fled the country or, worse, raped another vulnerable child at knifepoint.

Two days later, my detective sergeant (DS) from my own Major Incident Team (MIT) got in touch. He told me he'd been contacted by a senior officer on Operation Span, demanding that I hand over my work mobile phone. I immediately became upset because the implication was clearly that I had done something wrong when I knew categorically I hadn't. I'd had that phone for thirteen years and it was my job phone, my Family Liaison Officer phone, not an Operation Span phone. Why would they want it so badly? It felt as though someone was trying to silence me.

Nothing seemed to make sense any more. I'd been

sidelined on the Operation Span investigation because I'd stuck my head above the parapet and had voiced genuine concerns, and then I felt I'd been frozen out of the investigation. I just wanted to do my job properly, to uphold my promises as a police officer, but now this. I was beginning to wonder if maybe I knew too much. I also knew that by taking my phone away, I'd become even more isolated as my friends and colleagues would have no way of contacting me either.

In spite of how insecure and isolated I was feeling, I decided there and then that I wouldn't let them take the phone away from me and I told the DS this. Although trembling inside, I stood my ground. There was no way anyone was going to take my phone – it was a lifeline to the very families I had been employed to protect. He said he'd have to report my refusal back to the Operation Span hierarchy and I said that was fine, he was only doing his job.

Following my refusal, my detective inspector from MIT came to visit me, so I explained my situation to him.

'I'm not handing it over,' I insisted. 'I've done nothing wrong and what I'm seeing here shouldn't be happening.'

We talked for a while and, to my great relief, the DI interceded on my behalf and I was allowed to keep my phone. Although my own team were both fantastic and supportive, my last days on Operation Span had felt like I was back in my probation.

About a month later, on 4 August, I received a text from Lorna to tell me the girls didn't want anything more to do with the police because they didn't trust them, they only trusted me. It seemed what had happened to me was now happening to the family. The contents of this message came as no surprise to me as it was where I had feared the road was leading anyway because of the way the girls were being treated, but it was still a very low moment.

She'd texted: 'The girls are saying they are not doing any more [with the police] till you come back because it's not the same but X [the name of the other officer] said you wasn't doing your job proper. He said you were finished on this job, but Amber told him you are the best and it doesn't matter how long it takes, she will wait for you.'

I was horrified that any officer would make such critical comments about a colleague to a witness. Enraged, I reported the matter to the detective chief superintendent. It was obvious that they'd tried to pick up the pieces with Ruby, but it hadn't worked. Lorna and her girls were – and always would be – loyal to me and, for that, I will always be grateful.

Later that month, I finally received a phone call from DCI Scotson. We spoke for more than an hour, discussing Operation Span, Lorna, the girls, the decisions made and all the other issues that had given me months of sleepless nights.

'None of this makes any sense, boss,' I said. 'We worked so hard for seven months to bring this family on board and they've put their lives on hold to help us in every way they can. Why are they being treated this way? I just can't understand it.'

'Look, Maggie,' the DCI said eventually, taking a deep breath, 'you've not said anything I don't agree with. But the reality is that you're just a constable. In the police, senior officers make the decisions and as a DC, you do as you're told, simple as that. You carry out orders – you know that – and if you can't do that, then maybe you're in the wrong job.'

Although deep down I realised the truth of what she was saying, her words still shocked me to the core. As a police officer, I felt it was my duty to highlight gross neglect and failures where I saw them and paramount in my mind again were Chief Constable Peter Fahy's powerful words, telling us to 'challenge policies when we think they are wrong'. That was what I was doing here, even though it would have been much easier just to shut my eyes and walk away. I should not have had to raise concerns of this magnitude, they should have been dealt with by senior officers anyway. They should have been the ones standing up for these kids, not me. It was then that I realised I was a lone voice. However, I also knew my conflict of loyalty towards my SIO Sharon Scotson was over. As my boss, she was in a position to do something about this but, instead, she was giving me the party line and I'd been a police officer long enough to understand that. I also knew in my heart and without a shadow of a doubt that what was happening was wrong. My loyalty had to be to the children in Rochdale, not to any senior police officer demanding it of me, even if the suggestion was that if I didn't do as I was told, I would lose my job.

Truly, it was a lightbulb moment. Being a good, honest and ethical police officer was all I'd ever wanted to be and it had been a job I'd done to the absolute best of my abilities. I believed it was the main reason I'd been headhunted for this role on Operation Span in the first place and now I was an uncomfortable thorn in the side of Greater Manchester Police, but one that was not going to go away, not this time.

*

By now, I couldn't eat or sleep, but I knew that if the Operation Span hierarchy wasn't prepared to stand up and do right by these kids, then I myself had to. I was off work again and was referred to Occupational Health, where I confided in my former nurse and friend, Amanda. Once again, she gave me the strength to return to work and my own team, having decided I was going to voice all my concerns to the newly appointed Head of the Public Protection Unit, Detective Chief Superintendent Mary Doyle, an officer I had previously worked with on a few high-profile cases.

I'd started to feel not only bullied, but intimidated too, so during a two-hour meeting with DCS Doyle on 27 October 2011, she told me she understood what I was saying, that she had witnessed similar situations in other places she had worked, that the old boys' network was still alive and kicking, but she would get to the bottom of what I was saying. Ecstatic, I left that meeting believing, finally, someone in a position of power who I trusted was taking these concerns seriously and was going to do something. I can't begin to describe how elated and relieved I felt on that day.

I sent DCS Doyle an email confirming some of the main issues discussed at our meeting, but as the days passed and I didn't hear anything, I began to feel unsettled. I eventually chased her up and, eighteen days later, got a reply in which she reiterated her pledge to sort things out but also told me that she was going away for a month and would ask Sam Haworth, the original Operation Span SIO, to deal with me. The letter also said that I could once again take up my status as FLO.

In all honesty, I was devastated and had no doubt I was being fobbed off, particularly regarding the reinstatement of my FLO status. It seemed like a 'carrot and stick' situation so, having thought about everything, I decided not to mess around any further and, just three days later, took the scary step of emailing the Chief Constable of GMP – Peter Fahy – directly, outlining the basis of my concerns and requesting a meeting.

I told him I'd decided to stand up for what I saw as an injustice which also had the potential to bring the force into disrepute if it became public. I also said I had been motivated by his powerful article 'Doing the Right Thing' that had made such an impact on me. I had real faith this time that my concerns would be taken seriously and addressed by him and I awaited a reply with bated breath.

It seemed fate stepped in again when the very next day *The Times* ran a big spread, by reporter Andrew Norfolk, all about the explosion of grooming gangs in the Midlands and the North. The article described a 'catalogue of failure' by police and care agencies to prevent teenage girls from being groomed and raped by Asian men. In it, Norfolk highlighted numerous cases of abuse and even interviewed some of those who'd been raped. But despite his efforts, which had been on-going for many months previously, still no-one was being brought to justice for such horrific crimes.

These articles pulled no punches. They described in chilling and graphic detail how these girls were being abused, and who was doing the abusing. One girl told how she'd jumped from a bridge over the M1 in a suicide attempt because she was being sexually exploited but no-one would take her seriously. This article, and the others Norfolk wrote, fired me up.

It was exactly what was thought and feared – that Pakistani men were sexually abusing and exploiting white girls on an industrial scale. Suddenly this was national news and I knew from the shocked reactions that I'd have public concern behind me; I was fired up and ready to take on the establishment. All I could think of was the victims, the generations of girls who'd been raped and abused by these men. They were looking to the police, looking to us as detectives, to lock up and convict these men who'd ruined their lives. But we weren't doing that. Instead, it felt as though the job was being contained before the lid blew off it.

The day after the media storm I was devastated to receive a bland email from the chief constable, once again being fobbed off, telling me that if lessons needed to be learned, the force would learn them and that my concerns would be looked into. He was in charge of GMP, the last stop, the one person who I truly believed would be outraged when he heard what was happening and would put things right, but this was not to be. I felt my world crashing down around me as reality set in and this final door slammed shut in my face.

Detective Chief Superintendent Darren Shenton, Head of Serious Crime, was eventually nominated to look at the issues and discuss my concerns, and although he too tried to delegate it back down the ranks, I stood my ground. By then I'd suffered months of sleepless nights over the apathy in Operation Span and I was worried that time was running out to change things before the case reached trial, but I decided enough was enough and refused to be silenced. The DCS said he had only half an hour to spare, totally inadequate for a serious discussion such as this, but I went along anyway.

During the meeting, he too reminded me that I was only a constable, that policy decisions were made by senior officers whether I liked it or not and, with a wagging finger, warned that as a serving police officer, I should be 'very careful what I chose to do with the information I held'.

The DCS followed up our brief meeting with an even briefer email in which he acknowledged the Crown Prosecution Service had confirmed Amber was not a suspect over anything. Unbelievably, he went on to say Amber had never even seen herself as a victim – a clear contradiction of everything she'd said in her months of recorded interviews and Vipers. The DCS also said, 'there was little evidence that Amber had been a victim prior to her being sisxteen years of age.'

I was totally flabbergasted by that last remark. If Amber hadn't been a victim, why on earth had she been identified by the Greater Manchester Police hierarchy right from the start as a key victim? Why on earth had the chief lawyer in the Crown Prosecution Service spent two months confirming her as such, and why had we been putting all our energies into getting her to talk to us about what had happened to her? It was just ludicrous. DCS Shenton stated that he was happy that all processes had been followed properly and that the right decisions had been made. He ended his email with the following remark:

> You raised an issue within our meeting in a tone that suggested that if you were not happy with the outcome of our discussion that you would have to consider your position and what you did with your information. This gives me cause for concern and I want to remind you of your responsibilities as a police officer who comes into possession of information during the course of their duties and what they can use that information for.

This felt like a written version of the veiled threat he had delivered verbally in our meeting and I realised senior officers had closed ranks, leaving me completely alone. But I was also angry: I knew full well what a police officer's responsibilities were and I felt it was a shame that GMP didn't take these responsibilities as seriously as I did. Initially, I had thought it had been individual neglect on Operation Span, but now I was beginning to see it reached much further than that. The DCS's reply, and his closing remarks, made it very clear I had nowhere left to go within GMP so I contacted the Police Federation, the body that represents rank and file police officers, and asked them to refer me for independent legal advice.

*

In January 2012, I spent two hours with a solicitor nominated and paid for by the Police Federation and outlined my concerns to her. The lawyer seemed astonished at what had happened, but gave me two pieces of advice. The first was that I must officially lodge a grievance complaint. To me, a grievance felt like a sign of weakness – that I couldn't deal with things – and I'd be written off as a 'moaner', hence I had never done it before. The solicitor said a grievance was the only way to ensure there was an official record that I'd highlighted my concerns. Her second piece of advice was that I must give her my file of evidence so she could review it and advise me further.

When I told the Police Federation about the lawyer's advice their reaction couldn't have been more negative. They saw it as the end of the matter so the lawyer had to write to the Federation to outline her advice and it was at this point that the Fed withdrew their support. They said I had to hand all my evidence to them, which they in turn would give to the internal force solicitors. Needless to say, I refused: my trust was gone.

The Fed rep had agreed to help me prepare my grievance, but she didn't turn up for the meeting and then cancelled another appointment, so I prepared and submitted it with the help of my amazing friend and colleague, Pat Martin, a detective constable in the Major Incident Team, without whose support I doubt I would be still standing today. Incredibly, and despite every new obstacle placed in my way, I was still hoping that by putting everything down on paper, and by going through the official channels, something would be done to put the situation right before the case went to trial.

In my grievance paper I said that I took my police Oath

of Attestation very seriously and that I was proud of the work I'd done. I added this:

> I have tried vigorously to defend the principles that I vowed to uphold in my Oath, but in doing so I have personally been subjected to such horrendous treatment that it is no exaggeration to say that it has cost me my career and caused me many months of stress. My trust in GMP has been totally destroyed by both individuals and the organization.

I also said that 'Operation Span made commitments and promises to victims through me personally, which we have failed to honour. This will have long-term consequences for these victims, and also for me personally, as I too have been deceived and my own personal integrity and honesty has been massively compromised through no fault of my own. In the interests of GMP and the future victims of CSE [Child Sexual Exploitation], I have tried, in good faith, and to the best of my ability, to bring these matters to the attention of senior officers without resorting to the grievance procedure, but the attitude I have encountered leads me to believe that the organisation has no desire to acknowledge or address these failings. The organisation is hiding behind confidentiality and data protection, but as a public service we must be transparent and accountable.'

I then addressed my grievances over the handling of Operation Span, saying: 'I honestly believe that GMP are knowingly failing in their duty to properly investigate the horrendous crimes of Child Sexual Exploitation, and as a result we are allowing offenders to escape justice and failing to protect the most vulnerable in our society.

'Ultimately, I would like to see working practices and attitudes in relation to the investigation of Child Sexual Exploitation completely overhauled so that we have more success in bringing offenders to justice. On Op Span we had a very real opportunity to send out a powerful message that this kind of crime would not be tolerated, but sadly, I believe that opportunity has been wasted.'

I continued: 'The personal consequences for me in choosing this course of action have been immense. In doing my duty to highlight what I initially believed was individual neglect, but now appears to be organisational neglect, I realise that I have committed what is in effect professional suicide as the organisation does not appear to want to address these issues, and I will be labelled as a "troublemaker", although that could not be further from the truth.'

I added: 'I believe I had no choice but to pursue this course of action, as I have witnessed behaviour which is not befitting a police service, and which fails to protect the most vulnerable members of our society. To try and conceal wrong and ultimately I have to answer to my own conscience. I know that despite the difficulties I have faced, all I have tried to do is the right thing for present and future victims of these crimes at the hands of a very organised crime group. I firmly believe that should this get into the public domain, the public would agree with the course of action I have taken, as do many of my colleagues on Op Span, but who are too frightened to speak out the way I have.'

I also warned that I was seeking legal advice to make a protected disclosure in the public interest as I was left with no alternative but to believe there was a deliberate attempt to conceal the truth and silence me personally.

In other words, I was getting ready to blow the whistle.

*

I was still working as a detective within my own amazing team on a murder, but I wondered where I would go from there. Away from the job, I became a hermit. My kids were worried about me as I just couldn't talk of anything else. During the daytime I went through the motions but at night I would lie awake for hours trying to make sense of what was happening...and I couldn't. It just was unbelievable.

I would go for long walks with my son Steve almost every Sunday, and we would try to make sense of it all. My daughter Vicki would arrange for us to do things with my new little grandson Jake (born December 2011) and this was the light in the darkness. My kids were there for me as always, by my side.

I was referred to Occupational Health and my lifesaving nurse Amanda was there to hold my hand and support me too.

But I was in a mess. By March 2012, I couldn't sleep and could barely eat, yet I was still going into work: something had to give. I began to get regular dizzy spells and when these happened, I'd have to grab something solid so that I didn't collapse. One afternoon, I was by the photocopier at work and turned around suddenly. The next thing I remember was waking up on the floor, surrounded by a host of concerned faces. I'd blacked out and, finally, everything had literally come crashing in around me. One of the lads drove my car home while another colleague took me straight to my doctor. I could barely walk into the surgery, so poorly was I at that stage.

My GP took one look and told me she was signing me off work: 'Have you had any other symptoms besides what happened to you today?'

I thought back. I told her about all the dizzy spells I'd been having over previous weeks that I'd put down to lack of sleep, that I wasn't eating and was having heart palpitations. I also told her about my struggles to have my concerns at work heard and the toll that had taken on both my physical and mental health.

'Well,' she replied, taking out her sick notepad, 'I'm signing you off work for a month.'

'With what?' I asked, pulling my jacket back on.

'I'm signing you off with severe work-related stress,' she said. 'Your body is telling you it has had enough and I'm telling you to go home and rest!'

So, it had finally happened: the stress from Operation Span had ground me down to the point where I was unable to function or do the most basic things, such as stand up, eat or sleep. I'd been shut down, frozen out, gagged, threatened with the removal of my phone, ignored, fobbed off, bullied, and now I'd finally collapsed with the stress of it all. But if the powers that be thought they had me beat then they were wrong, because I wasn't out, not by a long chalk. In fact, I was only just beginning to fight back.

Chapter Sixteen
The Trial

> ❝ If you want to know
> what someone is like,
> look at how they treat
> someone who can do
> nothing for them ❞
> — Goethe

For a month I just stared at the TV, barely able to sleep, eat, walk, go out, socialise or talk on the phone. I was in the depths of despair. My husband had died and so had my granddaughter. I'd felt forced to walk away from a job in which I was very much needed by a vulnerable family. I had no income. I was ill, I had bills and a mortgage to pay, and I was on the verge of losing my family home of twenty-eight years.

I was at a very low ebb, yet I still couldn't help feeling that a great injustice had been done in Rochdale and, somehow, I needed to right this wrong. My mind kept going over and over the same ground, trying to figure out what had happened and why Greater Manchester Police seemed happy to discard the months of powerful testament of a young victim. None of it made sense. I'd reached out to the chief constable and the Police Federation and been rejected by both. I felt that what I was saying was not only common sense, it was what a police officer should be doing. We had children telling us they'd been raped on a daily basis yet a major investigation seemed to be turning a blind eye. From a starting point of twenty-seven identified victims at the very outset of Operation Span, we were now left with accompanying just three victims to court, two of whom were from the original 2009 Rochdale inquiry, plus Ruby. Every other one had been cast aside, for one reason or another, and to me that was scandalous.

I wondered if it was me. Was I going mad? Was I losing the plot, not seeing what was obvious to others? I questioned myself over and over again. Then I went back to my doctor, who thought I might be depressed. I was, but only over the injustice of what had happened. For the only time in my life I was prescribed antidepressants and I took them for a few days. I was due to go away to Turkey, where I hoped I might be able to clear my head, and told myself that I wouldn't take them while I was abroad, but if I felt the same when I returned, I would continue this medication. Before I went away, I was called up to two interviews regarding my grievance report that I'd filed at the beginning of February 2012. I was hoping I might be listened to and understood during these interviews, but nothing more was said and so I went away, wondering what might come next.

Away from home, I did a lot of thinking. With the help of good friends, the sunshine and a slower pace of life, I concluded that I didn't believe in the job any more. I hadn't become a police officer to simply walk away from a vulnerable family who needed our protection and help. I realised that I too felt I'd been 'used' by GMP, in the way that many officers of the lower ranks are used. I was just a pawn in the 'game' they'd talked about. I had dared to question senior officers and was now paying the price: their ranks had closed. Stress and despair had caused my vision to become so clouded, I could not find a way through the fog. Now that mist was clearing and suddenly I had 20/20 vision again. And no, I never did resume the antidepressants.

*

During this period the public inquiry into the Hillsborough disaster of 15 April 1989 was on-going and there were daily updates on TV. The disaster happened during an FA cup semi-final between Liverpool and Nottingham Forest, when Liverpool fans who had gathered outside the ground were allowed into an already overcrowded pen. The resulting crush killed ninety-six people – the worst stadium disaster in history – and the ramifications of that afternoon continue to this day. I watched and thought about the families of the ninety-six, and their decades-long fight to get to the truth, despite attempts by senior police officers and officials over all those years to conceal the truth. Their efforts and tenacity impressed me and I thought, *I don't want to be sitting here in twenty-five years' time, not having stood up for what I believed.* I had no idea how I'd do it, and I was terrified of going to prison for it, but I was determined one way or another, I would make my voice heard. However, I couldn't say anything for the moment, and for a very good reason:

while I'd been off the job, eleven men had been charged with various offences. Now, at least a few of these abusers were being brought to justice, but it could have been so many more. And many more victims could – and should – have been encouraged to come forward and give their evidence. The trial was scheduled for May 2012 and, just before it, I received the document that made up my mind, once and for all, that I would speak out about this whole investigation and the treatment of vulnerable victims to anyone who would listen.

This was the findings of my grievance procedure following my initial complaint and the two subsequent meetings I'd attended in March 2012. Surprise, surprise, it found there was no case to answer. According to Greater Manchester Police, Operation Span had not knowingly failed in its duty to properly investigate child sexual exploitation, no promises had been made to use Amber as a witness and I had not been bullied or intimidated in any way. I had, apparently, been slow to get results from the family (although everyone knew and understood that I had to go slowly in order to get them on board in the first place) and that I was more concerned about the welfare of the family than I was about the investigation at large. GMP also said it had never given any assurances that Amber would be used as a witness – in other words, I was talking complete nonsense.

Basically, they'd cherry-picked my complaints but totally ignored the overwhelming majority of my disclosures. Naively, I hadn't audio recorded the meetings, but there had been a minute-taker there from HR, who had recorded everything verbatim. Later, I requested a copy of those minutes, even using the Freedom of Information Act, but was unsurprised to be told all the minutes had been lost.

In a way, I expected the result I got. Having spent the previous months demanding answers to questions senior officers didn't want to hear, it was no surprise to hear that all my concerns had been ignored. Additionally, there were judgements made about Amber and her viability as a witness in court, in exactly the same way as those judgements had been made about Holly in 2009. It was said she was 'too dangerous and volatile to use as a witness' and that she was 'extremely negative and at times hostile about other complainants/witnesses'. It was concluded that Amber could not be considered 'a witness of truth', i.e. someone who could be relied upon to give 'the truth, the whole truth and nothing but the truth' in court. To me, it seemed clear that despite everything that had been said from the outset of Operation Span and the criticism directed at Rochdale CID about their treatment of Holly and Amber in 2009, Op Span had repeated the very same failures, the only difference being that this time they had failed Amber and the other two dozen victims instead of Holly, yet the same judgements and justifications were again being made, which to me were completely unjustifiable and shot to pieces a police officer's duty to remain 'impartial'.

Having spent so much time with this frightened girl, the picture these statements painted seemed to be that of someone else entirely. My position would be to let Amber give evidence in court, to allow her to stand up against her abusers and tell of everything that happened to her. Then it would be down to a jury to decide whether she was telling the truth. Evidently, the Crown Prosecution Service and GMP saw it in another way entirely. However, this wasn't quite the end of this story.

Amber's evidence was deemed useful after all, yet somehow she couldn't be trusted to deliver it in court. Instead, the CPS had decided to put her on the indictment – in other words, to list her as an offender under her real name – so that what she had said could be used in court. And to cap it all, they were keeping this secret from the very person they were indicting: a young girl who had done nothing wrong. This meant she would not be arrested, would not be informed, would not be cautioned, would not be interviewed, would not have access to legal representation and would have no chance of defending herself. I thought this was an abuse of process. It was most certainly against everything that I believe the law is there for, which is to protect the innocent. Quite apart from anything else, the basic premise of the law is that everything that is said without being under caution is inadmissible in court. I have never, either before or since, heard of anything like it in my life, nor has any lawyer, barrister or professional I have approached since. I also believe the reason Amber was denied these basic human rights was because by keeping it secret, they could basically say anything they wanted – because she had no one there to challenge anything. I also firmly believe that any defence team worth their salt would have had it all thrown out at the first hurdle.

In short, we were almost at the trial date and there was a late realisation that without Amber's evidence, the whole case could fall apart. Yet the police had alienated her beyond belief, making it impossible to now bring her back on board as a witness, so the prosecution decided to secretly portray her as a defendant.

Under UK law it is everyone's absolute right to know if they are being accused of a crime and what they are being accused of, so they have an opportunity to defend themselves. That legal right extends to even the worst offenders, the likes of the Yorkshire Ripper or Fred and Rose West. Yet, here we had a fifteen-year-old child victim of the most horrific abuse, designated as such by the top lawyer in the CPS, who was now having her months of video interviews as a victim used against her in court, and where she was secretly being described as an 'older madam' or paedophile.

Everything Amber had told the police had been as the victim and witness she was, not as a perpetrator. But time was ticking and now, only a few weeks before the trial, the prosecution had decided it needed her evidence, but at this late stage this was the only way Amber's evidence could be used in court. She had been excluded from the prosecution, so everything she had said in her video interviews would now be deemed inadmissible in court unless she were there to deliver her evidence herself and be available for cross-examination. Because of how she had been treated by the police and the CPS, it was now far too late for that so the only other way her evidence could be used was if she was portrayed as one of the gang – a defendant. This seemed like a tactical option to me.

I'd never heard anything so screwed-up and bizarre in my entire life. To me, it felt like wickedness beyond belief to first acknowledge at the highest level that Amber was purely a victim, then encourage her over a period of months to relive her terrible experiences on the record, *then* discard her like an oily rag – and finally, to add insult to injury, place her alongside her abusers as an offender just to shoehorn her evidence into court and not tell her this was happening.

At this point I would like every reader of this book to stop right here and consider the full implications of this. Consider if the police decided you had committed a heinous crime, but you were never told and you never had a chance to defend yourself. Imagine that terrifying prospect for one moment and then realise that this is exactly what the CPS did to Amber.

I asked myself, *Is this lawful? Can you really be indicted as an offender without your knowledge?* My police and legal training taught me that any suspect has a right to know what is being said about them and a right to legal representation. Furthermore, under the Human Rights Act, Article 6 says that 'everyone is entitled to a fair trial and a public hearing', yet Amber and her family were being kept in the dark.

To say I was incandescent with rage is an understatement. I could not say anything to Amber or her family because I knew to do so might jeopardise the trial that was now underway and the last thing I wanted was to be responsible for setting these paedophiles free. But this was the moment that I decided, once this is over, I'm coming for GMP and the CPS. I could no longer reconcile my duties as a police officer with the way senior management had acted. I saw a wrong, pure and simple, and now I was determined to right that wrong.

I did not attend the trial – I was still off work, having collapsed – instead watching the coverage on TV and reading about it in the press. Lorna, Amber and Ruby's mum, was not allowed into the court. She has since said they told her she might be called as a witness, and therefore was not allowed to hear her daughter Ruby give evidence, although I firmly believe that was just a 'ruse' used to prevent her from hearing the terrible things being said about her children in court – to which I know she would have loudly objected. That could not be allowed to happen as I believe it would have caused the trial to collapse. The case was largely built around Holly, plus one other victim, and Ruby – but Ruby would be giving evidence solely against the abuser who made her pregnant at thirteen (DNA evidence having been obtained from the foetus). Incredibly, not one of the other men she had named as having abused her was ever charged with any offences against her. Why was the man who had sex with a twelve, then thirteen-year-old child and made her pregnant, where we had a foetus, where paternity was one hundred per cent proven, never charged with rape? What more could possibly be available to prove the offence of rape? Ruby was and remains furious about the fact he was never charged with rape, and can't understand why, and nor can I. She is also outraged that the other men she named as having raped her were never charged either. Today, now in her early twenties with a children of her own, she understands far more that she was failed.

My personal opinion too is that the charges brought against other offenders were insufficient, but the CPS in their wisdom are responsible for deciding what charges are brought and trafficking is a much easier offence to prove and perhaps therein lies the real answer.

＊

The trial, which concluded in May 2012, attracted the attention of the far-right and there were often noisy protests outside Liverpool Crown Court from groups like the British National Party and the English Defence League. Unsurprisingly, it was a volatile situation and I take my hat off to those who took the witness stand against a dock packed with their alleged abusers. I was sad that there weren't more perpetrators or victims in court or giving evidence by video link – and, of course, that Amber wasn't being given the chance to be heard – and in a way that did not mark her down as one of the accused.

The court heard how the men had plied their victims with drink and drugs so they could 'pass them around' and use them for sex. The jury were told the abuse took place at two takeaways in Heywood – Tasty Bites and The Balti House (by the time of the trial, both were under new management), as well as on the moors, in taxis and in flats all over Rochdale and across into Yorkshire – and had involved men aged between twenty-four and fifty-nine. The court heard that one teenager had been forced to have sex with 20 men in just one night, while another told how she'd been so drunk when she was raped by two men that she'd vomited 'over the side of the bed'. Another said she'd been beaten and forced to have sex with 'several men in a day, several times a week'.

The prosecution barrister told the jury: 'No child should be exploited as these girls say they were.' But the defendants argued they were not aware the girls were underage.

Liverpool Crown Court was told about Ruby, how she'd become pregnant by one of the defendants. I was later told by journalists that Amber had been portrayed in court as an older 'madam', even though she'd been a child only four months older than Holly. She'd been represented as a 'woman' who brought kids along to be abused. The 'Honey Monster' nickname was rolled out again and Amber hadn't been referred to as a victim of these men. That made my blood boil. By putting her on the indictment sheet, her reputation had been trashed, even though she too had been a victim and always would be.

Thankfully, the jury chose to believe the word of the girls and, on 8 May 2012, nine men were convicted and jailed. All those convicted were found guilty of conspiracy to engage in sexual activity with girls under the age of eighteen. The men – eight from Pakistan and one from Afghanistan – had treated the girls 'as though they were worthless', Judge Gerald Clifton told the court. He added: 'Some of you, when arrested, said it [the prosecution] was triggered by race. That is nonsense. What triggered this prosecution was your lust and greed.'

Shabir Ahmed's ('Daddy') defence barrister said his client objected to being 'tried by an all-white jury', saying Ahmed believed his convictions 'had nothing to do with justice but result from faith and the race of the defendants'.

Sentencing him to nineteen years, Judge Clifton called Ahmed an 'unpleasant and hypocritical bully', who had ordered a fifteen-year-old girl to have sex with takeaway worker Kabeer Hassan (his nephew) as a birthday treat.

Hassan was sentenced to nine years for the rape of Holly and three years, concurrently, for a conspiracy conviction.

Mohammed Sajid ('Sajje'), thirty-five, was handed a twelve-year sentence after being convicted of one count of rape, sexual activity with a girl under sixteen and trafficking for exploitation. He was also told he'd be deported back to Pakistan at the end of his prison sentence.

Taxi driver Abdul Aziz, the man known as 'Car 40' or 'Tariq', was given nine years after being convicted of trafficking for sexual exploitation. Aziz was said in court to have taken over as the main trafficker of the girls.

Adil Khan, forty-two, was convicted of trafficking a child within the UK for sexual exploitation and conspiracy to engage in sexual activity with a child and was given just an eight-year sentence.

Abdul Rauf, known as 'Cassie', was sentenced to six years after being convicted of trafficking a child within the UK for sexual exploitation. Rauf, forty-three, a married father-of-five and a religious studies teacher at a local mosque, asked a fifteen-year-old victim if she had any younger friends. He also drove some of the girls to other men, who would use them for sex.

Mohammed Amin ('Car Zero'), forty-five, received five years for the conspiracy charge and for sexual assault.

Hamid Safi, twenty-two, of no fixed address, but originally from Afghanistan, was convicted of trafficking girls for the purposes of sexual exploitation and given a four-year jail sentence. Safi had sneaked into the country on a lorry in 2008 and had claimed asylum. He was also told he would be deported back to Afghanistan at the end of his sentence.

Finally, Abdul Qayyum ('Tiger'), forty-four, of Ramsay Street, Rochdale, was given a five-year jail term for conspiracy to engage in sexual activity with a child.

Another man, Liaquat Shah, was cleared, the jury being unable to reach a verdict on the conspiracy charge.

Qamar Shahzad, thirty, was found not guilty of conspiracy and acquitted.

'Daddy' had not been named at the time of the first trial as he had a second trial following on from the first about an unrelated matter, but in June 2012, a month after the initial Rochdale grooming trial, Shabir Ahmed was also convicted of thirty counts of rape against another young girl in that case.

It is worth mentioning too that it is quite normal in the UK for offenders to serve only half of their sentences due to prison numbers, so by early 2017, all but two of the abusers ('Daddy' and 'Sajje') were free to once again walk the streets of Rochdale. In addition, four of these offenders have also been granted millions of pounds of tax payers' money to fight deportation back to Pakistan.

At the end of the court case, I sat alone in my living room and cried in disbelief as I listened to Assistant Chief Constable Steve Heywood standing on the court steps and delivering his speech to TV crews and the world press

'This has been a fantastic result for British justice,' he said. 'These victims have been through the most horrendous of crimes and I just want to commend their bravery in relation to the ordeal they've had to go through, a long number of weeks in court, and they've had to go through a lot of trauma.

'In relation to the offenders, I condemn them from the

highest level. These are the most vulnerable in our society and they have been preyed upon by adults who should know better.

'I would also like to thank my officers for the professionalism and dedication they've shown in a very complex inquiry. And this is the first time in UK history that we've had trafficking in the UK. It is a new offence and will be seen as a significant way forward in tackling child abuse. I would also like to thank the CPS and our barrister for the professionalism they have shown under considerable pressure, not just internally, but externally.'

Here was the very officer who had been in charge of force Child Protection, back in 2004 at the time of Operation Augusta. I clearly remembered sitting in his office that year, speaking to him about that case. This comment, and his knowledge that offences perpetrated by Pakistani men against young white girls had been going on for all those years before, without anyone being brought to justice, made me so angry and even more determined to make my voice heard. Had he and other senior officers acted back then to stop this tide of abuse, then I had no doubt things would not have escalated to the scale they were now at – instead, he had been promoted to assistant chief constable.

I'd never doubted what I'd seen on Operation Span was wrong: I knew it was wrong, and I felt that if I didn't speak out, what kind of message would that send to my kids? I thought about in the years to come, after I'd gone, when all this would become public. What would my kids think of me? They'd wonder why I hadn't stood up and said something, because that's how Norman and I had brought them up – to always tell the truth and to stand up for what you believe in. I decided I couldn't just sit there, do the job and keep my mouth shut. I had to speak up because it was my duty. I recalled how the police had wanted to take my phone away from me, how they'd wanted to silence me so that no one would ever know what had gone on behind closed doors. But, at the end of the day, I had to look at myself in the mirror, knowing I had done my best and this was another light bulb moment for me.

*

After the trial, there was the inevitable fallout and usual paper exercise and back slapping. The Parliamentary Home Affairs Select Committee chaired by MP Keith Vaz asked senior police officers and council representatives to explain what had gone on in the town. Sara Rowbotham, as manager, was sent at the last minute by her employers to represent the Crisis Intervention Team (CIT). She told the committee that she had made 103 referrals to police and social services between 2005 and 2011, and that despite the convictions, sexual abuse was still going on in Rochdale.

There had been only nine convictions.

I wanted to tell the Select Committee what had happened from my point of view. I still hoped someone would want to know the truth and it seemed this committee was the only place left to go. But although I requested to be allowed to appear in person, my request was refused. I was told I couldn't attend. Instead, I was allowed to contribute a brief report, which I did, but when the final report was eventually published in June 2013 very little of my information had been used. It was another blow, but at least a professional like Sara Rowbotham had spoken to the committee and corroborated what I'd been saying all along – that these crimes had been taking place for years, with no one doing anything to prevent them.

In November 2012, Rochdale Metropolitan Borough Council apologised for failing to address child sexual abuse properly and for not protecting the girls. A twenty-nine-page report into the child sexual exploitation scandal had found 'deficiencies' in the way children's social care had responded to the victims' needs and these deficiencies had been caused by 'patchy' training of frontline staff. It said social workers, police and prosecutors had all missed opportunities to stop a child exploitation ring abusing young girls in the town. However, the ex-chief executive of Rochdale Council told the Home Affairs Committee that he knew nothing of the abuse until the men's arrests in 2010.

I was still off sick and considered what had happened to Amber a deep injustice. It seemed the only way I'd be heard was if I resigned. I was very nervous of going public, but I knew that as a serving officer, I just couldn't take this drastic step. If I was to take the risk and speak up – which I was going to do, despite my fears – I would have to resign.

In October 2012, I did just that – finally leaving the job I'd loved and been so passionate about. Men who had abused these girls were still walking the streets and I felt that prosecutors had failed to use evidence to convict other men, who were still out there and a risk to other children. The job had been contained, evidence ignored, and other victims had effectively been silenced by not having their accounts logged or crimed on the police systems. In fact, of the dozens of allegations of rape by in excess of at least two dozen men which had been disclosed by just Amber and Ruby alone, incredibly, only one had been officially recorded – and this was the one where we had the foetus. A cynic may say the only reason for that is because they couldn't just 'lose' a foetus and, consequently, that is the only reason that particular crime was recorded and not buried like the vast majority of the others.

I had to make someone listen and take my evidence seriously. First, though, as a civilian I had to make a very difficult journey to Rochdale and stand on the same doorstep that I'd stood on in December 2010. I knew, at the very least, I would be viewed with as much suspicion as I had been back then. I might even be told to go away and never come back. If that should happen, I would understand why: Lorna and her family had been let down appallingly and for them I might very well represent that failure. Yet I needed to explain why I hadn't been in touch. I needed to say that I'd been prevented from speaking to them – in short, I didn't want them to feel I'd abandoned them too. I'd expected them to feel angry that they'd been cheated by the judicial system. And I also wanted to tell them what I'd so far been forbidden from saying – that Amber had effectively been treated like a criminal in order to get her evidence into court.

Chapter Seventeen

Return to Rochdale

> 6 I don't go by the rule
> book... I lead from the
> heart, not the head 9
> — Princess Diana

It was now October 2012. Finally, after many months of worrying and waiting, my last day in service dawned. For months I'd sat at home on my own, still trying to figure out why everything had gone so wrong, and why it only seemed to be me who considered that a great injustice had been done. Everyone else, from the chief constable down, had hailed Operation Span as an outstanding success. No doubt the Home Office were pleased too; some offenders were in prison; three girls had had their say. Everything was tickety-boo and back to normal. No need for further questions, thanks, the Greater Manchester Police force has done its job and we can all move on.

Well, *I* couldn't. I'd nearly gone out of my mind over this and because I'd been signed off sick, I'd not been back to the job I once loved. I knew I was a good officer who had tried to do the right thing by everyone I'd ever come across. The list of commendations in my file attested to that. And, irony of ironies, there was even one for Operation Span. For obvious reasons I hadn't bothered to attend that particular exercise in back-slapping.

Friends and family must have been sick to the back teeth of me going on about it so much, but I needed their reassurance that I wasn't going mad. They all agreed with me – a terrible wrong had been done to Amber and her family, and the proof of the pudding was that the vast majority of their abusers were still walking the streets of Rochdale as free men. I talked to my GP and my nurse at Occupational Health and they felt exactly the same. What had happened was disgusting and people couldn't believe what I was actually telling them. Inside my head, I had all this mess going around, wondering why the police weren't seeing it the same way I had. I'd tried the Police Federation, the Children's Commissioner and the Independent Police Complaints Commission that was (now called the Independent Office for Police Conduct). But not one of these organisations would support me in that fight. The IPCC said they couldn't help me because I was still a serving officer and the Children's Commissioner considered that GMP were actually doing a good job. One of my Major Incident Team (MIT) colleagues who I was still in touch with me said, 'I get what you're saying, Maggie, but at the end of the day, they've made the decisions. This is your job, so just come back to work, get your bum on the seat, take your wage and go home.'

But no, I couldn't do that for one minute. That isn't who I am. I couldn't just sit there quietly, saying nothing while waiting for retirement day. I couldn't make any sense of why no one seemed to see this injustice or cared about helping me. I knew I was completely on my own and that I would have to fight this thing myself. And I would have to start at the sharp end – which came as soon I was out of the police service for ever.

*

It was like déjà vu. A cold, wintry day on a bleak council estate near Rochdale. A path leading through a scrappy bit of front lawn and up to a battered door. Nothing seemed to have changed since I was first here in December 2010, yet everything had. After that first knock at the door, my life and the lives of the occupants living here changed irrevocably in less than two years. There was no going back for any of us. And here I was, an unemployed civilian as apprehensive of making this call as I had been on the day I first arrived, as a proud detective with a brief to bring a vulnerable family into a complex and harrowing investigation.

The door opened and a familiar, weary face peeped out. Her shocked expression quickly turned to one of contempt. I gulped nervously, even though I had expected a hostile welcome.

'What do you want?' Lorna snapped.

I was about to reply, but she silenced me with a pointed finger.

'Where the bloody hell have you been? You told us you'd be there, but you weren't.'

'Listen, Lorna,' I said, holding up my hands in a gesture of surrender, 'can I please come in and talk to you? Just let me sit down and explain to you what's happened.'

There was a pause. Lorna looked me up and down, just

as she had done that first time. I knew her well enough to know what she was probably thinking – *Silly cow, coming around here full of apologies…* And who could blame her?

I waited for the sound of the door slamming in my face. Instead, she opened it wider, stepped aside and swept her arm in the direction of the hallway. Lorna was, and always will be, a decent person at heart and if I only lasted five minutes, she was, at least, prepared to hear what I had to say.

I took a seat as she sat down on the sofa opposite me.

'Look, Lorna, I've been forbidden from getting in touch with you,' I began, trying to find the right words. 'I'm really, really sorry, but I've given my job up over this.'

Her eyes widened. 'You did what?' she said.

'I resigned from the police because of what I saw happen with your girls,' I said. 'I think it's disgusting what's gone on. You've all been abandoned. And I'm here to say how deeply sorry I am that it's happened. I'm angry and I'm outraged. We've all been betrayed – me, you, Amber, Ruby. Especially Amber. And I couldn't stay in the job, not after that.'

I took a deep breath and felt my cheeks flush. Lorna was silent for a moment, then she stared me full in the face. She'd always known how much my job had meant to me and how hard I'd worked to get justice for her girls.

'Maggie, I had no idea,' she said. 'I thought you'd deserted us, just like everyone else.'

I shook my head.

'I know,' I said, 'and that's why I came here today...to explain.'

Lorna told me that Amber had just given birth to a

second child, who was only a few weeks old. I knew that I would be facing a very difficult conversation with her. Nevertheless, I had to do this.

'Can I see Amber, so that I can explain?' I asked.

She nodded. 'Yeah, I'll take you. Give me a minute, I'll just go and get my coat.'

On the way, I explained more about my reasons for not being in touch and for resigning.

Lorna nodded again. 'I'm glad you've come to explain, Maggie,' she said. 'Our Amber's furious – she thought you'd just cleared off and forgotten us.'

The level of that fury was evident when we reached Amber's house and knocked on the door. She didn't mince words: 'What the fuck do you want?' she snapped as soon as she saw me.

'Amber, can I come in?' I said, trying to stay calm. 'Let's sit down and I'll tell you what's been happening.'

Amber looked at her mother. 'It's alright,' she said, 'she just wants to tell you what's happened. And that she's not a copper anymore.'

'What?' said Amber. 'You're not in the police? Why not? What happened?'

'If you let me in, I'll tell you,' I said and, with that, she ushered us into her living room. Again, I went through my explanation of what had gone on and why I felt I had no choice other than to resign from the force. Amber sat there cradling her baby in a state of disbelief as she listened to what I had to say.

'So, what's been happening with you?' I said finally. 'Has anyone been to see you?'

'Nowt's happened,' she said. 'No one's been to see me.

I've not had a conversation with the police. They came to pick up Ruby. She went to court about the baby and all that, but no one *ever* came to see me and there's never been any explanation, and you'd not been in touch either.'

I sat up in my chair and clasped my hands together, resting my elbows on my knees.

'I'm so, so sorry, Amber, but I was forbidden from making contact.'

Amber's face scrunched up in disbelief.

'Why not?' she said.

'I was under orders,' I said. 'I couldn't do anything that might cause the case to collapse.'

Amber nodded. 'I understand that,' she said.

'There's something else...' I continued, once again searching for the right words.

Amber nuzzled her face against her baby's cheek and looked over at me expectantly.

'What? What is it, Maggie?'

I cleared my throat. I couldn't believe that no one had told the poor girl what I was about to tell her. It was nothing short of inhumane to have kept her in the dark for so long.

'You don't know this...well, I don't think you know this... but are you aware that they put you on the indictment – on the charge sheet – as one of the gang of paedophiles?'

Amber's mouth fell open as she stared at me in complete shock. It was quite clear the poor girl didn't have a clue. It had all been done in total secrecy because the last thing the police and the Crown Prosecution Service had wanted was for it to get into the public domain.

Amber's voice suddenly broke the silence.

'Oh my God, it all makes sense now!' she said, putting a hand against her mouth. Then she burst into tears. All the months of pent-up fear, hurt and anger came tumbling out at this sudden revelation. I understood her emotions completely, as they were the same emotions I felt too and I threw my arms around her as she sobbed, hugging her, reassuring her until she was all cried out.

Now it was my turn to ask questions.

'What? What is it?'

'It all makes sense now – everything makes sense.'

'Why? What do you mean, Amber?'

She rose to her feet, placed her sleeping baby in its crib and began to explain that she'd been in court the previous week.

'Court? Why?' I asked.

'It was the family court,' she said. 'They're trying to take the children away from me.'

'What? Why?'

'I dunno why,' she said. 'Or I didn't know why until you just said that. Now it all adds up. That's why I'm being treated as a criminal. Jesus, I can't believe this...'

Amber explained that in late September 2012, just days before her baby had been born, Social Services had turned up on her doorstep, unannounced, and said they were going to take both her children away from her. Then they'd taken her to the office, where she said she felt terrified and alone. By this time, her eldest child was two years old and there had never been any issues with him or her care of him.

'They said that when my baby was born, they were

going for full care orders and I'd lose both of my kids,' she said. 'I didn't have a clue what they were on about, or why they wanted to do this.'

Once again, I couldn't believe what I was hearing. Amber's children were her life and without them she had nothing. She'd already been prevented from going to college because of the previous 'madam' arrest. She had no friends because she could no longer trust anyone and was practically in hiding from the world as if she'd done something wrong when all she'd ever been was a victim of child sexual exploitation. The only other people who she now trusted to be in her world were her partner, her mum and sister.

'The following week, I went into labour,' she said, 'and travelled to the hospital. But as soon as I'd given birth, someone from the hospital came in and put a tag on my baby.'

Amber's eyes again began to fill with tears at the memory of it, so raw and so recent.

'They told me I wasn't allowed to take my baby out of the hospital because she was going to be made a "Ward of Court".'

'So, they did this on the instructions of Social Services? They tagged the baby?'

'Yep.'

I looked over at Lorna, who shook her head in despair. No wonder they were both so angry when I turned up. For myself, I was utterly disgusted that after everything they knew, Social Services could come in and do something so despicable to a newborn baby and its mother. Tagging it like an animal. What a despicable act by an organisation who had let down this girl in the most appalling ways possible. I didn't think they could get any worse, but I was wrong.

'I was laid there in hospital while Social Services were trying to get an order to take the baby away from me,' Amber continued.

'So, what happened?' I said, interrupting her.

'Well, that was it...'

She explained that after two days a manager or someone at the hospital had questioned the decision and had asked Social Services where its authority was to prevent mum and baby going home and to show her the documentation to prove there was a risk of the child being harmed.

'The nursing sister was really angry,' said Amber. 'She asked to see some paperwork and Social Services had to admit they didn't have it – they didn't have anything.'

Thankfully, once the hospital had questioned it and realised Social Services had no legal right to keep Amber's baby there, they removed the tag and Amber was told she was free to leave with the child. However, a social worker called at her house afterwards and from then on stayed for hours each day, watching her.

'I was a complete nervous wreck, Maggie, but I didn't know what I'd done wrong,' she said. 'I was terrified I'd lose both kids and you know my kids are my world. It just wasn't fair. I couldn't enjoy being a mother, I just couldn't relax. Why is it always me?'

Within a week, Amber had to appear at the family court, her week-old baby in her arms. Of course she'd been unaware that she'd been named on the indictment sheet and was totally baffled why she was even there.

'I told them, Maggie. I said, "I've never hurt my baby. I'm a good mum."'

Amber had to sit in court and listen while a similar set of allegations to the ones police had interviewed her about in 2009 were read out. The same unfounded allegations that had resulted in no charges and no further action being brought against her. The CPS had declared her a victim, nothing less. Then she had been put on the charge sheet and, suddenly, in the eyes of Social Services, she was now a child abuser.

'The mother [Amber] represents a risk of sexual harm to the children in that she has significantly skewed sexual boundaries,' a Social Services report to the court said, 'and a child in her care is at risk of being sexually exploited or of being exposed to the sexual exploitation of others.'

These allegations were outrageous and baseless. And if they were based on anything, it was on the purely 'tactical' decision taken by the CPS at the last minute as the only way to allow them to use all the critical evidence she had provided in the trial – a tactic she had no knowledge of whatsoever until I told her. Amber was a good, loving mother and yet Social Services were even maintaining that she was still being exploited in January 2011. This was after Operation Span had started and getting on for two years since the abuse had finished. So much for the quality of their research...

Thankfully, the judge had his eyes wide open and complete sympathy for her situation and had asked Social Services why he had the mother of a seven-day-old baby before him in his court.

'The judge was lovely,' Amber recalled. 'He told them there was no evidence that I was a bad parent and I shouldn't have been there. He actually told me, "You go home with your baby."'

The judge demanded that if Social Services were determined to pursue this, they should bring more evidence to court. Meanwhile, Amber would have to sit at home and worry for a whole month until the next hearing.

'Don't worry,' I insisted. 'I'm completely disgusted by what's happened to you. We're going to fight this and I'll help you.'

*

If I couldn't get justice for Amber during Operation Span, there was plenty I could do now I was a civilian. Quickly, I contacted a solicitor and got her some legal representation under the Legal Aid scheme. I also told him what had happened to this poor girl. I wanted the solicitor to use all my information and evidence and pass it to the family court to support Amber's case and offer her some defence. To sum up everything, I wrote a long statement, which was presented to the court.

A month later, Amber was at court again, only for the judge to send her home once more. However, Social Services had already placed her children on the Child Protection Register for a whole year. In the meantime, she was told that both the police and Social Services had visited her friends and associates to try and get them to say that she was a 'bad girl and mother'. It was a 'fishing trip' but, unfortunately for them, none of Amber's friends or associates were prepared to bite. Not one person said anything negative to police or Social Services about her; in fact, one of those who was called upon told her unwelcome visitors to 'fuck off'. To me, it felt like a major spot of arse-covering. They'd labelled her a criminal by putting her on the indictment sheet and now they had to try and get that label to stick – only it didn't, because Amber was, and still is, a great mother. It had been shocking to see such treatment of a poor, defenceless girl.

*

One day, Amber turned to me and asked why these things had been done to her.

'I sat there for hours and hours trying to help them,' she said, 'so why are they doing this to me, Maggie?'

I had no answers, and I still don't.

Amber also spoke to me about the grooming trial.

'I knew Ruby was going to court because she told me,' she said, 'but I didn't understand why they didn't use me. I blocked it out, to be honest, because it was just too painful. I didn't speak to anyone about it, although I did feel good that the men were on trial for what they'd done to us so that justice was done to them. I'm just upset that they never used my evidence...no one told me they weren't going to include me.'

'So, how did you hear about what had happened to them in the court case?' I asked.

Amber looked up at me.

'I found out about the verdicts on the news, like everyone else.'

It had been beyond belief that she'd found out at the same time as everyone else. Ruby had also found out about the verdicts on the news, too. In short, they'd been treated like shit.

At the end of a full twelve months of having Social Services turning up on her doorstep, Amber's nightmare and fight to keep her kids finally came to an end. The judge had repeatedly asked Social Services to show him evidence that Amber was a bad mother and that her children were at risk. But Social Services had nothing, so the judge, God bless him for ever, dismissed the case. Social Services had pitched a case that she had 'colluded' with the men who had abused these girls. However, it had failed to mention that Amber had been a child victim herself. In fact, they failed to even say how old she'd been at the time of the abuse – just fifteen, and still a child. It was as though it had targeted and singled her out when she was nothing but a child victim herself. The judge had informed Social Services in no uncertain terms that if they ever tried to bring Amber back into the family court in the future then the case must be brought before him because he had full knowledge of it. Furthermore, he said that if he had retired by then, he must still be made aware so he could inform the new judge of the full facts of the case.

It was quite obvious to me that the judge had seen this for what it had been – someone, somewhere, had set out to target Amber and discredit and tarnish her reputation. But for once, and against all the odds, she'd won. It is to her absolute credit and strength of character that she not only managed to survive those horrific twelve months, but came through them an even stronger and more resilient girl.

*

Around the same time as I called round to see Lorna and Amber, I'd also made my second important decision: I was going to speak out publicly about the case and so I decided to approach the BBC's *Panorama* documentary programme. Very quickly, they replied, saying they were interested in what I had to say and a meeting was arranged in London with multi-award-winning producer Joe Plomin, who listened carefully as I went through the whole story.

Like me, he was completely horrified by what I told him and determined to make a programme about what I had disclosed, so he went back to the BBC to make his pitch. A few weeks later, he called to say he was really disappointed that *Panorama* had decided they were unable to take on my story. However, the reason was nothing to do with the quality of information that I held: the Jimmy Savile scandal was just breaking and the BBC were right in the thick of it for not having acted against him before his death. At this moment the saga of Rochdale wasn't the right fit for *Panorama* because they didn't feel they could take on another sexual scandal at that exact moment in time. Joe also said the only other programme he felt would do a thorough job was BBC Radio 4's flagship current affairs programme, *File on Four*.

'These people will do your story justice,' he told me. Joe passed over my details and, in November 2012, a producer called Sally Chesworth came to see me. Immediately, she was very interested in what I had to say and could see there was an important story to be told. The programme was commissioned and I spent the next three months working with Sally, taking her through the whole story and introducing her to the girls and Lorna, whom she interviewed. This was the first time all three had spoken publicly about their ordeal and they were understandably very nervous. However, in the time I'd been working with her I'd got to know Sally well and I trusted her for her empathy and professionalism. I knew *File on Four* had an outstanding reputation so I introduced Sally to the girls and Lorna, and was there to hold their hands during their interviews with her. All they wanted was to be heard and to prevent anyone else going through what they'd experienced. Sally was understanding and totally professional at all times, doing her homework carefully and not pressuring her interviewees in any way.

I was delighted that a reputable programme like *File on Four* was taking these issues seriously, but shortly before the programme was due to be aired, I started to fret. Everyone involved in the Rochdale story would be listening; not just victims and their families, but police and Social Services too. One question nagged me constantly – 'What if I go to prison for speaking out?'

I'd seen first-hand how Amber had been treated. What if someone decided I too needed to be silenced?

I spoke to Sally about my concerns and before the programme was broadcast, the BBC paid for me to seek advice from an independent solicitor in relation to becoming a whistleblower, how I'd be protected and what I could say. He advised that once I'd made it public, there were no guarantees I would be protected and that I must make my decision bearing that risk in mind.

In spite of my fear, I wondered if I'd found myself on the wrong side of the law but in my mind still was the Hillsborough scandal, where the cover-up and lies told at the time were finally exposed thirty years after the event. I knew that I couldn't live with myself unless I spoke out.

Moreover, I didn't want my kids to learn the real truth in thirty years' time when I was no longer around and wonder why their mum had remained silent. In the end, that was the deciding factor for me. But first, I called all my children together: they needed to know in clear terms what might happen to me if I blew the whistle on this whole sordid affair.

'Listen, kids,' I said, 'you know what's been happening and that I'm ashamed of what I've seen. I've decided I have to speak out.'

My children were naturally worried.

'Are you sure this is the right thing to do, Mum?' Matt asked me. He worried a lot about whether I would be arrested and prosecuted for telling the truth, and still does.

I nodded. 'I couldn't live with myself if I sat by and said nothing. There are some things in life that are so important that we just have to stand up for them, whatever the risks, and this is one of those things. It's just too important not to.'

'Well, in that case, you do the right thing and we'll back you,' they agreed.

I'd never felt prouder of my children than I did in that moment because they had no doubt what had happened was wrong and they vowed to stand by me. Their absolute belief gave me the strength I needed to carry on. I thought that if I was ever locked up then I would spill my guts, because people needed to know the truth. It didn't matter what personal cost that might be to me. If I was to be charged and put on trial, so be it. I'd have my day in court and say everything I needed to say in front of a judge and jury.

So I accepted the risk, put my fear out of my mind, but

before the programme aired on 31 March 2013, I flew out to India for three weeks alone, joining a small group of independent travelers on a spiritually themed tour of the country. I had watched the film *Eat, Pray, Love* and I felt I needed to try to mend my soul, look ahead and try to recover in some way.

I had decided I would stay away when the programme went out. I didn't know what the public response would be, nor did I know whether Greater Manchester Police would arrive at my door with a van to arrest me. I also needed space to think about where I might go next and what I'd do.

I had no grand plan, I just wanted the public to know the truth.

*

My backpacker's trip to India, which took in many of that vast country's spiritual places of interest, gave me time to reflect, gather my thoughts and try to repair my soul. On the day of the broadcast, I wondered whether this moment would be the end of the road for me. But at least it was out there and in the public arena.

If they locked me up now, I'd had my say.

At this point I also felt broken, thoroughly exhausted with it all. There was no one to speak to because I didn't know another officer who had been through the same thing – someone who had witnessed something wrong and spoken out publicly against it.

I knew *File on Four* had done a very thorough job. The interviews with Ruby, Amber and Lorna were harrowing, but at least now they were being heard. Holly's father, Jim, told the programme about the police informing him in 2009 there had been 'no reliable prospect' of convicting those accused of raping his daughter – despite clear DNA evidence – and that the case was being dropped. I'd been interviewed at length and was able to convey some of the shock and horror I felt at what had happened on Operation Span. A statement from the CPS claimed that although Amber had been put on the charge sheet, she had been 'treated as a victim throughout' – a clearly contradictory statement that made no sense at all.

For balance, Chief Constable Peter Fahy – now *Sir* Peter Fahy following his knighthood in June 2012 – was interviewed. He said that victims such as Amber 'consented' to sex with their abusers and that such victims would be under pressure from the defence, should they be taken through the court process.

Of me, he said that he had spoken to me many times about my concerns and that it was important that 'officers maintain their objectivity'. Perhaps he had somehow forgotten that he had refused to meet me and he still hasn't ever met me to this day! Ironically, even he conceded that young victims of this kind of abuse needed to be treated more fairly and sympathetically. MP Keith Vaz and the then Director of Public Prosecutions, Keir Starmer, agreed that the failings of police and Social Services to deal with victims properly was a wrong that needed to be corrected. To me, this was just more propaganda. Words are easy, but what was really needed were action, resources, commitment, integrity, human decency and honesty, which throughout my long and lonely journey to this point had been in very short supply.

I knew there would be a strong response and it was overwhelmingly in favour of the stand I'd taken. Suddenly, everyone seemed to want to know about the real story of the Rochdale child abuse scandal and why certain victims had been favoured over others. My phone didn't stop ringing as request after request for interviews poured in. At the time I resisted most of them as I needed to take stock and come to terms with the fact that, suddenly, I'd become the centre of attention as a whistleblower.

A few days later, BBC Radio's *Woman's Hour* covered the story. Unfortunately, I was still in India and couldn't take part, but the chief constable of GMP was again interviewed and said the usual platitudes about this being a difficult case and that lessons could be learned. Again, he said that I'd become too involved with the family and too emotionally involved, possibly because of the bereavements I'd suffered. It seemed to be a case of 'Go away, you silly little girl, and let the grown-ups get on with the real work'. His words made me angry because they made me sound as though I'd lost the plot and now they were trying to shoot the messenger – me. But even while I was dodging the bullets coming from GMP, I was proud that because of what I'd said the genie was now out of the bottle and the public were fully aware of what had really happened in Rochdale.

Chapter Eighteen

Three Girls

❝It always seems
impossible until it's
done❞
– Nelson Mandela

Gradually, I gave in to requests for interviews. No one was helping me with all the media requests. I simply followed my instincts and travelled my own path, telling the truth. The story of my fight for justice was featured in *The Sunday Times* and *The Telegraph* newspapers, among many others, and I was even interviewed by the legendary John Humphrys on BBC Radio 4's *Today* programme – and survived the encounter!

The girls were supportive of me taking this public stand and giving them a voice by retelling their stories in the media. We established a deep trust through the relationship we'd built up and that was why talking to the media about Rochdale was (and still is) a massive responsibility for me. The girls' abuse cannot be undone and they have dealt with it. What they were angry about then (and still are today) were the unforgivable failures of the police and the Crown Prosecution Service to do the right thing by them after they'd selflessly agreed to help.

Public interest in this story was high, so when I received a call soon after the *File on Four* programme from a familiar voice, I shouldn't have been entirely surprised. The caller was Simon Lewis, a talented TV producer with a lot of credits to his name. I'd first met up with him several years previously when he'd wanted to make a drama-documentary on the Gooch Gang and the subsequent trial. I'd been heavily involved in the investigation and family liaison for two years on that job, and so I was the 'go-to' officer who could introduce the production team to all the families involved.

Unfortunately, for various reasons the drama-documentary hasn't yet been made. My brief flirtation with TV seemed to be over. I knew that Simon, along with executive producer Sue Hogg and director Phillipa Lowthorpe, had made the excellent drama *Five Daughters*, about five young women murdered in Ipswich in 2006, which came out in 2010, but I'd had no more contact with him since.

'I'll not beat around the bush, Maggie,' he said, after we'd exchanged the usual pleasantries. 'We've seen and heard everything you've said about Rochdale and we think we could make this story into a factual drama for the BBC along the lines of *Five Daughters*.'

Simon told me that it would be the same team – he, Sue and Phillipa – who would work on the drama and that he'd very much like to talk to me at length about it. I filled him in with some of the background and then he asked if the team could come up to Manchester to meet me.

I knew, given this team's track record in TV, that any drama they made would be watched by a lot of people. If it told the story in the way I hoped it would, that could only be a positive thing. So, I agreed to meet them, no strings attached, and a few days later we were sat in my front room, looking at all the evidence and information I'd gathered. It was obvious they were keen and a follow-up phone call a day or so later confirmed this.

'We'd very much like to make this drama,' Simon said, 'but we really need your help. You're the one who can bring on board all the major players – the girls, their parents, the CIT people. We really need these people so that we can put together a script and find a production company to make it.'

At that point, an alarm bell rang: I was being asked to bring these still-vulnerable and betrayed girls into a situation where they would have to re-live all their harrowing abuse once again with the result that, having considered everything, a production company might just say, 'Thanks, but no thanks.' It was a kind of mirror image of what had happened with Greater Manchester Police and the Crown Prosecution Service. I could not put these girls through all that, just for them to be let down and abandoned once more. There was no way I could agree to this and I told Simon how I felt.

'I cannot bring these girls on board without a commitment from the BBC that the drama will be made,' I said.

I could hear Simon's intake of breath as he prepared to reply.

'There's no way the BBC will do that, Maggie,' he said. 'Not without sight of a script. And we need the girls and everyone else with us so that we can create that script.'

'In that case, I think you'd better find someone else to help,' I said, 'because there's no way I'm putting them through all that again.'

'Well, I can put the question to them,' Simon said, 'but I think I already know what the answer will be…'

*

For two months I heard nothing more, assuming that Simon had indeed been correct, so when he phoned out of the blue and asked to see me again, I was surprised and intrigued. The team came up to visit and they almost bounded through the door in their haste to tell me something they were clearly very excited by.

'Maggie, it's the most amazing news,' said Phillipa. 'The BBC have never done this before, but they've committed to making this drama without first seeing the script. They know how important this story is, which is why they've taken this step.'

I took a deep breath. The BBC had committed. Now it was up to me to make my choice. I knew that a lot of work went into the making of such dramas – months, maybe even years of it. I would be working closely with a scriptwriter to hone the script and using all my powers of persuasion to get the key people on board.

'Okay,' I said, 'I'll do it. But I want a proper contract from the BBC and, when it goes out, I want a standalone credit as the programme consultant. I want some acknowledgement that I've helped to tell these girls' stories and to show the world what happened to them. And I want that in writing.'

It sounds like a grand demand, but to me it was very

important that this was honoured. I'd put my principles and beliefs before my career and I wanted to show GMP and the CPS that what had happened to these kids was plain wrong and that the whole country agreed with me.

The contract was duly arranged and drawn up and, once I signed it, I plunged into my new role with a massive amount of enthusiasm. The talented scriptwriter, Nicole Taylor, started spending a lot of time with me, going through all my information and, together, we identified the people we felt would be best placed to tell the story in the most honest and hard-hitting way possible.

There was Amber and Ruby, of course. And Holly. Lorna also. And Sam Haworth, the first SIO on Operation Span and Ian Hynes, the force interview advisor. From the Crisis Intervention Team there was Sara Rowbotham. All these people had to come on board, otherwise there would be no drama. That was a huge responsibility and I hoped I could use all my powers of persuasion to make this work.

At first, Amber, Ruby and Lorna weren't sure. There was no question that they'd been through the mill enough times as far as telling their stories went. They had no desire for fame or notoriety as a result of any TV programme. They wouldn't even be paid, as that would go against BBC rules. There was very little in it for them other than by re-living the horror of what they went through, they would make millions of people aware of what sexual grooming is and how grooming gangs operate, and so force the authorities to sit up, listen and take notice.

Time and again, I asked myself, *Is this really in their best interests?* And while I knew how hard it would be to talk again, my instincts told me that if this issue wasn't exposed fully then it would simply continue. Gently, I steered Lorna and her girls towards this conclusion. They really were pivotal to the success or failure of this project and without them, the full story couldn't be told. Eventually, after many conversations and primarily because they once again put their trust in me, they gave their permission and allowed their story to be told in all its painful detail. I was blown away by their courage and determination to try to make sure that grooming and sexual abuse didn't happen to any more vulnerable girls.

My conversations with Sara Rowbotham were harder. As the representative of an organisation which had collated information on the abuse of girls in Rochdale in the years before Operation Span, I felt she and the CIT workers must be included in some way. For me, their story would corroborate the fact that police had known about these abusers for ages, but had sat on their hands and done nothing. I rang Sara, told her what was happening and she agreed to meet me for tea. During this first meeting she was adamant she didn't want to be involved. She had too much going on in her life, she said, and helping out a TV team would only add to what was on her plate.

I didn't go in hard on her; I could see what the whole Rochdale scandal had affected her too. We'd come to it from very different directions but she knew what had gone on and so did I, and in that, I saw we had some common ground, although we had approached the situation in very different ways. She'd also met Victoria Agoglia, the girl whose picture had featured in the Operation Augusta report. I felt she could add something to the drama, another perspective. Subsequently, we met four or five times and eventually I persuaded her to meet the team.

Another difficulty was recruiting Holly. The situation was complicated by the fact that, at this point, Holly's book, *Girl A*, had been published. She'd given her side of the story in a very hard-hitting way, but again poor Amber had been portrayed badly and all the 'Honey Monster' accusations were doing the rounds. Personally, I was very upset by what had been said about Amber in the book and I knew Holly's father, Jim, had always been hostile towards Amber. He, in turn, most likely knew how I felt about Amber and Ruby, and although I was prepared to call him and talk about the drama, I didn't expect it to be an easy conversation.

Fortunately, a meeting I had with the-then Rochdale MP Simon Danczuk provided the help I needed with Jim. Simon was one of the very few public figures who'd stuck his neck out about sexual abuse, not just in relation to what happened to the girls and the authorities' catalogue of failures, but also when it came to former Rochdale MP Cyril Smith and the abuse he had carried out at the Knowl View children's home – the institution Lorna's now-deceased son had been placed in. He had been a very vocal critic of GMP's handling of child sexual abuse and in some ways I saw him as an ally in that fight. There had been a discussion about including Simon as a character in the drama, so I went to see him and his researcher, Matt Baker. The two had written a book about Cyril Smith – *Smile for the Camera: The Double Life of Cyril Smith* – and were naturally interested in what I had to say. After a two-hour discussion, Simon said he needed to leave and, as he got up, he started laughing.

'What's funny?' I asked.

'It's you,' he said. 'God help Peter Fahy if he thinks you're a woman who's lost the plot!'

After Simon left, Matt and I had continued our discussion and he told me he knew Holly's family, including her dad. I said I'd like to get Holly and her father on board, but doing that might present some difficulties.

'Leave it with me,' he said, 'and I'll have a word.'

Soon after, Matt contacted me with a number: 'He'll speak to you,' he said, 'and I'm sure it'll be fine.'

So I called Jim and we chatted for hours. He seemed an educated, articulate person and shared a similar outrage at what had gone on, and how failures to protect victims in the first place had led to the huge growth of abuse in the town and right across the north of England. Obviously, we differed hugely in our perception of Amber. Whereas I see her as just another child victim of these men, as Holly's father he needed someone to blame for what ultimately happened to his daughter and he chose to blame Amber. Notwithstanding that, we met several times over the ensuing weeks and months and he told me his family would cooperate with the drama. Having never met her, I very much wanted to see Holly, but although she was asked to take part, she declined, and to this day I am sad that I have never met or even seen this important person in the whole sorry story.

*

Months and months went by. I helped Nicole Taylor in every way I could to get her head around this complicated, controversial story and was now at the stage of introducing the production team to those who were being interviewed, a lengthy and intense process where I held the hands of the girls and Lorna during each and every meeting, and this took over my life for almost another three years. My focus was always on exposing the failure of the authorities and supporting Amber and Ruby as they told their stories. Although my own journey through the nightmare of Rochdale occasionally reared its head when in conversation with others, I didn't seem to be in a position where my own story was being put on record. I was led to believe that I would contribute my story when everyone else's had been gathered.

The early drafts of the scripts were starting to come through and, hour upon hour, I sat reading them, voice-recording amendments, supplying all the background material and making suggestions where I thought the script might be veering away from what actually happened. This was a very difficult job but, finally, in the summer of 2016, I was told the script was ready and that there would be a read-through at a film studios in Bristol. On this occasion, I would meet the entire production crew, the actors playing myself, Sara Rowbotham and Lorna (Lesley Sharp, Maxine Peake and Lisa Riley respectively) and I would also be introduced to the girls playing Amber, Ruby and Holly.

I always knew that whoever played Amber would have a real task on her young hands, because this girl had been treated very differently to everyone else and a lot of my purpose in taking part in the drama was to show how badly the authorities could treat a child like her. Phillipa took me into a room in the studio complex to meet the three young actors who were playing the girls – Molly Windsor

(Holly), Liv Hill (Ruby) and Ria Zmitrowicz (Amber). For a moment we stared at each other in silence. And then I looked at Ria, this young actress who was to take on such an important but complicated role.

Our eyes locked and I couldn't tear mine away from hers as we stared at each other intensely. After what seemed a lifetime, the intensity of my stare made Ria jump up, burst into tears and run out of the room. I think the emotions involved were so strong at that moment because it was very odd to come face-to-face with these young people who had such vital roles to carry.

Ria came back in and apologised for crying.

'It's fine,' I said, hugging her. 'I understand. This whole story is very close to my heart, you know, and you've got the most difficult part to play.'

She nodded as I explained how Amber had been treated so differently and what I hoped she would bring to the part. Ria totally 'got' Amber. They met when I took Amber to watch filming and Ria could see how shy she is. She felt the same protectiveness towards her as I do.

After this came the read-through, attended by all the actors, crew, the scriptwriter, production team, etc. At least fifty people were assembled in that huge room and Phillipa introduced every person in turn. However, when she came to me, instead of saying who I was, she quickly moved on to the person next to me. I was upset and slightly confused, and the moment passed, but I have wished ever since that I'd spoken up, introduced myself and explained my role. I'd never been in an environment like this before and didn't really know how to react. Perhaps I was being over-sensitive, but I felt quite hurt and tearful at the time.

I spent a day with Lesley Sharp and I liked her. I think she is a really talented actress but, if I'm honest, I don't think she quite portrayed me in the way I see myself. The Maggie Oliver of the drama came across as somewhat cooler and distant than I am, not as much of a fighter. I'm also a lot more touchy-feely – in some ways I'm closer to the character that Maxine Peake played (although Maxine portrayed a character that combined the roles of several different people in CIT, not just Sara Rowbotham herself, who was the manager). This came across in the scene I watched when I attended filming in Bristol, which was the one where Sara meets Maggie for the first time and tells her to 'fuck off'. The real Maggie would have told her to fuck off back, but that wasn't how it was portrayed. I sent the team an email to say that what I'd seen had upset me and they told me that by not responding, Maggie comes out of the scene more strongly. I accepted their explanation with misgivings. There was also the scene which showed Amber's Viper, which doesn't reflect just how many hours that process took, nor the overwhelming trauma of it. I guess in the end though it's a drama and can only reflect a tiny portion of the truth. It was the compromise necessary to educate the public about the horrors of grooming.

*

When I first saw *Three Girls* in a special viewing for me and my kids in a Manchester hotel room, my feelings were that while it reflected some of the story, it hadn't gone nearly far enough. In some ways it had let the police and the Crown Prosecution Service, in particular, off the hook, especially in the way Amber was first treated as an offender, then a victim, then an offender again. I knew this would be complicated to tell and I felt the drama team had centred the story more around Holly because her abuse was an easier storyline to follow. I also felt that my passion for this case, and all the time and effort I'd put into bringing the family into the investigation, plus what I'd gone through personally as a result, hadn't really been brought out. I was sad and disappointed, but I also understood that it was a drama and, as such, the production team has the final say in how events are portrayed. That said, I did insist on a few changes and some wording at the end, which was incorporated.

Amber and Ruby saw the drama soon after and Ruby stormed out of the viewing room because she considered that her sister had come out of it badly. Amber was quiet – she didn't want to upset anyone, but I knew she was hurt because she and Ruby felt that their abuse hadn't been documented properly and didn't make clear the full extent of the sexual abuse they had both suffered, which was at least equal to that which Holly had endured. Yet both girls selflessly signed off the script and the final cut so that it could be broadcast. They knew, as did we all, that while it didn't quite paint the full picture, it was nonetheless a very powerful piece of television indeed and would bring what they and many other girls went through to a mass audience and perhaps prevent other children having to suffer as they had. Lorna too felt that Amber had been done an injustice and that caused her pain, but they all recognised the importance of getting the story out to educate the public and inform other children in a bid to prevent them going the same route into Child Sexual Exploitation.

When broadcast as a three-part mini-series in May 2017, *Three Girls* was the most-watched programme on TV. Some nine million people saw it and the reviews were universally good. I'd hoped that, through the BBC press office, I would be asked to do a lot of promotional interviews but it seemed that Maxine Peake and Sara Rowbotham were put forward for the lion's share. I did do one with Nicole Taylor for *BBC Breakfast*, but that was it, so I arranged some interviews myself and although the BBC press office wasn't happy, I did them anyway. I also had to fight to get my name and role as the programme consultant used as a standalone credit (they were planning to list me among the other contributors). Luckily, I had my contract and this was all I had asked for, so I stood my ground over this one and got what I wanted.

In fact, I did get my chance to say what I really wanted to a TV audience not long after *Three Girls* was broadcast. During the making of the drama, I was told by the drama producer Simon that the BBC wanted to do an accompanying documentary about the Rochdale child abuse scandal that would be broadcast the day after the last episode of *Three Girls* went out. This would be a hard-hitting investigative documentary really digging into the issues I'd fought to highlight for so long.

The director of the documentary would be world-renowned documentary maker Henry Singer, an American whose credits include *The Falling Man* (about the 9/11 attack) and *Baby P: The Untold Story*, which looked at the scandal around the death of seventeen-month-old Peter Connelly, and more recently, The Trial of Ratko Mladic about the 'Butcher of Bosnia'. The producer would be Rob

Miller. Both men were keen to meet me, Simon said, and as usual, I agreed. If I could tell the story of how the Rochdale victims were abused and betrayed, in the way it needed to be heard, I'd talk to anyone.

So, I met Henry and Rob and was very impressed with them both. Henry was very clear that he didn't want to re-tell the story that had formed the basis of the drama. He wanted to go back, right back to the late 1990s, when MP Ann Cryer was fighting to highlight what she'd seen and heard in her West Yorkshire constituency, although she was being ignored by everyone. Henry wanted to prove that for decades blind eyes had been turned to this particular type of abuse and was I able to point him in the direction of those involved.

Again, I agreed to approach the key participants and recommended that Sara Rowbotham come on board to help find those girls whose stories had never been recorded by police, and never had their day in court, mainly because Crisis Intervention were the agency the girls had regularly visited for condoms. There was one of our original Operation Span victims in particular, whom we'll call Daisy. She was failed in the most horrendous of ways and I thought she had a powerful story to tell. However, Henry called one day to say Sara had told him Daisy had moved on and shouldn't be approached.

'That's strange,' I said, 'because I'm sure she has a lot to say and I think she'd like to be part of this. I feel strongly that, either way, she should be the one to make that decision.'

Through Lorna, I eventually tracked Daisy down, we talked and although she'd been very badly damaged as a result of her experiences, she wanted to be part of the documentary. As it turned out, she was an excellent interviewee. She had a lot to say about what happened to her, although, unfortunately, there was only time to include the tiniest part of her story, which in all honesty would fill a book of its own.

Henry and Rob were very decent, ethical and generous human beings and they showed a lot of empathy towards the victims they interviewed, including Amber and Ruby. Everyone involved in the documentary, titled *The Betrayed Girls*, was kept informed at every stage and treated with the utmost respect.

For reasons best known to the BBC, *The Betrayed Girls* wasn't broadcast the night after the last episode of *Three Girls*. Instead, it was shown two months later in July 2017. There was speculation that it was the victim of rivalry between the Drama and Documentary departments and perhaps *The Betrayed Girls* did suffer for not being part of the impact on the public that the drama had created. However, it was an incredibly strong piece of work and because it gave the story a much wider context and greater backstory, I felt it reflected events in Rochdale in an even more hard-hitting way than the drama, if that were possible.

*

Fast forward a year... *Three Girls* always had 'award-winner' stamped all over it and so it proved. In 2017 and 2018 it took a whole host of honours at the Royal Television Society awards and at the Broadcasting Press Guild and Broadcast Awards ceremonies respectively. The big one, though, was the BAFTAs. It was up for six awards, including Best Mini-Series, Best Leading Actress and Best Supporting Actress. I very much wanted to attend the ceremony – well, come on, who wouldn't? – and when the nominations were announced, I asked Simon about getting a ticket. He made noises about the BBC having a limited budget for such events and that the team weren't sure how many tickets they'd get.

'I have to say,' he said, 'that I'm not sure you'll get a ticket, Maggie.'

'Simon,' I replied, 'I don't care if the BBC pay for my ticket or not, but one thing's for sure: I am going to those BAFTAS, come hell or high water. I want to be sitting on that big, round table with my posh frock on, and if I have to pay for my own ticket, so be it, but I intend to be there! So, you just let me know what's what.'

I was determined not to be pushed out of this. Even if I had to be in the public seats I'd be there. Call me a diva, but I'd put years of my life into that drama and it just wouldn't have happened without my efforts. I wanted to be there to represent Amber and Ruby, Lorna and for all the thousands of other girls who'd been through hell and back.

Simon eventually confirmed that I would be on the guest list, so I booked my hotel and train ticket to London and some of the actors I'd met during filming picked me up en route to the South Bank. I had a terrific night in my beautiful dress gifted to me by the kind and generous designer Mark Melia and, of course, the drama won two BAFTAS for Best Mini-Series and Best Leading Actress went to Molly Windsor, who played Holly. It was also nominated for Best Supporting Actress, for Liv Hill's depiction of Ruby.

On top of this, the drama went on to win three BAFTA TV Craft awards for Best Editing (Fiction) – Una Ni Dhonghaile, Best Director (Fiction) – Phillipa Lowthorpe and Best Writer (Drama) – Nicole Taylor.

Although it was impossible for any of the girls or their families involved in either the drama or documentary to attend any of the awards ceremonies, I really wanted to mark the occasion in some way, to thank them for their bravery in allowing their stories to be told. I wanted them to share in the celebrations too so, in August 2018, I decided to hire some vehicles and take the girls, their families and all their kids for a day out. My son Danny drove one car, my mate San another, and I drove my own car and we all descended on Gulliver's World theme park for a summer's day out. I think the park staff must have wondered what on earth had hit them, but it was a day filled with sunshine, fun and laughter, and a well-deserved escape from all the sadness they had been through.

I think it's fair to say that I had some issues with the content of the drama and that I had hoped it would go further than it did in relation to police and CPS failures. I also understand that the team had editorial control and they made the programme they wanted to make. But, and it's a big 'but', having experienced working with a TV drama team for four years, and going through everything we did, if I was asked to do the whole thing again, the answer would still be yes. For all that we went through, it was worth it, because if the general public didn't know what grooming gangs were before *Three Girls*, they certainly did afterwards. The authorities can never again claim that what girls like Amber, Ruby and Holly experienced is in any way a 'lifestyle choice'. Without that drama, we wouldn't be where we are now, with the authorities and police at last being forced to take claims of sexual abuse and grooming seriously, and without as much judgement of the victims. *Three Girls* has been a springboard for change and although I know I'm very close indeed to the events in Rochdale, I do feel that in some way the drama has vindicated what I've done and given it some meaning. I feel very pleased to have been involved and extremely proud of what we have achieved.

Chapter Nineteen

Big Brother and Beyond

❛ Fill your life with experiences, not things. Have stories to tell, not stuff to show ❜

— Buddha

Stepping into a media storm is bewildering for anyone not used to such levels of attention, but I knew I had to take these steps if I wanted my voice to be heard. In order to continue as a campaigner for truth, justice, women's rights and young victims of abuse, and as someone who will hold officials to account for their failings in these directions, the platform I need requires that I'm 'known'. And if by being known I can do some good, then I have to stick my head above the parapet.

As I've mentioned, before *Three Girls* I had already started to enter the public arena by way of newspaper articles, contributions to discussions about child sex abuse on radio and TV, and public speaking engagements. I'd often get phone calls from researchers and journalists wanting an interview or a comment, and I'd just deal with these myself.

After the drama, things were different. I was being asked to do lots of things, including making appearances on talk shows – in short, I was becoming something of a minor 'celebrity'. And, if I'm honest, I felt way out of my depth. This wasn't a world I was used to. I'm an ordinary person who found herself in an extraordinary situation and just tried to do the best I could with the resources I had. When I took my Oath of Attestation and joined the police, in my wildest dreams I couldn't have imagined that I would end up as a character in the most talked-about BBC drama of the year and as a spokesperson for victims of child sexual abuse who have been failed terribly by councils, social services, police and the Crown Prosecution Service.

It was the actress Lisa Riley, who played Lorna in *Three Girls*, who suggested that I might need an agent to help me with all the media attention and she recommended her own agent, Phil Dale of Q Talent, as someone I might be able to work with. By this time I'd already been on ITV's *Loose Women*, a show I have always loved and one that does a great deal of good as far as presenting women's issues in a positive light goes, and I was thrilled to make an appearance on it as an ordinary woman who spoke out about what she saw as an injustice. The response was overwhelmingly positive and I seemed to have struck a chord with the millions of women who watch this show; ordinary women, mums who were outraged at what had happened.

When I met with him in October 2017, Phil was enthusiastic about working with me and asked me what kind of things I'd be interested in doing.

'Well,' I said hesitantly, wondering what I might accidentally sign myself up to, 'I'm open to anything really. I won't do anything I don't believe in, but I'm always prepared to listen and have a go.'

'Okay,' he said, 'I've got a few ideas so give me a bit of time and I'll get back to you.'

In October 2017, he rang again. 'Listen, Maggie,' he said, 'something has occurred to me. How would you feel about going on *Celebrity Big Brother*?'

'Really?' I couldn't believe what I was hearing.

'Yeah, why not?' he said. 'Why don't you come down to London and I'll set up a meeting?'

'Okay, if you think so,' I replied, stunned. 'I'd love to meet them.'

I put the phone down, still dazed. Then I thought, *Why not? It will probably come to nothing anyway, so I'll just go with the flow and only worry about it if they offer it to me.*

So, I travelled down to London and met Phil. I found him to be a nice, friendly, laid-back guy, who put me at my ease straight away. He introduced me to one of the bosses from the Celebrity Big Brother Team at Endemol, a lovely lady and her colleague, and we had a great chat. I told them all about what had happened in Rochdale and about myself and my own life experiences, Norman and the kids. I was told that because 2018 was officially 'Year of the Woman' and one hundred years since women got the vote, their idea was to have an all-female line up in the house. This appealed to me, and while I was still apprehensive at the prospect of being observed twenty-four hours a day in the *Celebrity Big Brother* house, I really hit it off with the team and had the impression they liked me too and understood where I was coming from. To be honest, I had only ever watched the odd episode in the past, which was perhaps a good thing!

One of my biggest worries was what my kids would think. Actually, I half-knew what they'd think – that Mum had lost the plot and such exposure could destroy me. Nevertheless, I'd have to have the conversation with them at some stage, so on the quiet I told my daughter Vicki that I'd been in talks with them.

'Oh my God, Mum!' she said, frowning and clearly thinking, *What on earth is my mum getting herself into now?* 'Are you mad? You've got a good reputation to protect. This could totally destroy that.'

I reassured her that I'd made no decision and in any case I hadn't even been asked yet. I also told my best friend, San, and she went into meltdown too – and said it was a hell of a risk. In fact, it was the risk element of the show that attracted me. I wanted to show that a woman of a certain age who had been properly through the mill could reinvent herself and do something like this. That I hadn't been destroyed by all my difficulties, but instead had found a way through them and embarked on a new and exciting adventure.

At the beginning of December, Phil finally called me. They wanted me to go on the show! I was in shock. 'Wow,' I said, 'that's amazing. But just give me the weekend to think about it, will you, Phil?'

So, I sat down and pondered. What was the worst that could happen? I'd have no control over how I'd be portrayed and I might come across badly. Never one to run away from a challenge, though, I thought, *If you don't do it, if you say 'No', how will you feel in a year's time? Will you regret it?*

I realised that I probably would. I know I'm not a bad or horrible person and that I wouldn't be one of those who would fall out with people and cause lots of arguments. I'd go in with an open mind, be myself and hope it might be a platform for me to say a few words about what had happened in Rochdale and life in general.

So, I phoned Phil and with a pounding heart told him 'yes'. Then I went away for the weekend with my friend San and told her I'd accepted it. The two of us sat there through two sleepless nights, alternately laughing, then having panic attacks about this crazy decision I'd made while drinking copious amounts of wine. When I came home, I told Vicki, but asked her to keep it quiet from the other kids until December was out. I was due to go into the house right at the beginning of January and I didn't want the subject dominating or ruining Christmas for them. I was particularly worried about what my Steve would say: he's protective of me and would be upset if he thought I'd be damaged by appearing.

The day after Boxing Day, I finally told Danny and Matt. They were understandably nervous for me, but otherwise fine, their one and only request being that I didn't jump naked into the hot tub! Then I messaged Steve and asked him to come over from where he lives in Chorlton. He arrived the day after, looking very worried.

'What is it, Mum?' he said. 'Are you ill? Please don't say you're ill.'

'No, I'm not ill,' I said, 'but I do have something to tell you and I'm sure you won't agree, but I've made my decision and I'd really like your support, if possible. I've been asked to go on *Celebrity Big Brother* and I'm doing it.'

He just stared at me, like he'd been hit with a lightning bolt. Then he burst out laughing. 'Oh my God, Mum,' he said, 'I thought you had a serious illness or something! Is that what you wanted to tell me?'

I nodded.

'So, what do you think?' I asked.

He paused, letting the shock wear off and turning over in his mind the news I had just delivered. I waited nervously and, finally, after what seemed a lifetime, he said, 'I'm not sure I agree with it,' he said, 'but I really can't stop you. I've just got two pieces of advice: don't get drunk and remember that no one in there actually gives a fuck about you!'

So, I had been given the cautious if nervous blessing of my four kids and, with that, I set off on a new adventure with a sense of excitement mixed with pure panic.

*

On New Year's Day 2018, I was picked up in a big limo and was on my way, accompanied by my best mate, San and my daughter Vicki. Excited, terrified, apprehensive, entering unknown territory, I had no idea who would be there or what to expect, other than the bits I'd seen on TV. On the way down, I posted letters to Amber and Ruby and some of my other Rochdale girls. I hadn't been able to tell them I was coming on the show, but I wanted them to know that I was going on because I intended to use my appearance as a platform to highlight what had gone on in Rochdale and speak out about the situation around grooming and sexual abuse.

After two days locked in isolation with my wonderful chaperone, I did the obligatory entrance interview with presenter Emma Willis, giggling all the way through it to hide my nerves. I emphasised that I was just an ordinary person who had spoken out about something I felt very strongly and passionately about. Then I said this: 'I really wanted to tell my Rochdale girls I was coming on because the last thing I want is for them to feel let down by me. They're very close to my heart and I have written them a letter. So, girls, you'll be getting a letter tomorrow morning! Father Christmas is bringing you a letter!'

Then, after one last hug with San and my beautiful daughter, who had decided to support her mother's crazy decision, I walked down the famous stairs into the house and into a room of five women. I recognised only one of them – former politician Ann Widdecombe. The world of celebrity isn't really mine, so I do apologise to India Willoughby, Malika Haqq, Ashley James and Rachel Johnson for not knowing who you were initially!

The other contestants entered, one by one. I recognised Amanda Barrie from *Coronation Street* and I got on particularly well with actress Jess Impiazzi. We ending up having a real mother-and-daughter relationship which has evolved into a friendship. Slowly, we began to settle into life in the house. I had no game plan, no ambition to be the eventual winner – I just wanted to have some fun, be a part of the whole thing and, hopefully, air a few issues about what I'd seen and experienced. And we did talk. I was asked about my work and what I'd done in Rochdale and we had some really interesting conversations long into the night.

After a few days we were taken by surprise by the

arrival of men – so much for the 'Year of the Woman' concept! We were joined by Shane Lynch of Boyzone, *Love Island*'s Jonny Mitchell, social media content creator and comedian Dapper Laughs (Daniel O'Reilly), dancer Wayne Sleep, Andrew Brady (*The Apprentice*), R&B singer Ginuwine (who I inadvertently called 'Dynamite' to his lasting amusement!), footballer John Barnes and drag queen Courtney Act. Again, there were a few blokes I didn't know, but everything settled down and I got on well with everyone – except for one person.

From the start I could feel that Ann Widdecombe didn't like me. It was an absolute personality clash. We had a couple of heated debates about sexual abuse in the Catholic Church and I felt she always took a dispassionate yet moralising view of everything. This is her way, and she's well known for her opinions, but even so I found her hard to get along with. She was the only housemate who never once mentioned Rochdale or asked me what had gone on there, despite the fact she had served as Shadow Home Secretary for some years. I was polite to her, but I knew I'd never be able to change her mind about anything. That said, I admire her for the way she's reinvented herself after a life in politics and will go on shows like *Celebrity Big Brother*, no matter what people think about her.

We had daily tasks to complete, which were based around the Battle of the Sexes and were lots of fun. Tasks such as getting dressed up in 1950s outfits and going to work on a production line, walking round and round the garden in little cars and other silly challenges. One of the games we played was where the men had to lie on beds and be hooked up to machines which simulated labour pains. Us girls were in hysterics as these big butch men rolled around until they finally gave up and took off the sticking plasters which attached the wires to their bellies. It was funny and it was only a game, but Ann didn't see any humour in it at all. I happened to be sitting next to her and she made no secret of the fact she found the whole thing disgusting and immoral. In fact, she was so displeased that in the live nominations the following night, she said that if Ashley James and Jess Impiazzi, who were laughing hardest, were not immune from eviction, she would have no hesitation in nominating them and she actually made Jess cry.

Life went on in the *Celebrity Big Brother* house in its own weird way. As I've said, I particularly enjoyed spending time with Jess. One night as Ginuwine sang his Magic Mike hit 'Riding My Pony' in the talent contest, John Barnes pulled me up from my seat and we had a bump'n'grind-style dance together. It was hilarious and, according to my kids, the press and TV were full of it the next day – the trailers ran something like 'Watch Maggie grinding with John Barnes'. All day, my kids were in bits, wondering what I'd done and whether I'd made a big fool of myself. Vicki said she had a twenty-four-hour anxiety attack wondering what her mother had done this time! But it was all just good fun and had been a real laugh – and I promise that I wasn't drunk!

A couple of weeks later, we had an eviction session. Dapper Laughs was up for eviction but when he and Ann won a 'Driving School' task, he also secured himself the chance to win immunity from eviction so there was now the option for him to replace himself and substitute someone else instead, and it was up to him and Ann to decide who that would be. And she nominated me, accusing me of enjoying the pain the lads were going through when they'd done the 'labour pains' challenge. Now, the whole show is only a game but that really upset me. I would never stand by and enjoy watching anyone in pain. In fact, the truth is the polar opposite. And I did say this to Ann. I was particularly unhappy because to me, she represented a political system that had stood by and watched while young girls went through hell in places like Rochdale and Huddersfield and did nothing about it. I'm not saying she was directly responsible for any of that, but I did take great exception to being accused of revelling in others' pain when I'd spent a lifetime trying to alleviate people from it and given up so much in the process.

From that moment on a black cloud descended on both me and the rest of the house. I knew none of the others would have nominated me, but I also knew they had much bigger social media followings than I did and they'd get the support from the public that I couldn't really muster – I wasn't even on Instagram or Twitter until I went into the house. I wasn't feeling great at all and I didn't sleep that night. In fact, Wayne Sleep and I sat in the kitchen most of the night, reminiscing about life and Princess Diana, who he had famously danced with, and putting things into perspective. The reality is that in such a close environment, the tiniest thing can become blown out of all proportion, but my housemates were fantastic and getting to know them all was one of the highlights of the entire experience for me, and many have become friends for life.

The following day, I took myself off into the garden and, in that moment, I really did think my world had fallen apart. It started to sleet, enormous hailstones like boulders bouncing all around me, and as I curled up in the gazebo, I pulled a blanket over me to keep out the cold and hide from the cameras. I was alone and feeling quite down, when at that precise moment I looked up into the sky and, to my amazement, saw a huge rainbow arching perfectly across the garden where I was sitting. It was a completely magical moment.

That's Norman, I thought immediately, *he's looking down on me and he's saying, 'You silly old bugger, get a grip! It's only a game show, what's the big deal?'*

And as I looked skywards, underneath the big rainbow a smaller one appeared, but no less vivid. *That's our Macie Moo*, I thought, *up there with her grandad*. It is the only time in my whole life when I have ever seen two perfect rainbows together at exactly the same moment and I took it as a sign. Once again, as had happened so many times before in my lowest moments, Norman had come along to help me, to guide me along the right path, and with that I thought, *Come on, Maggie, pull yourself together. It's just a bloody game show, remember what you've been through in your life. Get a grip!*

With that, I started to pull myself together and as some of the others noticed me sitting outside on my own, they began to come out and join me in the rain. Dapper came out with Jess, Andrew, Jonny, Ashley, Wayne and Ginuwine, and he improvised a really funny play that we all had parts in, which had us all in stitches. His antics took the heat out of the situation and so I pulled myself together, said my goodbyes and prepared to leave with an open heart and a big smile.

*

I guess I'd been an unusual choice for a *Celebrity Big Brother* contestant, not being a 'celebrity' in any conventional sense of the word. But I had absolutely loved every minute of my time in the house and will be forever grateful to my agent Phil and the *Celebrity Big Brother* team for giving me such an amazing life experience and also for editing me kindly throughout. I felt it had given me a platform to say some of the things about Rochdale and what happened to the girls and me. I was only upset at the way I'd had to leave and this came out during my live exit interview with Emma Willis.

'I have been very outspoken, I'm only on *Celebrity Big Brother* because I spoke up about what was going on in Rochdale,' I said. 'And I spoke out about that because I felt that generations of girls were subjected to a lot more pain than that [the *CBB* labour game] over a period of years.

'For me, Ann [Widdecombe] was in a position of influence as Shadow Home Secretary in the Houses of Parliament when [former MP] Ann Cryer was banging on doors and trying to get MPs to deal with that abuse. So, for Ann to make that nomination, based on the fact that she said I could watch pain, is completely hypocritical. It upset me. I turned my life upside down because I saw pain that was unacceptable.'

Undoubtedly, it was a controversial thing to say and maybe Ann bore the brunt of my feelings towards politicians of all stripes who really have failed to take any notice of what's been going on in places like Rochdale, but I don't regret it. I feel politicians have, at the very least, been totally complacent about such things and it's taken people like me and others to stand up and point out these fundamental wrongs. If it takes me going on *Celebrity Big Brother* to say it, and get that message out, then so be it. In fact, I'd be very keen to go on more shows like that, not because I want to talk about it all the time, but because when I do talk about it, more people sit up and take notice. And that can only be good.

That said, I did talk a lot with the housemates about other serious issues facing our country when I was in the house. Subjects such as poverty, homelessness, religion, racism, the whole failing criminal justice system, human rights and, of course, Rochdale, but very little of it actually appeared on TV.

When the show wrapped there was an after-party for everyone involved, contestants and crew, and I met the woman who was responsible for editing all my material because, of course, everything you say and do, twenty-four hours a day, is filmed. She told me she admired everything I'd said about Rochdale because she'd been a teacher in her former career and also the Child Protection lead at the school she'd worked in. She actually started to cry as she told me she had fought desperately to include more of what I was saying, but couldn't get it past the legal department onto the screen.

'Don't worry,' I said, 'it's not a problem. I've been on here and people will now know me better and want to hear what I have to say.'

*

As soon as I came home I went to see Lorna, Amber and Ruby. They are a big part of my life, and they understood why I had done it. We all want the changes that are so badly needed. They support this journey, at every step, and have sacrificed their own feelings in many ways for the greater good. A couple of weeks later, I decided to take a week's holiday – just to mend my head after such an intense experience on the show. A very good friend of mine from Turkey, Jules, had rented a house in Barbados so I splashed out and went to join her there. I was on a remote beach when it started to rain and a couple nearby invited me to share their umbrella while the shower passed. The woman looked at me closely for a few seconds, then said: 'I know you – you're the Rochdale police lady who's just been on *Celebrity Big Brother*!'

I was a bit taken aback as I hadn't had much of this kind of recognition before. But it did lead to a conversation about grooming and everything I'd been involved with, so it proved the point that going on the show was a force for good in terms of highlighting these issues and this has since become an almost daily occurrence. Whether I'm in Primark, at the airport, on a beach or in a bar, total strangers approach me all the time to talk, to take a selfie or just to say, 'Hi, Maggie' – and I love it! Without exception, everyone has had only nice things to say and ordinary people feel the same way as me: that what was going on was wrong, plain and simple. This alone has made me feel this journey has been worthwhile and has totally restored my faith in humanity, knowing that decent people believe what I believed. So why is it that those in positions of power didn't see that too, or rather chose to turn a blind eye and allow generations of vulnerable children to continue to be abused on an industrial scale? People like senior police officers, many governments regardless of party, the IOPC, the CPS, Social Services, councillors and many more too numerous to mention.

*

Celebrity Big Brother opened up a whole new world for me and, in June 2018, I was shocked but delighted to be invited to present an award with the lovely Brooke Kinsella, actress and anti-knife crime campaigner, at the British Soap Awards televised live on ITV to one of the biggest TV audiences of the year. It was great to spend time in the Green Room with her and everyone else who goes to such events, people I had only ever seen on TV before. For me, it's a little bit of sparkle in a life that has often been overshadowed with dark and troubling events and I relish the opportunity of getting into a nice frock and having a bit of fun and glamour. If we're honest, we all like a bit of that now and again, and it's good for the soul, and thanks to the kindness of talented Liverpool designer Mark Melia making me two beautiful dresses for both the BAFTAs and the Soap Awards, I truly felt like a princess going to the ball. I was even named eleventh Best Dressed Celebrity at the soaps – how surreal is that?

I have attended ceremonies at the Houses of Parliament, met many inspirational people and was even included in a list of Incredible Women who have made a difference, alongside such icons as Kate Adie, Mo Mowlam and even Emmeline Pankhurst. All unexpected, but nevertheless amazing. I continue to appear on TV and radio and carry out speaking engagements, telling my story, and as an activist speaking out about women's rights, human rights and much-needed changes to our failing criminal justice system. In 2018, I went to lots of events to mark International Women's Day and now I've even had my first professional stage role, playing The Enchantress in the pantomime *Beauty and the Beast*.

What matters to me most, however, is helping to make real changes. Over the past eighteen months I have been working with esteemed human rights lawyer Harriet Wistrich and the Centre for Women's Justice (CWJ), exploring potential legal challenges to hold senior police officers to account for their failures in the Rochdale case, something I truly believe is necessary to ensure we do not see a repeat of such horrific failures in future.

CWJ (www.centreforwomensjustice.org.uk) is an amazing organisation set up by Harriet Wistrich to deal with cases in which women are being failed by our criminal justice system and is supported by eminent lawyers, barristers, academics and activists. In 2018, Harriet won two ground-breaking cases: one in the Supreme Court, in which she won a judgement against the Metropolitan Police for human rights violations in respect of their failure to properly investigate John Worboys, the Black Cab Rapist. Separately, but as a result of the same case, she brought a judicial review of the Parole Board and government in the High Court challenging the decision to release him. The parole board had, unbelievably, sanctioned his release after he had served only eight years in prison. Harriet successfully challenged the decision in the Supreme Court and this has resulted in a complete review of the way these decisions will be made in future.

I am still angry that a grave injustice was done to Amber

in naming her on the indictment without her knowledge and without saying too much at this stage, CWJ is currently looking into both her case and others. It is also fair to note that a barrister who works with the Centre has said that in all her professional experience, she has never before known of anyone to be treated this way without their knowledge, unless it was an offender who had absconded. I feel it is a complete breach of human rights and I am determined that, one day, this will be recognised as such.

I have also done quite a lot of public speaking, including at Fresh Start – new beginnings (www.fsnb.org.uk), a charity that works out of Ipswich, Suffolk, and provides therapeutic help for children who have been sexually abused. This is a wonderful organisation set up by an amazing woman called Diana Porter, MBE, and it's exactly the sort of work that gets my heart pumping. Their fundraising manager is a real gem called Patsy Johnson-Cisse. These people understand exactly what I'm saying about child sexual abuse and I'm in total admiration of the work they do. I would really like to see this kind of work replicated right across the UK so that children everywhere have the chance of being able to talk to someone and slowly come to terms with what's happened to them and, although still in the early stages, I intend to replicate this charity first in Rochdale, as The Maggie Oliver Foundation. The dream would be to have branches of this amazing organisation throughout the UK so that every child victim of abuse can have the support so desperately lacking in our country. A big ambition, but one I hope can be achieved.

I was even asked if I'd be interested in standing as a councillor in Rochdale, as former CIT manager Sara

Rowbotham has done. I considered it, but decided it wasn't for me. This is primarily because I can only do what I do because I'm completely independent and no one can tell me what I can or can't say. In a way, you can't not be political in times like these, but I'm certainly not party political in any way and would never be drawn into doing or saying anything I don't believe in just for 'the good of the party'. In my experience there has been far too much of that over the years and far less of a down-to-earth, common sense and honest approach. If I stand for anything, it's that: a non-biased, non-political way of addressing vital issues such as child sexual abuse and making sure that the powers that be are both aware of what's going on and will be held accountable for their failings. There has been too much 'us and them' in this country and too many vested interests looking after their own, covering up for them when things go wrong. This is what I want to address and change, and I welcome the opportunity to go on programmes such as *CBB* and *Loose Women* which reach out to wide and varied audiences, to inform the whole country about the truth.

Epilogue
The End of the Beginning

Not long after *Three Girls* was broadcast, I received a panicked phone call from Amber at 1am. Rochdale is not a huge place and people know each other. Someone, in their kindness, had put a picture of Amber's house on Facebook with the caption, 'This is where the Honey Monster lives'. I told her to call the police straight away and tell them she was in danger. She did that, but when police looked on the system, they could find no record of her being a victim so they refused point-blank to go out and protect her.

Of course they couldn't find any reference to her being a victim because all the evidence she gave was never placed on the system so the fact that she cannot get assistance from the police is another consequence of the crimes committed against her, and many of the other children, not being recorded. This was one of the many issues I highlighted in my report to the Home Affairs Select Committee in 2013. It was one of the very few issues they acknowledged and referenced in their subsequent report but, as can be seen, the consequences of police failures to record these horrific crimes are far-reaching and catastrophic.

Another horrendous consequence of not prosecuting Amber's abusers is that she has to endure the reality that many of these men are still living in Rochdale and walk the streets freely. Only this week she has told me that one of them works in a takeaway close to her house and that she sees many of the others when she is out with her children. In fact, on one occasion in 2018, she was visiting a friend in a house in a cul-de-sac and her little girl was playing outside in the street with the other kids. Amber came outside to leave and was brought to a total standstill because there, right in front of her, stood one of her abusers staring directly at her little girl. He looked up and saw Amber, then calmly walked to his car, smirking as he got in and drove away, knowing full well who she was and that he had escaped justice in spite of what he was guilty of.

In this day and age, that is simply wrong and it is this type of injustice committed against victims that I'm fighting against and dedicating my life to. The police officer (or officers) who decide not to go out to a vulnerable woman they know full well has been the victim of sexual abuse – because an award-winning, three-hour TV drama has been made about it – need to be held accountable. But at the moment, they're not. Unfortunately, policing has entered the world of politics, which appears to drive every decision made, large or small.

In my opinion, chief constables and other high-ranking

police officers are no longer the impartial forces of law and order. It seems that if you are promoted to superintendent or above, you can freely let go of your conscience and move smoothly up the ladder. The higher you go, the better you seem to be rewarded for protecting those above you, i.e. the politicians, some even receiving knighthoods for their 'loyalty'. Meanwhile, cuts to front-line policing seem to go through without a squeak and the public continue to wonder why they are being picked up for a speeding offence when nothing happens at all if they're burgled, or worse.

To my mind, senior officers should be doing the exact opposite of what they're currently doing. They should be demanding extra resources for tackling crimes like child sexual abuse, so they don't have to prioritise who they do or don't visit. If such demands are never made, we will continue to have a culture of policing just like the one we had on Operation Span, in which a dedicated team of front-line officers are prevented from arresting and prosecuting criminals because of decisions about 'priorities' made from the top. More lower-ranking officers should be speaking out about this, but in these times of savage cuts to policing, what choice do they have? If you've joined at eighteen and you're in the job for forty years, do you risk everything to speak out, or do you do as I was advised: 'Go into work, get your bum on the seat, do your job and take home your wage'?

Perhaps because I saw myself as a person first and a police officer second, a woman who had experienced many traumas in my life, I couldn't be indoctrinated in such a way. I couldn't not step out of the ranks and say something when I felt such injustices were being committed. I didn't care about the gang mentality. My job was to protect the vulnerable and do my job, and while I'm aware many police officers will think I betrayed the service, I'm not going to apologise for that. I had to blow the whistle and, as a result, I had no choice other than to resign. I couldn't have been sacked, but I'd have been buried away in a back office in a job I hated. Despite the horrendous consequences for me personally, my conscience wouldn't allow me to remain silent about what I consider neglect.

*

Andy Burnham is the Mayor of Manchester and the person who is now ultimately in charge of Greater Manchester Police. His job is to hold them to account. He gained public recognition, applause and praise while Shadow Home Secretary for the stance he took in the speech he gave to the House of Commons on 27th April 2016: the day after the Hillsborough inquests verdicts were delivered. He called for the fundamental reform of South Yorkshire Police, saying:

At long last justice for the ninety-six, for their families, for all Liverpool supporters for an entire city. But it took too long in coming and the struggle for it took too great a toll on too many. Now those responsible must be held to account.

*

I thought, *At last, here we have a politician who intended to hold senior police officers to account.* When he stood for election, I voted for him with high hopes. I hoped he would support those who 'blew the whistle' and hold those responsible for serious failures to account.

The unfortunate and uncomfortable truth is that Mayor Burnham, having been personally presented with credible and well-evidenced disclosures of police corruption, criminality and misfeasance at the highest levels within Greater Manchester Police by myself and two other police whistleblowers, in August 2018, has still neither responded to nor addressed these serious disclosures, more than eight months later, as I write. He has done the very thing that he criticised others for in his speech about South Yorkshire Police.

He spoke of three reasons why justice was delayed in Hillsborough. Firstly, a police force that has consistently put protecting itself ahead of protecting people. Secondly, collusion between the force and a complicit print media, and finally a flawed judicial system that gives the upper hand to those in authority over and above ordinary people. I believe by failing to address the incredibly serious issues we raised with him, as Mayor of Manchester, he is repeating the same failures he spoke out about as Shadow Home Secretary, and I feel very let down by him and totally disillusioned by his failure to address our concerns as a matter of urgency.

There was some acknowledgement of policing failure in Rochdale following a report in December 2013, but this only dealt with the mess that Rochdale CID made in the original investigation of 2008/09. A few junior officers got a ticking-off and there was an apology of sorts. Sir Peter Fahy said: 'The failings detailed in this report are unacceptable and we should never lose sight of the fact that we have let down some innocent victims.' However, this 'review' didn't go nearly far enough in my opinion and I find it utterly incredible that the Independent Police Complaints Commission didn't bother to even consider Operation Span or look at its failures too, the failures I was talking about right through 2011 up to the point I resigned in October 2012, and beyond. A handful of ordinary bobbies were blamed, but at least all the evidence they gathered in 2008/09 was placed on the record so that it could be used at a later date. Senior officers escaped a single word of criticism once again. I believe the reason there have been no other Baroness Jay-type 'Rotherham-style reviews' is because the truth is too horrendous for the authorities to let out of the bag, hence why they tried to keep the lid firmly closed.

As we know, in the 2010/11 investigation, Amber's months of interviews were more or less dropped into the circular filing cabinet – until someone decided they were useful after all and she was put on the indictment so her evidence could be entered in court. To this day, not a single person from Greater Manchester Police or the Crown Prosecution Service has been called to account for this, or for what I see as gross neglect to follow up on offers of help from many other abused girls. I would very much like to hear Nazir Afzal, who was the CPS's chief prosecutor for the North West at the time, explain clearly why the decision was made to overturn the original decision of John Lord, the Head of the CPS's Complex Case Unit, that Amber was purely a victim, particularly as he has been very vocal in claiming full credit for overturning the original CPS decision that Holly was an 'unreliable witness who had made a lifestyle choice'.

I and many others would also like to know who made the decision to put an innocent fifteen-year-old on a charge sheet and not tell her about it. The only person who has been punished is Amber – a victim right from the beginning. If that isn't wrong, I don't know what is, and I sincerely hope that no fifteen-year-old will ever again be locked up for being a 'madam', or secretly put on an indictment that lumps her in with a gang of paedophiles without even being told that was happening. If you're accused of something, you're entitled to know what that is and also entitled to a defence. The law says you are innocent until proven guilty and that needs to be shouted from the rooftops. We are not living in a police state, though given what Amber went through, you might be forgiven for thinking otherwise. There is nothing worse than being labelled a paedophile and to do that to a vulnerable child victim of paedophiles who was already on the Child Protection Register is wickedness beyond belief. Personally, I don't think I'll ever get over that. It shocks me to this day. This label has also overshadowed Amber's young life and to this day she feels she has to hide away from people, even though she has done absolutely nothing wrong. As I say, wickedness beyond belief... So to my mind, there has to be much more accountability. Apologies count for very little if the institutional failures of organisations like the police, local councils or social services continue unabated. If such organisations keep turning a blind eye to serious issues like child abuse and scapegoat children like Amber, who come forward to help them, they are clearly avoiding responsibility and should be held to account.

A handwritten note by Amber really hits home for me just how devastating the treatment she received was.

> College –
>
> on child protection register
> but i know mum was asking
> for help
> i was stopped from going college
> i was a danger to young people
> why????
>
> So left school.
> Sat home on my own
> no wage
> no job
> no support
> no friends
> lonely – frightened
> depressed.
>
> Then ████████ born was
> living with mum
> ████████ born and was put
> straight on child proctian
> register for emonibal abuse.

Where do these vulnerable girls turn if the authorities put in place to protect them don't help? Amber's isolation at the time is clear here:

In 2011, I tried to tell the chief constable of Greater Manchester Police that this was going on under his watch and for my troubles I felt I had no option but to leave his force. That simply isn't right and in future I would very much like to see figures in high authority take seriously the concerns of those serving under them, rather than take the easy option and try to discredit that person. And if they don't, and they are subsequently proved to be wrong, then I feel there should be severe consequences.

Where should someone facing the same situation as I faced go today? The honest answer is I don't know, because as my painful journey has taught me, every 'independent' body I approached was more interested in concealing the truth than addressing it. That is the terrifying, but inescapable reality.

Rochdale, Rotherham, Huddersfield, Telford, Oxford, Derby, Peterborough, Newcastle, Middlesbrough…the abuse of vulnerable children by grooming gangs in these and many more towns and cities around the UK was an inconvenient truth the authorities really didn't want to tackle. We will never know exactly how many children were abused, but given that there were at least 1,400 victims in Rotherham alone, it is quite possible that the numbers run well into the tens of thousands. Hundreds have now been prosecuted, yet many more still walk freely on the streets of this country. And new cases are emerging all the time, which isn't surprising because for years complaints of child sexual abuse by organised gangs were ignored. Even Nazir Afzal recently conceded that the Home Office sent a secret email to all police forces in 2008 directing them not to investigate the sexual exploitation of young girls across the UK. If what he says is true, and I have no reason to doubt it, it is clear proof that what I'm saying was no figment of my imagination but official Government policy.

In Baroness Alexis Jay's 2014 report into the Rotherham child abuse scandal, she stated: 'Over the first twelve years covered by this inquiry, the collective failures of political and officer leadership were blatant. From the beginning, there was growing evidence that child sexual exploitation was a serious problem in Rotherham. This came from those working in residential care and from youth workers who knew the young people well. Within social care, the scale and seriousness of the problem was underplayed by senior managers. At an operational level, the police gave no priority to CSE, regarding many child victims with contempt and failing to act on their abuse as a crime.'

This statement, sadly, could apply to almost every UK town and city plagued by child sexual abuse and is most certainly what I observed on Operation Augusta and Operation Span and which led to my eventual resignation. The people at the top saw a toxic combination of the ethnicity of the offenders and the status of vulnerable white girls from poor backgrounds and simply buried their heads in the sand. And not just on this issue. There is a class-driven 'them and us' attitude in the UK that stems right from above: they don't care about doing the right thing, they just tell you what to do, whether it's right or wrong. We only need to look at disasters like Hillsborough and Grenfell Tower, or the Jimmy Savile scandal, to see this in action. Amber was demonised because the authorities didn't want her to appear in court, yet needed her evidence. It was a tactical option; no one cared how it might damage her. And if they'd had their way, they'd have taken her children from her to justify their wickedness. The big question to be asked of these senior police officers, lawyers and politicians is, 'If this were your daughter, would you still have acted in the same way?' My opinion is that the answer would be a resounding 'no'.

In life, there are some things you have to accept and others you need to challenge. As a police officer, I was doing what I believed I was paid to do and when I challenged the status quo, I was treated as the enemy. So began a journey down a long road of loneliness, fear and disillusionment that led to my understanding that I, along with the victims, had been 'used'. To this extent, I've never been able to have any 'closure' and that is why I continue to fight for victims' rights – in a way I'm deflecting all the hurt and harm I've suffered and putting my own struggles into helping others. Thousands of kids like Amber and Ruby have no one to fight their corner and I'd like to think that all my years as a police officer are not wasted as I take up a campaigning role on their and others' behalf.

Having said all that, since Rochdale progress has been made in terms of identifying offenders, charging them with the more serious offences they should be charged with and locking them up for longer. In October 2018, twenty men from the Huddersfield area were jailed after an investigation into a grooming gang. Unlike Rochdale, however, most of these men were charged with and convicted of rape – an encouraging sign that the police and the CPS have toughened up on such offenders. Yet it was heard that again the authorities took many years to do anything about complaints being made and that other perpetrators were never identified and therefore are still walking around freely. That is wrong and police should be making more effort to act much quicker and bring such abusers to justice. A 'representative' sample of offenders in court is not good enough – they should all be standing in the dock. My belief is that if police and the CPS are determined to pull in as many offenders as possible, and on the strongest charges, these girls may not have to go through the ordeal of giving evidence in a trial because there won't be a trial – the evidence will be so overwhelming that the defendants' barristers will advise them to plead guilty and get a deal on the length of sentence. It's a lot of work, but I feel it would be worth it.

I hope I can take some credit for the majority of the country at least now knowing what grooming is and that the authorities can no longer blame children for the abuse they've suffered. Personally, I can't see myself ever letting go of this issue. In a way I'd like to, as undoubtedly it has taken its toll, but every time there is a new case of gang abuse or a development in the Rochdale story, I'm approached for a comment and I feel it's my duty to give that comment. I have a circle of truly amazing friends and family and I enjoy the lighter side of life, like going travelling or appearing on shows like *Celebrity Big Brother* and in a panto but, inevitably, I come back to the serious issues that occupy my life virtually every day.

I would like to talk more about the things that are close to my heart, like grooming and abuse, but also around poverty, homelessness and drug addiction and the outdated laws surrounding this – issues that really need looking at and tackling. I'm a person who cares about other people and it doesn't matter if it's abused children or homeless people in Manchester city centre or those trying to deal with drug addiction – we cannot turn a blind eye to any of these things. I would maybe like to go down the documentary-making road to examine such issues because I have a social conscience, I'm passionate about what I believe in and I have a strong sense of right and wrong. I would like to be involved in some way with an international charity too, trying to advance children's rights for girls all over the world and draw attention to the horrific injustices faced by them.

I also want to speak out for women who feel they shouldn't be limited by age as to what they do, where they go or what they talk about. I'd like to be a kind of positive role model for women to believe in themselves, jump into each new adventure that comes along, travel the world, embrace life and be brave. This is not a rehearsal and I believe that if you keep fit, active and interested in life, the world's your oyster.

For Amber and Ruby, I feel that their children are now their worlds and in this way they have been able to at least come to terms with their difficulties. There has also been public acknowledgement, through the drama and the documentaries, that they've been failed. How they've been failed cannot be put right, but in allowing their story to be told, they have helped educate the country into the realities of grooming and child sexual exploitation, and saved thousands of other girls from going what they themselves went through. They are proud to have done that and I admire them from the bottom of my heart for having the courage to put their pain and suffering out there. Without them allowing that to happen, we simply wouldn't be where we are today.

These girls will always be part of my life and in a way

they are like surrogate children to me. Barely a month goes by when I've not talked to them on the phone or been up to see them. Obviously, I can't do that for all the victims in the Rochdale case, or those from other areas, but I am hoping to set up an organisation or a charity in Rochdale which does make sure all victims of abuse are listened to and supported. And to help them understand that what has happened to them is not their fault. Prosecuting offenders is very important, obviously, but it's not the whole story. Education is the key to all this; educating young people about grooming and abuse, educating adults that abuse exists within the confines of their communities and needs to be addressed, educating the authorities that political correctness should play no part in who gets the blame for grooming and abuse. We should all be working together to achieve this.

To this end, in early 2018, I helped to launch *Loose Women*'s campaign called 'Never Too Late to Tell' together with Sammy Woodhouse and Saira Khan, both survivors of childhood abuse themselves. Victims of childhood sexual abuse are encouraged to consider speaking out to help start the healing process and the campaign is there to help any woman, or man, who has experienced sexual assault or rape at any point in their life. In 2017, Saira broke down on *Loose Women* after bravely telling how she'd been molested by an uncle at just thirteen. It was a secret she'd kept for decades, in large part because of the veil of secrecy surrounding this subject within her community. Sammy had been groomed at just fourteen by a man ten years her senior – Arshid Hussain – and had been subjected to brutal beatings even when she was carrying his child at just fifteen years old. In 2016, Hussain was jailed for thirty-five years for abusing girls in Rotherham and Sammy has since become a vocal campaigner for victims' rights.

I'm proud of this campaign because, by doing it, we are continuing the debate and by talking about it, we are educating people. We have to continue with that voice to bring about change and then we really will put a stop to this. Without that, we never will. Since the campaign began, many others have spoken out and we have of course had the worldwide #metoo and #timesup campaigns, so perhaps the tide is finally beginning to turn. There is, after all, strength in numbers.

I am also now in the process of establishing my own charity, The Maggie Oliver Foundation, to offer help, support and advice to the survivors of abuse in Rochdale, intending to emulate Diana Porter's amazing charity Fresh Start – new beginnings in East Anglia. Diana has agreed to become one of the trustees with me, for which I am very thankful. This is just another way I hope to put back something into a young community destroyed by the failures of the authorities to protect it. I hope that the public who know me will trust me and support me in this. My dream would be to ultimately replicate this in every town and city throughout the country where children have had their young lives blighted in this way. An unrealistic dream, perhaps, but one that I am determined to achieve before I die.

If going through this process has taught me anything, it's that I have rarely trusted anyone to do anything on my behalf ever since I was a child. All I have is my voice and my conscience and I'm not afraid to speak out, stand up, be counted and fight for what I believe is right – even if that means losing everything. And I urge others to do the same. If you see something you know is wrong, say it. Stand up and be counted. Unless people are prepared to step up to the mark, public bodies will continue to get away with massive failures in secret, because the whole establishment is created to cover up such neglect. Blowing the whistle is a huge mountain to climb, not least because to be heard, you also have to be prepared to face up to your greatest fears, challenge authority, endure unimaginable stress and survive it. And be ready to deal with the media. You need the press to tell your story, but you also have to know what you're getting into when you make that first call to a news desk or TV station. It's scary and if people feel they aren't able to go through with it, then I totally understand. But where possible, don't be a bystander – there are enough of these in life. For me, everything I went through to tell the real story of the Rochdale child sexual abuse scandal has been worth it. I am beginning to see some light at the end of the tunnel, but I was in that tunnel for a long time. I only wanted the right thing to be done by the victims of the abusers and it just escalated from there.

I am not a special person – I am just an ordinary woman – and all I ever wanted to be was a good wife, mum and police officer. When I joined Greater Manchester Police in 1997, I swore my oath and I took it seriously from my first day in the job to my last day as a serving officer. I hope that by standing up for what I believed to be right, I carried out my duty with integrity. The police oath is printed at the very beginning of this book, if you'd like to read it again. I'll let you be the judge.

Acknowledgements

There are so many people who I would like to thank for holding my hand, listening to me, encouraging and believing in me since I resigned from Greater Manchester Police that I don't really know where to start…

First of all: to my husband, the love of my life, my soulmate. I have felt you beside me many times on this long and lonely journey, holding my hand, guiding me and giving me the strength to carry on. My love is eternally yours.

To my four amazing children and partners, for your never-ending patience, kindness, support and belief in me, through the darkest of days. I am so proud of you all, and I love you with all my heart. I hope that when I am no longer here and you remember me, you think of fairness, caring, integrity and perseverance.

To my very best friend in the world, Sandra, who has held my hand and listened to me every day. I don't know where I would be now without all your love and support and I feel blessed that we met that fateful day ten years ago. I'm sure you could have written much of this book for me!

To all my treasured girlfriends, but especially Linda, Sharon, Karen, Alana, Pat, Joanne, Victoria, Jules, Debs, Becca and Amanda, who have travelled this road with me too, and who must have thought many times that they wished I would just shut up and stop going over the same old ground, you have my admiration for your patience!!

A million 'thank-yous' to every single person who has read my story or spoken to me in the days since I exposed this scandal. You have restored my faith in humanity and given me the courage to carry on fighting to change our broken criminal justice system, and provide care and support for survivors. There is still a long way to go.

To the BBC and teams behind both *Three Girls* and *The Betrayed Girls* for all your hard work creating the drama and documentary, both of which shocked the nation and shone a spotlight on some of the issues.

To Sally Chesworth and BBC *File on Four* for helping me take the first life-changing step into the unknown.

A big thank-you goes to the talented Tom Henry who has worked tirelessly and under great pressure to understand this complex story to help me write it and make it accessible to the readers.

My heartfelt thanks and appreciation must also go to my lovely editor Kelly Ellis at Bonnier Books UK, whose trust, perseverance, encouragement and belief finally convinced me to write this book. You just understood me, Kelly, and for that I will be for ever grateful.

But the final word of thanks must go to all of 'my girls' in Rochdale. Amazingly brave young women, survivors of the most horrific sexual abuse who were further abused by the failures of the authorities. Despite all your pain, I am honoured and humbled that you put your trust in me and allowed me to speak to the country for you. Not once, not twice, but time and time again, in selfless acts, just to try to prevent other children from being failed as you have all been. I consider you my 'extra' children, my extended family, and I know our lives will be for ever entwined. Your bravery fills me with awe, and I will always be here for you when you need me, no matter what.

Maybe the reason I understand you is because we are similar, we are all survivors who have come through the bleakest of times. Perhaps I was meant to join the police, perhaps it was written in the stars all along, just so that I could expose the terrible scandal I witnessed as a serving police officer and give you all a voice.

As you were all written off, so was I. Considering my age, my rank, my gender, my fear, the threats, the power of the police and their juggernaut of a PR machine, everything was stacked against me being heard. But what do you do when everything is stacked against you?

You keep going
You don't stop
You never give up
You keep fighting on.

And that is the message I would like to leave all my readers with.

**THE IMPOSSIBLE IS POSSIBLE. YOU JUST HAVE
TO BELIEVE IN YOURSELF!**

Afterword

The Maggie Oliver Foundation
Transforming pain into power

www.themaggieoliverfoundation.com
JustGiving: The Maggie Oliver Foundation

Thank you for reading my book. It's a story from my past that very much needed to be told and now I'm looking to the future...

The Maggie Oliver Foundation is the next chapter of my journey. I am setting up a nationwide network of community centres that will provide much-needed support, advice and mentoring as well as access to psychological, counselling and legal help for survivors of abuse from all communities who have nowhere else to go.

My first centre will, of course, be in Rochdale where this journey began. This centre will 'Transform Pain into Power' for all those forgotten and neglected by the powerful in our society.

If everyone who watched *Three Girls* and was moved by the story of these children contributed just £1, think how much help my centres could give to the most vulnerable in our country. So, I am asking if you would consider donating what you can to my foundation? Without funding, I cannot achieve this goal, but I give you my word that every penny of your donations will help make a difference to many damaged young lives.

FOLLOW ME ON:
Instagram: @MaggieOliverUK
Twitter: @MaggieOliverUK
LinkedIn: Margaret Oliver
www.maggieoliver.co.uk

THE JOURNEY CONTINUES...